BASIC EDITING

A PRACTICAL COURSE

THE TEXT

NICOLA HARRIS

The Publishing Training Centre
45 East Hill, Wandsworth
London SW18 2QZ

This edition © The Publishing Training Centre/UNESCO 1991

First published 1991
Reprinted with corrections 1992, 1995, 1999, 2003

British Library Cataloguing-in-Publication data
Harris, Nicola
    Basic editing: a practical course
    1. Publications. Copy-editing
    I. Title
    808.02

    ISBN 0-907706-02-9 Text
    ISBN 0-907706-03-7 Exercises

Typeset in 10/13 pt Palatino

Printed in Great Britain

Contents

Acknowledgements

My first and greatest debt of gratitude is to Judith Butcher, not only for her helpful advice on this course but for her book, *Copy-editing* (Cambridge University Press, Cambridge, 3rd edition, forthcoming). I was lucky enough to begin my editing career shortly after the publication of the first edition in 1975. Her rational, sensitive and explanatory style and comprehensive coverage have made the book a valued companion both in those early days and in later years.

The second great debt is to Liz Bland, long-time freelancer and friend, who got me into all this. She it was who first devised the three-day Copy-editing Skills course at Book House, from which this fuller course grew, and she recommended me as one of the tutors. Several of the exercises in this longer course originate from her and I'm grateful for her unfailing encouragement and comments on the text.

Thanks are due to Dag Smith, whose persistent advocacy of a 'book of the course' eventually made me take up the challenge; to my co-tutors, Joan Angelbeck, Harriet Barry, Gillian Clarke, Tim Fox, Mike Hauser and Barbara Horn, who have commented thoughtfully and pertinently on early drafts. I am grateful too for helpful input from Meg Davies, Hilary Frost, Mary-Claire Hailey, David Hill, Sue Hughes, Ros Spry, Lesley J. Ward and Anne Wilcock. Finally, my thanks go to Sage Publications, particularly to Stephen Barr, for sympathetically tolerating absence of mind as much as body over the year and a half it has taken to put the course together.

Each of the publishers I have worked for – the International African Institute, Basil Blackwell, Longman and Sage – has contributed different strands to whatever expertise may be found in the book, as well as a fund of examples for the exercises. Most particularly, I am grateful to the freelance editors who have broadened my knowledge of how others operate, to the authors who constantly bring unexpected challenges and rewards, and to those I have helped to train, who have at the same time taught me a great deal, and forced me to think about the whys and wherefores of our craft.

It is conventional to end acknowledgements with a disclaimer that, for all the advice and comments, the final result is my responsibility, but it certainly needs to be said here. In several instances I have wilfully gone my own way, though trying to make clear, when I have done so, that opinions differ.

How to Use this Book

This text is designed for use with its companion volume of exercises, which constitutes an individual workbook. The course introduces you in a varied and, I hope, enjoyable way to the art and skill of editing.

The exercises range across many different subjects and around the globe; they relate to general, educational and academic publishing of both books and journals. Each exercise addresses a specific skill (while also giving practice in the skills already learned), step by step building up your confidence in handling the whole spectrum of editorial work. The aim is to impart sound techniques, instil sensible habits, tune your antennae to editorial concerns, and so lay the basis for the further practical experience that will make you a first-class editor.

The course may be taken in class or by self-tuition. If you are working on your own, you should find adequate preparatory hints and follow-up comments in the text to enable you to do all the exercises successfully. Occasionally, worked answers are given in the text, especially where they help to demonstrate marking technique. However, since there is rarely one 'correct solution' in editorial work, discussion is often more appropriate than answers. Try to avoid looking at the follow-up discussion before doing an exercise.

If possible, especially in the early stages, ask a more experienced colleague to look through your work and discuss with you any points you don't understand. Do hold on to your earlier work (even if you are not entirely satisfied with it): from time to time the text refers back to previous exercises to illustrate new points.

Minimal instructions are given at the beginning of those exercises that involve anything other than straightforward editing. The book of exercises can, therefore, be used in class independently of the text, which becomes simply the tutor's reference book. The fuller instructions that appear in italic in the text under 'Now do Exercise ...' would then form the basis of the tutor's spoken introduction to the exercise. Some of the more essential illustrations in the text could be made into overhead projector slides. In this way, class sets of the exercises can economically be combined with a tutor's and/or library reference copy of the text.

Written primarily to offer a sound basis for editors in their first publishing job, the course is equally suitable as a pre-employment introduction for those seeking in-house or freelance work. It may also be helpful as preparation for a switch from in-house to freelance work, which can lead you into previously unfamiliar areas of publishing.

Time allocation

Each unit (normally containing two or three exercises) may constitute one session, for example an evening. (If you are doing the course this way, note that Unit 1 is very short and best combined with the first exercise of the much longer Unit 2.) The units are further *grouped into fours* to make a varied but thematically related full day's work. The tougher sections usually come early in the day, so do persevere.

The course may therefore take thirty-six sessions or nine whole days (the Consolidation exercises being the final day's work). Ideally it should be taken during the first two or three months of an editor's career. Although an intensive course would be possible in a fortnight, one day a week is recommended as being less likely to give you indigestion.

My hope is that publishing firms that are committed to training will regularly set aside one day a week in the first months of a new editor's work schedule so that he or she may follow the course, perhaps appointing a colleague to help as necessary. In places where several publishers are gathered together, day-release schemes at a local college or training centre would be ideal.

Advance preparation

'Tools of the Trade', the first section of the book of exercises, spells out what you need, notably

- a good English dictionary
- either *The Oxford Dictionary for Writers and Editors* (often known as *ODWE*) or the paperback version, *The Oxford Writers' Dictionary*
- *Hart's Rules for Compositors and Readers*

These last two works are referred to throughout this text as the *Writers' Dictionary* (which equally denotes *ODWE*) and *Hart's Rules*. They are published by Oxford University Press and regularly updated.

You will find Unit 2 easier if you learn the proofreading symbols (pp. 4–5) in advance. True competence in using them only comes with practice, which the unit offers, but going through them beforehand should help you to absorb the techniques more quickly.

Variations

If you have never worked 'in house' at a publishing firm, you may be best advised to skip Unit 3 (on the production process) and go straight on to Unit 4, returning to Unit 3 whenever it is convenient. Make sure that you do so before tackling Unit 20.

If the course is taken in class, some of the exercises may be done in groups or in pairs to vary the pace. The exercises that particularly lend themselves to such group work have been marked with the symbol **G**.

Feedback

At the end of the volume of exercises you will find an assessment form. Please do fill it in: feedback from you, whether you were learning from the course or teaching with it, will help us to improve any future editions.

Addendum

Page

vi   *Hart's Rules for Compositors and Readers*, referred to throughout the text, has been completely revised. The new edition is known as *The Oxford Guide to Style* (Oxford University Press, 2002).

        The Oxford Guide to Style and *The Oxford Dictionary for Writers and Editors* are available as one comprehensive *Oxford Style Manual* (Oxford University Press, 2003).

20   Giles Clark, *Inside Book Publishing*, is now in its 3rd edition (Routledge, 2001).

34   Maeve O'Connor, *How to Copyedit Scientific Books and Journals* is no longer in print.

        Suggested alternative: Huth EJ et al. *Scientific Style and Format: the CBE Manual for Authors, Editors, and Publishers* (Cambridge University Press, 6th edition, 1995).

42   In addition to those listed: RW Burchfield, *The New Fowler's Modern English Usage*, revised by Ernest Gowers (Oxford University Press, 3rd edition, 1999).

        John Sinclair (ed) *Collins Cobuild English Grammar* and also *Collins Cobuild English Guides* (HarperCollins Publishers, 1991) – good for second-language users of English.

53   G.V. Carey, *Mind the Stop*, is no longer in print.

        Suggested alternative: R.L. Trask, *The Penguin Guide to Punctuation* (Penguin, 1997).

65   Casey Miller and Kate Swift, *The Handbook of Non-Sexist Writing for Writers, Editors and Speakers* is now in its 3rd edition (The Women's Press, 1995).

72   *The Chicago Manual of Style* is now in its 15th edition (University of Chicago Press, 2003, distributed in the UK by John Wiley & Sons).

79   *The Chicago Manual of Style* is now in its 15th edition. See above.

        How to Copyedit Scientific Books and Journals is no longer in print. See above.

90   *How to Copyedit Scientific Books and Journals* is no longer in print. See above.

152   Hilary and Mary Evans, *Picture Researchers Handbook*, is now in its 7th edition (Pira, 2001).

172   M.D. Anderson, *Book Indexing* is no longer in print.

        Suggested alternative: Nancy C Mulvaney, *Indexing Books* (University of Chicago Press, 1994, distributed in the UK by John Wiley & Sons Ltd).

177   M.F. Flint, *User's Guide to Copyright*, is now in its 6th edition (Butterworths, 2004).

200   In addition to those listed: *The New Fowler's Modern English Usage*. See above.

        Chicago Guide to Style is now in its 15th edition. See above.

        Book Indexing is no longer in print. See above.

UNIT 1

The Editor's Role

Why do we need to edit an author's work? Surely a professional writer knows how to present his or her material appropriately? As this book aims to demonstrate, however good an author may be, the editor has some role to play.

The purpose of editing is

- to help the eventual reader to understand
- to save the author from embarrassing errors
- to make everything clear for the typesetter

Editors in all spheres of publishing have to think about these three aspects in everything they do. Their work is usually (but nowadays not necessarily) done on an author's **typescript** (discussed in more detail in Unit 2).

Helping the reader

You need to check that the structure and argument are clear and coherent; that terms and abbreviations are adequately explained; that illustrations are relevant and helpful. Eliminate ambiguities, imprecise use of words, monotonous repetition and grammatical or spelling errors. You will also ensure that any references are complete; that any notes relate correctly to their indicators in the text; that tables and illustrations bear out and complement the text.

Working with the author

The editor acts as midwife to the book: the author has done the creative work, with all the anguish that that often entails, but may need some practical help in these final stages. A fresh eye may spot all sorts of minor problems of detail. Remember, though, as you gasp at his/her slips, how much the author has achieved in writing the book.

Sometimes the editor helps by improving the language: an author may have important things to say (perhaps in a technical field little known to others) but have difficulty communicating these ideas.

Cooperation is the keyword: make sure the author knows about and approves the changes you are making. For most projects, there will be a query stage in which you check various points with the author. It is a good idea to return the edited typescript (or a good photocopy of it) along with the queries to allay fears and avoid problems at the **proof** stage (which we look at in more detail in Unit 2). Phrase your queries as suggestions; discuss any major points of disagreement on the telephone or in person.

Marking up for the typesetter

If the typesetter can see immediately what is wanted, without having to read the text for sense, he or she will work more quickly and accurately. So you should identify ambiguous symbols and make your instructions and changes in wording as clear as possible.

You need to show the relative importance of different levels of heading and to identify matter that is to be displayed in a special way, for example long quotations. On these points your marking may be either a direct instruction to the typesetter or a briefing for the designer.

Consistency

In practice, editors spend much of their time imposing consistency. Why does consistency matter? The main reason is that variations in spelling, hyphenation, etc., may distract the reader from the argument or story. It is important to do this work when the project is still in typescript because amendments at proof stage are extremely costly. Authors who have ignored discrepancies in the typescript will often notice them in proof and want to make extensive changes.

A standard **house style** can be helpful. This, as

we shall see, is a publishing house's rule book, which sets out its preferences on alternative spellings, ways of treating numbers, dates, etc. Such guidelines can help you to achieve consistency, particularly if you work for the same publisher for some time. On the other hand, imposing a rigid style that requires numerous trivial changes can be time-consuming and induce unnecessary irritation in authors. Do take special care whenever the house style requires reversal of the author's system or usage: he or she will almost certainly notice in proof any instances you happen to miss.

The commissioning function

A commissioning editor (or acquisitions editor or sponsoring editor or publisher) is responsible for seeking out new authors, encouraging existing authors, devising new projects, negotiating contracts, assessing the quality of typescripts and advising on revision, and building up a coherent list of marketable books. He or she forecasts likely sales, balances them against costs and so decides on the viability of a project, the appropriate print-run and the price.

During the commissioning or development stage, wider questions such as the coverage of the book, its content and argument should usually have been worked out.

The desk editing function

All work on the typescript itself may be categorized as editing. It may range from rewriting (even ghost writing) and specialist checking of facts, through minor stylistic improvements, to the detailed work of ensuring consistency and correcting spelling.

Some editorial work may have been done by the commissioning editor, by the academic editor of a journal or by the volume editor of an edited collection. The desk editor (or sub-editor or copy-editor) is usually responsible for all remaining editorial work.

What is to be done – in particular, how much work on style improvement is worth while – may need to be discussed with the commissioning editor because of the time and cost implications. How far house style is to be applied may also have to be considered.

Some people draw a firm distinction between 'editing' and 'copy-editing'. The implication is that rewriting and improvement of the author's literary style lie on one side of the fence; detailed cross-checking and ensuring consistency lie on the other. I prefer to view these various activities as a continuum, all potentially the concern of the editor,

whose skill lies precisely in judging what level of 'interference' is appropriate for a particular book, author or market. Throughout the course, therefore, I use the term 'editor' rather than 'copy-editor' and provide practice across the whole spectrum.

Certainly where extensive style work or rewriting is necessary, it is sensible to edit first for style, then for detail (preferably having the script retyped, or disks amended, in between). Concentration on one aspect at a time simplifies the task. The two stages may then be undertaken by different people (whether a commissioning editor and a desk editor, or an editor skilled at rewriting and a copy-editor with an eye for detail).

This two-stage procedure may be practicable in school textbooks or reference books. In other fields, such as academic publishing, editing is normally a single operation and the editor has to look out for infelicities of expression and structural problems at the same time as doing the detailed checking.

Design

Some editors will work with a designer, or a production controller responsible for design; others will do all or some design work themselves. A production editor may do editorial, design *and* production work. All these functions are discussed in greater detail in Unit 3.

Proofreading

In addition to editing the typescript, you may be responsible for proofreading (checking the typesetter's proof against the typescript) or collating different sets of proofs. In Unit 2 we explore proofreading skills and in Unit 3 look at the different stages and processes a book may go through, before returning in Unit 4 to editorial work on the typescript.

Project coordination

For most people working as editors **in house** (in a publishing firm), a large part of the work consists in coordination of projects and liaison with other departments or individuals. This network of contacts is discussed in greater detail in Unit 3. You may be responsible for some commissioning aspects as well as desk editing; you may be organizing a team of **freelance** editors, proofreaders and indexers. In addition to work on the text and illustrations, you may be handling budgets and schedules. The aim is not only to produce as good a book as you can, but also to bring it out at the right cost and on time.

UNIT 2

Reading Proofs

We look at proofreading first, partly because most editors are given proofs to read before they embark on other editorial work and partly because learning the standard proofreading symbols establishes a sound basis for further work. Whether you are reading galley proofs, page proofs or output from a desk-top publishing system, you use the same symbols and the same techniques. (These different proof stages and methods of production are explained in Unit 3.)

Proofreading symbols

The main standard symbols (or marks) are listed on the following pages. Learn them carefully but have the list to hand whenever you are proofreading until you become fully familiar with the symbols. Life is very much easier if you learn them correctly from the beginning. If you have already been doing some proofreading, this is your opportunity to correct any bad habits.

The symbols listed are the 'new' standard ones (introduced in Britain in 1976). If you work for a publishing firm that continues to use the traditional symbols, you may be expected to follow suit. Nevertheless, you should **also become thoroughly acquainted with the new ones**, as they are widely used. Avoid learning a mixture of old and new. (See the end of this unit for more on the traditional symbols.)

When you are reading proofs, identify each error both **in the text** and **in the margin**. You may normally use both margins, as in the example shown below. Mentally divide the line you are reading approximately down the middle; mark corrections to the left half of the line in the left margin and corrections to the right half of the line in the right margin. (All corrections, however, should read from left to right: so, for the left half of the line, begin a short distance from the text and work inwards.)

As shown in the **example**, you should put an *oblique stroke* after each correction, unless it is already followed by an insertion mark (a **caret**). You include the oblique stroke even if there is only one correction on a line.

You will notice in the example that some of the typeset lines have much more space between the words than other lines. Such variations are inevitable

First table (upper)

Instruction	Textual mark	Marginal mark
Change damaged character(s)	Encircle character(s)	✕
Set in or change to italic	——— under character(s). Where space does not permit textual marks encircle the affected area instead	☐
Change italic to upright type	Encircle character(s)	↲
Set in or change to capital letters	≡ under character(s)	≡
Set in or change to small capital letters	═ under character(s)	=
Set in or change to bold type	∿ under character(s)	∿
Set in or change to bold italic type	∿ under character(s)	∿
Change capital letters to lower-case letters	Encircle character(s)	╪
Change small capital letters to lower-case letters	Encircle character(s)	╪
Invert type	Encircle character	⌒
Close up. Delete space between characters or words	linking ⌒ characters	( )
Insert space between characters	| between characters	⊤
Insert space between words	⅄ between words	Give the size of the space when necessary
Reduce space between characters	| between characters	⊤
		Give the size of the space when necessary
Reduce space between words	⋔ between words	⊤
		Give the amount by which the space is to be reduced when necessary
		Give the amount by which the space is to be reduced when necessary

Second table (lower)

Instruction	Textual mark	Marginal mark
Leave unchanged	- - - - - under characters	✓
Remove extraneous marks	Encircle marks to be removed	✕
Delete	/ through character(s) or ⊢⊣ through words	♂
Delete and close up	⌒ through character(s) or ⊐⊏	♂
Insert in text the matter indicated in the margin	⋏	New matter followed by ⋏
Substitute character or substitute part of one or more word(s)	/ through character or ⊢ through word(s)	New character or new word(s)
Substitute ligature e.g. ffi for separate letters	⊢⊣ through characters affected	e.g. (ffi)
Substitute or insert full stop or decimal point	/ through character or ⋏	⊙
Substitute or insert comma, semi-colon, colon, etc.	/ through character or ⋏	,/ ;/ ⊙/ (/)/ [/]
Substitute or insert character in 'superior' position	/ through character or ⋏	⅄ under character e.g. ⅄²
Substitute or insert character in 'inferior' position	/ through character or ⋏	⅃ over character e.g. ⅃₃
Substitute or insert single or double quotation marks or apostrophe	/ through character or ⋏	⁷⁷ and/or ⁷⁷
Substitute or insert ellipsis	/ through character or ⋏	...
Substitute or insert hyphen	/ through character or ⋏	⊢⊣
Substitute or insert rule	/ through character or ⋏	⊢⊣ Give the size of the rule in the marginal mark e.g. 1em⊢⊣ 4mm⊢⊣
Substitute or insert oblique	/ through character or ⋏	⊘
Wrong fount. Replace by character(s) of correct fount	Encircle character(s)	⊗

Instruction	Textual mark	Marginal mark
Move matter specified distance to the right*	enclosing matter to be moved to the right	(mark)
Move matter specified distance to the left*	enclosing matter to be moved to the left	(mark)
Take over character(s), word(s) or line to next line, column or page	(mark)	The textual mark surrounds the matter to be taken over and extends into the margin
Take back character(s), word(s) or line to previous line, column or page	(mark)	The textual mark surrounds the matter to be taken back and extends into the margin
Raise matter*	over matter to be raised / under matter to be raised	(mark)
Lower matter*	over matter to be lowered / under matter to be lowered	(mark)
Move matter to position indicated*	Enclose matter to be moved and indicate new position	(mark)
Correct vertical alignment	(mark)	(mark)
Correct horizontal alignment	Single line above and below misaligned matter	(mark) placed level with the head and foot of the relevant line

*Give the exact dimensions when necessary

Instruction	Textual mark	Marginal mark
Make space appear equal between characters or words	between characters or words	(mark)
Close up to normal interline spacing	(each side of column) (linking lines)	(mark)
Insert space between lines or paragraphs	or	Give the size of the space when necessary
Reduce space between lines or paragraphs	or	Give the amount by which the space is to be reduced when necessary
Start new paragraph	(mark)	(mark)
Run on (no new paragraph)	(mark)	(mark)
Transpose characters or words	between characters or words, numbered when necessary	(mark)
Transpose lines	(mark)	(mark)
Transpose a number of lines	3 / 2 / 1	Rules extend from the margin into the text with each line to be transposed numbered in the correct sequence
Centre	enclosing matter to be centred	(mark)
Indent	(mark)	Give the amount of the indent
Cancel indent	(mark)	(mark)
Set line justified to specified measure*	and/or	(mark)
Set column justified to specified measure*	(mark)	(mark)

Extracts from BS 5261: Part 2: 1976 are reproduced with the permission of BSI. Complete copies of the standard can be obtained from BSI, Linford Wood, Milton Keynes MK14 6LE. The marks alone are also available on a fold-out card.

in **justified** setting, that is, setting in which the right margin forms a straight vertical, just like the left margin. You would mark a correction only if words were exceptionally closely or exceptionally widely spaced (or if the space varied between the words on one particular line).

Technique

If you are reading proofs **against copy**, you will normally have in front of you a double-spaced, typed version (the author's **typescript**, as marked by an editor) and a **proof**, which looks more like a printed page. Your task is to ensure that the typesetter's version (the proof) accords with the original copy (the typescript).

- If you are right-handed, put the typescript on the left and the proof on the right. (If you are left-handed, put the typescript on the right and the proof on the left.) You will normally have a pile of proofs and a pile of typescript, so make plenty of space on the desk for turning the pages of each pile over methodically, avoiding any mix-up.

- Hold your pen over the word you are reading in the proof; slide a ruler (or piece of paper) down the lines of the typescript with your other hand as you read, in order to keep your place.

- Read every word in the proof, every letter in a name or difficult word – remember that proof-reading is totally different from reading for pleasure or skimming rapidly for information.

- Every sentence or so (every line, if sentences are long), look across from the proof to the typescript to make sure nothing (including punctuation) has been left out or added. Look particularly at names, numbers and technical terms to check that they are correct.

Colours for marking proofs

Although your main task is to look for errors introduced by the typesetter, you may also find problems not noticed earlier.

- Use red for errors made by the typesetter.

- Use blue for other necessary changes. In collating different sets of proofs you may need to distinguish between author's changes and publisher's changes, in which case you can use blue and black (unless black marking already appears in the proofs).

- The typesetter may have marked some corrections on the proofs already. The traditional colour for this was green but, since proofs are often photocopied, this may appear as black.

Your colour coding enables the typesetter to allocate costs quickly and fairly. Red (and green) corrections will be done at the typesetter's own expense. Blue and black corrections will be charged to the publisher. Most contracts between publisher and author allow for this cost to be set against the author's royalties (earnings) if it amounts to more than a specified percentage of the typesetting cost.

Now do Exercise 2.1

---

*The typescript is on the left-hand page and the proof is on the right. (Apologies to the left-handed.) When you have proofread the **first paragraph only**, look at the answer given on p. 10. Then finish the exercise before continuing to the review below.*

Review of Exercise 2.1

Turn to p. 13 and check your own work against the rest of the sample answer.

It is not possible to show colours here but boxed asterisks indicate the blue corrections. In general, when you are marking proofs you should not make unnecessary changes; so, for example, I would not insert 'in' before 'some' on proof l. 11 (it spoils the rhythm) or query the unusual but evocative 'millipede' on l. 2. You might similarly hesitate to change 'long' to 'far' (l. 19), as the repetition of this word (and others in the passage) is evidently a deliberate device to build up the palpable tedium. However, 'far' does express the meaning better.

Did you see that the typesetter had saved us from a further blue correction at proof l. 27 (copy l. 17)? Both this point and the one on l. 40 should have been picked up by the editor of the typescript.

You may also have marked ll. 26 and 51 for a **ligature** 'fi'. If you didn't, notice now that in each case 'f' and 'i' have been set as separate letters (as on a typewriter) rather than as the joined-up form (shown in the proofreading symbols) that is traditional in print. In practice, however, you can no longer expect this nicety from all typesetters and may have to accept separate letters if that style has been followed consistently.

Notice that full stops and colons are circled; other punctuation marks (such as commas and semi-colons) are not. This helps the typesetter to distinguish between them.

The 'substitute a superior' symbol $\mathcal{Y}$ similarly helps to distinguish a closing quote (inverted comma or quotation mark) from a comma. An apostrophe is identical to a closing quote but you will have noticed that in most printed typefaces opening and closing quotes curve different ways. Show this difference clearly in your correction marks.

Other symbols to practise particularly are *ш* (italic or sloping type) and *ψ* (roman or upright type). Make sure that in the latter your middle stroke is distinctly longer than the other two.

In the proof 'MAN' was (wrongly) set in **small caps**. Compare the 'M' with the 'M' of 'Morse machine' and you will see that small caps are the same height as a lower-case 'x'. (This is known as the **x-height**.)

You may have been surprised to find 'p.m.' marked (copy l. 32) as small caps. Lower case is more common today, although either form is acceptable.

Distinctions possible only in print

Distinctions such as that between small caps and full caps are possible only in typesetting or desk-top publishing systems, not on an ordinary typewriter or word-processor. In the typescript the author or editor has to show what is wanted by special marking. This section is about such technicalities, distinctions that cannot be checked until you see the proofs but need to be marked in the typescript (or indicated by a general instruction).

Hyphen, en rule and em rule

In most printed typefaces a hyphen (note that there is no technical term for it) is extremely short, much shorter than its typed version. It is used to connect words or parts of words in various ways: 'pre-eminent', 'the decision-making process', 'marriage break-up', etc.

An **en rule**, which is normally about twice as long as a hyphen, is used in several different ways.

■ Between words, it can be understood as 'to' or 'and': its function is to connect separate entities.

So, 'the Paris–Rome express', 'rural–urban conflict', 'the jazz–classical music boundary', 'a German–French trade agreement'. Can you see the difference in meaning between these examples and those given under hyphens?

Be careful about one particular case: although 'French–German trade agreement' takes an en rule, 'Franco-German' (or 'Anglo-American', 'Sino-Soviet', etc.) has to take a hyphen because 'Franco-' (like 'pre-') cannot stand on its own.

Some publishers have abandoned this distinction between a hyphen and an en rule between words but it does serve a useful purpose.

■ An en rule may also be used between numbers: 15–17, 35–40, etc. Example 1 on the next page compares an en rule (A) with a hyphen (B) in a range of numbers. Although the en rule is still generally preferred, either style may be used, provided you are consistent.

■ A **spaced** en rule can be used for a dash (see below). As you will see when you come to mark up a typescript, it is important to show that it should be spaced in order to distinguish it from an en rule between words.

An **em rule** is twice as long again. (The origin of the terms is that in many typefaces the en rule is the width of an N and the em rule the width of an M.)

■ An em rule is used for a dash, traditionally **closed up** (with no space before and after it). Some publishers now use a spaced em rule for a dash (because we are accustomed to seeing that space in typed text). Others, as we have seen, prefer a spaced en rule for a dash.

■ A spaced em (or 2 em) rule may indicate a blank (in place of someone's name or a swear word) or an unfinished sentence.

Spacing

Look at the examples on the next page of:

■ units/measurements (example 2)
■ people's initials (example 3)
■ page, figure, volume numbers (example 4)

You will see that some of the examples are closed up while some are spaced. The amount of space can be **variable** (changing like the space between all other words when the line is justified) or **fixed**. The standard space mark $\mathcal{Y}$ indicates that you want a variable space; in Unit 15 we look at how to ask for fixed spaces. In the typescript an editor has to make sure that it is clear whether spaced or closed-up

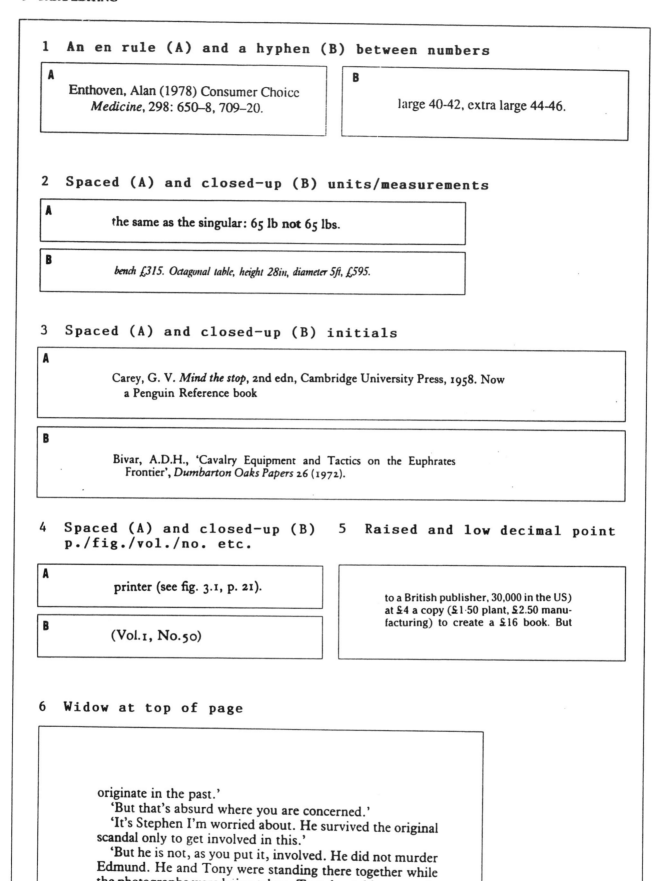

1 An en rule (A) and a hyphen (B) between numbers

A

Enthoven, Alan (1978) Consumer Choice
Medicine, 298: 650–8, 709–20.

B

large 40-42, extra large 44-46.

2 Spaced (A) and closed-up (B) units/measurements

A

the same as the singular: 65 lb not 65 lbs.

B

bench £315. Octagonal table, height 28in, diameter 5ft, £595.

3 Spaced (A) and closed-up (B) initials

A

Carey, G. V. *Mind the stop*, 2nd edn, Cambridge University Press, 1958. Now
a Penguin Reference book

B

Bivar, A.D.H., 'Cavalry Equipment and Tactics on the Euphrates
Frontier', *Dumbarton Oaks Papers* 26 (1972).

4 Spaced (A) and closed-up (B)
p./fig./vol./no. etc.

A

printer (see fig. 3.1, p. 21).

B

(Vol.1, No.50)

5 Raised and low decimal point

to a British publisher, 30,000 in the US)
at £4 a copy (£1·50 plant, £2.50 manufacturing) to create a £16 book. But

6 Widow at top of page

originate in the past.'
    'But that's absurd where you are concerned.'
    'It's Stephen I'm worried about. He survived the original
scandal only to get involved in this.'
    'But he is not, as you put it, involved. He did not murder
Edmund. He and Tony were standing there together while
the photographs were being taken. Tony has told me exactly
how it was.'

style is wanted. As proofreader, you must recognize the distinctions and check that they have been applied consistently.

For units of measurement (such as '60 km' and for 'p. 21', 'Fig. 3', 'Vol. I', etc., spaced style is still generally thought preferable. Even when these are spaced, however, some expressions are always closed up, for example '3.1', '3.2', etc. (to denote figures or exercises), '£16' (and other symbols for currency), 'p.m.', 'B.C.', 'i.e.' and similar abbreviations. (Butcher, *Copy-editing* gives a helpful list.)

On people's initials, opinions are fairly evenly divided, some preferring the traditional spaced style, some the more compact closed-up style. Others again might retain some space but omit the full stops between the initials.

Raised and low decimal point

In handwriting most of us put a decimal point above the line (this is called a raised or median point). On a typewriter this is not possible, so we have become very used to understanding a low point (an ordinary full stop on the line) as a decimal. Schoolbooks often use the raised point; others usually the low point. Needless to say, they should never be mixed as they are in example 5. (*Hart's Rules* favours a low decimal point for normal usage but raised for decimal currency; there seems little logic to this distinction.)

Lining and old-style figures

Again, there is a modern style and a traditional style for figures (numbers). Although this is not one of the distinctions specifically mentioned in the examples shown, several instances of each style are included.

- **Lining** figures (such as those in examples 1, 2B and 5) are all the same height (the full cap height), just as they are on a typewriter.

- **Old-style** (or non-lining) figures vary in height. Look carefully at the figures in examples 2A, 3 and 4. You'll see that some (such as 2) are the x-height (like small caps). Some (such as 6) have an **ascender** (that is, they rise above the x-height, like an 'h' or 'k'); others (such as 9) have a **descender** (a tail going below the line, like 'g' or 'y').

Some typefaces will only have one style of figure: in others you or your designer will be able to choose which to have. (Unlike the other points discussed so far, no specific marking is required in the typescript; a general instruction is sufficient.) The two styles are not usually found in the same book. (When this did happen in the example shown in Exercise 2.2 below, it was because correction lines for a new edition were set with lining figures and no one noticed until proof stage that the original had old-style figures.)

Now do Exercise 2.2 **G**

Widows

A widow is a short last line of a paragraph at the top of a page or column (example 6 opposite). Most publishers prefer to avoid these, although with **automatic page make-up** (division of the continuous text into pages by the typesetting machine) this can be difficult to achieve without additional expense. A line that is three-quarters of the usual length is acceptable. (Some would say that half a line is all right.)

Word-breaks at the end of a line

Most typesetting machines have an in-built **hyphenation program**, which determines where it is acceptable to break words when they will not fit on to a line. Since there are rival authorities on the subject (given in full at the end of this unit), proofs may not always conform to the system you expect.

In general, it is sensible to accept hyphenation decisions unless they are startlingly wrong or misleading.

The main principles are:

- At least two letters should remain on the first line; at least three letters should be taken over.

- *Collins Gem Dictionary*'s major criterion is that the first part of the word should not lead the reader to mispronounce it (and therefore find the second half unexpected). So, 'psycho-logical' is fine but 'psychol-ogist' and 'psy-chology' are preferred to the etymological break at 'psycho-'.

- The *Oxford Minidictionary* regards etymology (the derivation of the word) as the major criterion and would divide all these at 'psycho-'.

To complicate the issue further, Americans go by syllables (rather than pronunciation or etymology), regularly dividing between consonants, even in such cases as 'pos-sible'.

Answer to Exercise 2.1 (first paragraph only)

He sat down facing the huge chart with
all the lines and the millipede names of
slow stations alongside it. Nothing much
has happened. Nothing much would
happen. The traffic of the afternoon was
usual very slow and very sparse. Perhaps
from some side station near a mine, a
quiet line of open wagons with cracked
boards held together with rusty plates
and rivets would slide along the hot
rails to a languid stop some forgotten
place to wait for other slow days when it
would get ~~to be~~ shunted down to the sea
far away

Margin marks: r/ ; them/ ; was/ (5) ; (deletion symbol)/ (10) ; back and ; and left-margin marks d/, e/, >/, 9/, ⊙/

- Remember that each correction should be followed either by an oblique stroke (if you are substituting) or by an insertion mark (if you are adding). Never put the insertion mark *before* the letter or word to be added.

- Use (symbol) when you are deleting a letter or letters in the middle of a word. Use (symbol) when you are deleting a whole word, or the beginning or end of a word.

- Make sure that your correction in the margin is on exactly the same line as the error. The typesetter needs to be able to see immediately which line you are referring to.

- Fitting in several symbols relating to the same line is no problem in the right-hand margin. It can be more difficult in the left-hand margin. Start far enough out to the left to allow room for two or three corrections.

- Practise the deletion sign carefully as it is an awkward one. It originated in 'd' for 'delete' plus the oblique. (For this reason, some people find an additional oblique stroke following it redundant but most proofreaders do include one.) Refer back to the symbol list, rather than my marking, as a model for developing your own style. (Mine is based on older versions.)

Now do Exercise 2.3

---

*In this case no copy is provided: you are **reading for sense**. (It is helpful to have one person reading the proofs against copy and another, often the author, reading them for sense: each will spot different kinds of error.) Not having the copy, you have no way of allocating responsibility for errors, so just use a red pen. Keep the proofreading symbols in view, follow them accurately and position your corrections as carefully as you can alongside the relevant line.*

Review of Exercise 2.3

You **will have** found plenty of places where corrections are clearly necessary, even without having the copy to check against. (By contrast, in Exercise 2.1 there were several phrases that, although not following copy, made sense as they stood, and plenty of incorrect words that would go undetected by an automatic spelling checker.)

Amending l. 1 to 'seventeenth' (in view of the dates on ll. 5 and 13) is probably safe but it is better to raise a query. Similarly, query the discrepancy in the spelling of the surname on ll. 14 and 21. 'Somersetshire' (l. 2) should be 'Somerset'.

On ll. 1 and 2 'eighteenth-century farm' and 'old-fashioned house' are usually hyphenated, although the unhyphenated versions are possible if consistently used. (See Unit 10 for such hyphens.)

Where two errors occur together, they may usually be marked as one correction. For example, if you kept 'fifty' as a word on l. 15, changing l. 22 to match and adding the comma may be accomplished in the same proof mark:

70̶ tall   seventy,/

Whether or not you have someone to check your work, put this exercise aside until tomorrow. Then look at it again with a fresh eye.

■ Scan it to see what you have missed. (When there are so many errors together, few proofreaders will find everything.) Look out especially for whole areas you did not think about the first time – punctuation, perhaps?

■ Assess how far you have succeeded in making your corrections as clear as possible to the typesetter.

Smudges and broken letters

Since proofs are usually photocopied, some of the smudges may come from dust, etc., on the glass of the photocopying machine. If, for example, a smudge (or a hair, which makes a letter look broken) appears in the same spot on each page, it is probably on the photocopier and you do not need to mark it. If you are in any doubt, however, do mark the problem so that the typesetter can check.

Now do Exercise 2.4

This time you have the copy again (on the left), so remember to check regularly against it. Unlike either of the previous proofreading exercises, this is a genuine example of page proofs. For this reason, the typescript folios and proof pages do not match up exactly. Only check the sections of the proof for which you have copy.

Review of Exercise 2.4

Even this genuine example contains more errors than the average set of page proofs. When you are proofreading good typesetting, it is important not to switch off, assuming all is well – that is bound to be the moment when the typesetter and his or her proofreader lost concentration too. Did you find fourteen red (typesetter's) errors? (This does not include two blobs and a broken letter that you may have marked.) If not, look again.

The typesetter saved you from one error by ignoring the comma that the editor forgot to remove after 'viable' (copy l. 23). Notice that the editor removed one split infinitive, 'to not do' (copy l. 14) but left 'to largely exclude' (copy ll. 10–11) because it is part of a direct quotation. Such quotations should not be altered or made consistent with the rest of the text. (Split infinitives are discussed more fully in Unit 7; quotations in Unit 11.)

In Unit 12 we return to the use of 'their' on copy l. 20. It should not be 'corrected' here as this style may have been used deliberately throughout.

Additional commas (in blue) might be helpful on proof ll. 61 (before 'for'), 62 (before 'and') and 73 (after 'co-residence'). However, such changes should have been made at the editing stage. Correction at page proof (the stage reached here) is disproportionately expensive. Whether you can afford such niceties will depend on the overall level of correction and the budget.

(If you are already accustomed to the author–date reference system, discussed in Unit 19, you may have spotted that the date and page number on copy ll. 7 and 11 would be better together. Again, you might not be able to afford to correct this in proof.)

In Unit 4 we return to look in detail at the editor's marking on the *typescript* in Exercises 2.1 and 2.4. The importance of spotting problems at that stage should be clear by now.

Gappy and tight lines

Because there were so many corrections in Exercises 2.1 and 2.3, there was no point in marking lines where there was too much space between words. In each case, the whole passage would be re-run and you'd see a corrected **revise proof**. That would be your opportunity to make sure that the end result was pleasing.

Uneven spacing is often a particular problem in justified setting (explained on p. 6 above) when the **measure** (line length) is narrow, as in Exercise 2.1 (The Morse Machine). Often the best option may be to have a gappy line (or even additional space between letters) rather than divide relatively short words.

In **unjustified** or **ragged right** setting (where the right margin is left uneven), there is no problem about gappy or tight lines because there is a standard space between all words. This is why it is often used when setting to a narrow measure, for example for the blurb on the jacket flap.

In unjustified setting the usual convention is to avoid word-breaks altogether, so some lines may be very much longer or very much shorter than the average. The overall shape can often be improved at proof by taking a word or two over to the next line or back to the previous one. Alternatively, the designer may specify a minimum length of line and allow occasional word-breaks in order to achieve it.

Traditional proofreading symbols

The current marking system is followed in this book. You must, however, also be able to recognize the traditional abbreviations as they are still widely used. In the new system, all the marks are symbols; in the old system, you put similar symbols in the text but amplified them in the margin by using abbreviations of English (or Latin) words.

cap	capital
l.c.	lower case
s.c.	small caps
ital	italics
n.p.	new paragraph
f.o.	full out (no indent)
r.o.	run on
#	space
t.b.	take back
t.o.	take over
trs	transpose
stet	'let it stand' (keep original, ignore my mark)

Further reading

The British Standards Institution is contemplating a further revision or perhaps reconciliation of the proofreading symbols, so look out for any news of this. The present standards are:

BS 5261: Part 2: 1976
BS 5261: Part 3: 1989

The latter deals particularly with mathematics, as we shall see in Unit 15.

The two (sometimes conflicting) authorities on word-division are:

Collins Gem Dictionary of Spelling and Word Division (Collins, London, 1968)

The Oxford Minidictionary of Spelling and Word-Division (Clarendon Press, Oxford, 1986)

Hart's Rules also has a section on the subject, in broad (but not complete) agreement with the *Oxford Minidictionary.*

Answer to Exercise 2.1 (excluding first paragraph)

After a while it was possible not to be
aware of the noises of the fans. on the   15
Morse machine there was a long Roll
that could only raise thoughts of people
going irretrievably crazy at the long end
of the Telegraph. Maybe also the famous   20
rattle of men preparing too die. In a
while, when it was no longer possible to
ignore the rattle/the MAN tapped back
one for silence, then taped out the
message, 'Shut up.'   25

The roll came again, definitely insis-
tent. The maniac at the end of the line
has grown indignant. (Another rap.
Short silence.) Then the man asks in
half/conciliation, 'Who be you?'   30

A roll now, very long and very sense-
less. But at the very end it carries a
signature, 'Obuasi.'

That at least was some thing, and
should deserve a reply.   35

The man held the Morse knob again,
lightly: 'Hello.'

With amazing spede the answer
comes back, this time entirely coherent,
decipherable at the last. 'Why do we   40
agree to on go like this?' Then again the
rattle.

The question was repeated several times,
alternating with long answered rolls on
the machine. To stop himself form   45
cutting the sound in anger, the man
turned and watched the fan, but then
another feeble useless movement would
happen and the blades would be drawn
though another arc Only a long hour   50
later did the noise finally stop—4:30
p.m.

* Blue corrections

UNIT 3
The Production Process

With some trepidation, in this unit I attempt a brief overview of the production process in an extremely diverse industry. If you are already working in a publishing house, this may help you to see how your function fits into the overall process.

Project development

As we saw in Unit 1, the process of producing a book begins with the author and commissioning editor. Sometimes, for example in fiction, the author may write the book first and then (with or without the help of a literary agent) look for a publishing house to accept it. At the other end of the spectrum, for example in school textbook or **trade book** (glossy adult non-fiction) publishing, a commissioning editor may have an idea for a book and then seek out an author (or team of authors) with the appropriate expertise to write it. Between these extremes lie numerous other scenarios. For example, in academic publishing, an author might write a proposal and a commissioning editor shape it into something more specifically adapted to the market.

Whatever the project's genesis, there are likely to be assessment stages during its development. The outline proposal and/or drafts of the typescript may be sent to specialists for **readers' reports**. There may be extensive discussions or workshops involving authors and editors to decide the precise coverage, kind of illustration, etc. At the same time the project's financial viability will be assessed through market research, on the one hand, and estimates of costs, on the other. It may go through approval procedures and committees at the publishing house. The author may be asked to revise the work extensively, recast both content and style, recheck facts, etc.

Editing the typescript

Some editing may be done on drafts during the development stage (by in-house or freelance staff)

but the bulk of the editorial work normally begins with the arrival of the author's final typescript. The flow chart and network diagram opposite outline the production process for a fairly simple book.

As we saw in Unit 1, the amount of editing required may range from extensive rewriting to a brisk check on consistency. A **cast-off** is usually done (by the editor or by a production controller) to determine the likely **extent** (the number of pages in print). Casting off involves reckoning up the number of words or characters on each page (or on an average page) of the typescript and converting that into the number of words or characters on a page set in a particular type size, estimating the space needed for tables and figures and making an allowance for material still to come (such as the index). If the extent turns out longer than expected, the editor's tasks may include cutting.

Editing often gives rise to queries to be answered by the author (or sometimes by the editor, using a library). As we have seen, whenever possible, the edited typescript (or a good photocopy of it) should be sent back to the author with the list of queries, to make sure that he or she approves of the editing before money is spent on typesetting.

Showing the author the result of the editing and clearing up queries may sometimes be done at galley proof for books going through that stage (see below). If extensive rewriting has been done, for example, it may be easier for the author to see the results on a galley proof than to try to work out the effect of handwritten additions. Amendment of galley proofs is less costly than amendment of page proofs, though still to be avoided where possible.

Authors' disks

Many books in certain areas of publishing are now presented by the author on computer disk. In other areas, the author's material will be **keyed** (typed) on to computer disks in house before editorial work starts.

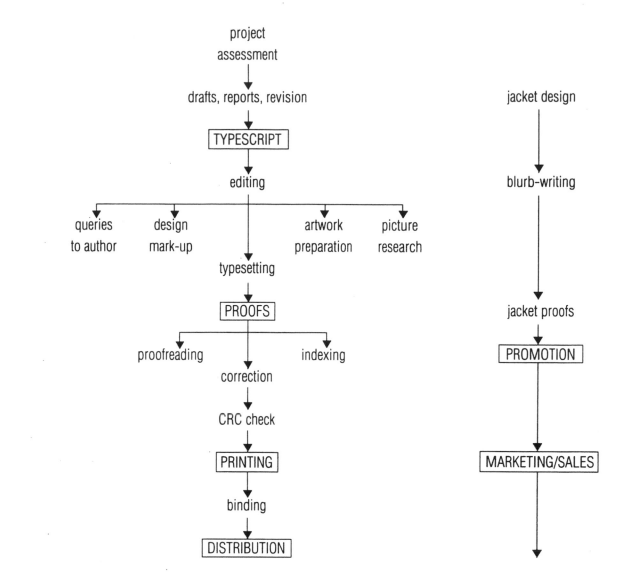

Flow chart of the publishing process

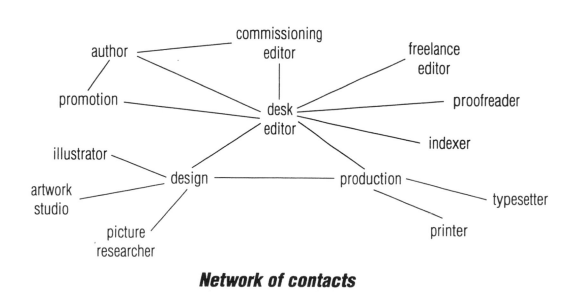

Network of contacts

This simplifies global changes (for example standardization to 'USA' rather than 'U.S.A.' or ensuring a space after 'p.' for page references). On the other hand, it sometimes means that the editor has to become familiar with codes (for example for accents and special symbols) before being able to check the text adequately.

Much the same editorial technique applies whether you are working on a typescript or on a **hard-copy printout** from a disk. If, on the other hand, you are **editing on screen**, the skills of communicating your meaning to a typesetter become irrelevant: you are making the changes yourself. In all cases, however, the content of the editorial work to be done is the same.

It is always important to have a version of the disk or hard-copy printout that retains the author's original, in case there are disputes about editorial changes and in case something is inadvertently deleted.

If you are working on hard copy, ensure that you have an *up-to-date* printout. Authors sometimes send in a printout that does not include their last-minute alterations to the disk; equally they sometimes write changes on the printout that have not been made on the disk.

The labour cost of correcting the disk (if the author does not take on that responsibility) may mean that you have to limit editorial amendments if the method is to be cost-effective. You may, for example, decide not to convert the text to your usual house style. Certainly it is crucial to weigh carefully the decision to use an author's disk according not only to the complexity of symbols and layout but also to the standard of writing and consistency. Ensure that authors are given clear guidelines on preferred styles early enough for them to incorporate them on the disk from the beginning.

Design

Book design involves specifying typefaces and sizes and the typographical treatment and spacing of different features such as headings, **extracts** (long quotations), tables and boxes.

The editor may simply be expected to **code** the various design features (levels of heading, etc.) so that a designer can quickly decide on their typographical treatment. The designer may then do a detailed **typographical mark-up** of the typescript. Alternatively, or as well, the designer may provide a **typesetting specification** (type spec) for the typesetter to follow, using the editor's coding of the typescript.

In some fields, for example in an academic journal or series, a standard typographical design may be followed. In that case the editor (rather than a designer) may be required to do a detailed mark-up, either as he or she goes along or as a separate operation. Alternatively, because the style is standard, simple coding on the typescript, together with a type spec (and perhaps specimen pages), is often sufficient.

More complicated books will not usually conform to a standard design but will need individual attention. In some publishing houses this design role may still be combined with the editorial role. As with the rewriting and detailed editing discussed in Unit 1, if you are wearing the two hats, it makes sense to go through twice, in this case once to edit (coding as you go) and once to finalize the design.

We look at straightforward coding in Units 4–5 and at more detailed matters of design in Units 24–5.

Illustrations

The illustrations are assembled either before or during the editing stage.

- Technical figures (diagrams, graphs, maps, etc.) may need to be drawn, by a finished artist (one preparing camera-ready **artwork**) or an artwork studio. Sometimes the author is able to provide figures in a state suitable for direct reproduction, but usually he or she only provides **roughs**.

- Creative artwork (original drawings of people, animals, etc.) may need to be drawn by an illustrator, usually following the author's or editor's brief, first as roughs, then as final artwork in black-and-white or colour. In children's books the author and illustrator may collaborate from an early stage and present the final typescript and illustrations together.

- Photographs (prints or transparencies) may need to be obtained, perhaps by a **picture researcher**, from photo libraries, art galleries, etc. Alternatively, a photographer may be commissioned to shoot photographs specifically for the book.

We return to these topics in Units 26–8.

Proof stages

The text, tables and figures may go through one or several stages of proof. The diagram opposite shows two possible routes.

- Fiction and many academic books, where text is in a single column per page and the number of tables and figures is moderate, normally go direct

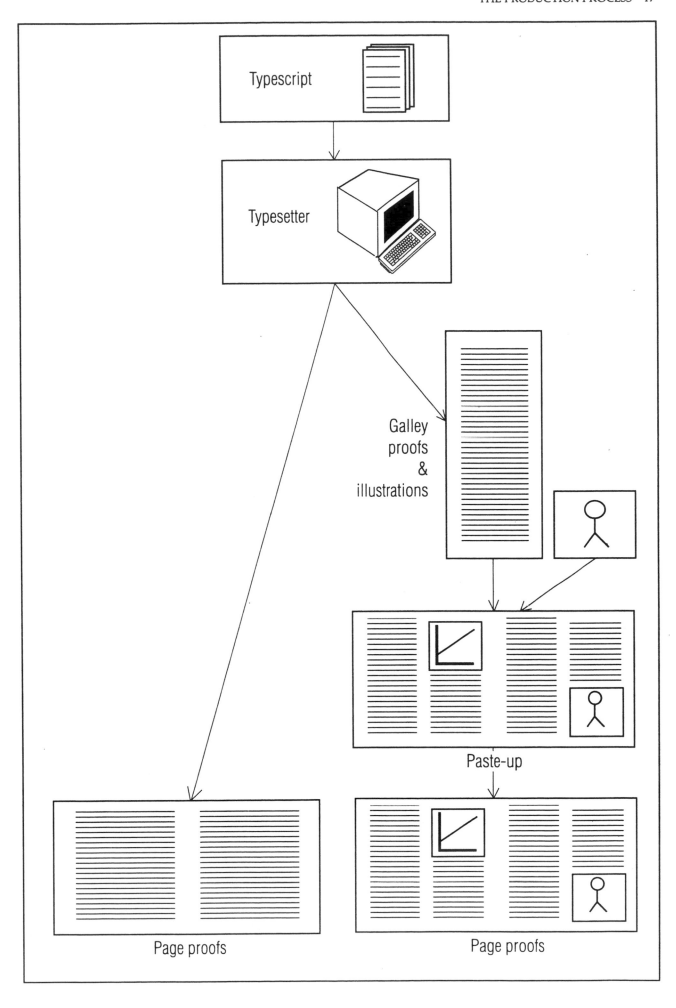

Typescript

Typesetter

Galley
proofs
&
illustrations

Paste-up

Page proofs

Page proofs

to **page proof** from typescript (usually slotting in already drawn and proofed figures; sometimes leaving measured spaces for them).

■ More complex books, especially those set with two or three columns per page and/or highly illustrated, may first require **galley proofs** (long sheets of text not yet divided into pages). These will be proofread and checked against the designer's typographical specification.

Then the designer may do a **rough paste-up** (taking into account any changes marked in the galleys). This consists of copies of the typesetting and illustrations pasted on to page-size **grids** to show the typesetter how to make up each **double-page spread**. The editor (and/or author) may be asked to cut or expand text to fit the pages, as we shall see in Unit 20.

Sometimes illustrations will be drawn after paste-up so that they fit into the spaces available. The **sizing** of photographs (determining appropriate sizes at which to reproduce them) may be done at this stage too. The typesetter then makes up page proofs.

■ Alternatively, especially for shorter books, you may have galley proofs, then revise galley proofs (with all the corrections made), and the designer will use the original **bromides** (or **repro**) – the shiny end-product of the typesetting machine – to do an exact paste-up in order to create **camera-ready copy (CRC)**.

At the first proof stage, whether it is galley or page, the proofreader checks that the original copy has been followed, as you did in Unit 2. At later checking stages the proofreader usually only has to read **correction lines** (the particular lines or paragraphs altered) and ensure that the specified layout has been followed.

At any of these stages your task may be to **collate** proofs. This means creating a single **marked set** of proofs, often using the set marked by the proofreader and transferring on to it, say, the author's marks. In the process you may need to exercise your judgement on which blue changes (whether the proofreader's or the author's) are really necessary and worth the expense.

Whatever route is taken, whether direct to page proof, or galleys and paste-up, there is usually a final opportunity to check the CRC or film from which the book will be printed.

Proofs of **halftones** (photographs, artwork with complex tints, etc.) and colour illustrations often come separately. The originals will be sent to the printer, with correctly sized copies in the CRC to show their position.

Desk-top publishing systems

As the diagram opposite shows, the whole process can be significantly simplified with a desk-top publishing (**DTP**) system. The DTP can generate text, tables and a range of computer graphics for figures. It can also make up all these elements into pages in several columns. Programs are available for scanning halftones and producing creative artwork. The advantages of a DTP are greater freedom of design, and speed and simplicity of page make-up and of cutting and expanding text to fit.

Index, captions, acknowledgements

The index is not usually compiled until page-proof stage, when the final page numbers are known. The work may be done by the author or an indexer (often freelance).

Captions are sometimes not written until paste-up stage, when the space available and the precise illustrations to be included are known.

Seeking permission from copyright-owners to include lengthy quotations or to reproduce illustrations should begin as early as possible but, again, may not be finalized until page-proof stage.

We look at all these in Units 28–30.

Even workings

For economy, it is usually important to fit a book within a multiple of 32 or possibly 16 pages. This is because most (though by no means all) printing is done in 32-page signatures (or sections). Each **signature** consists of a large sheet folded again and again to make 32 (or 16 or 64) pages. So at paste-up or page proof, the **prelims** (preliminary pages such as the contents list) or the **endmatter** (the index, etc.) may have to be squeezed or spread (to avoid too many blank pages) to fit an even working.

This is partly why it is helpful (at least in books going directly to page proof) to use roman numerals for prelims, only starting the arabic numbering at Chapter 1. Arabic page 1 always has to be a **recto** (a right-hand page). Subsequent odd pages are all rectos and page 2 is always a **verso** (as are all subsequent even pages).

Since, therefore, there must always be an even number of pages in the prelims, saving a *single* page may not help. It is usual to start most items in the prelims on a recto. So, if space is short, you can often save a whole **leaf** (recto and verso) by moving a one-page item on to a verso. Prelims are discussed in greater detail in Unit 31.

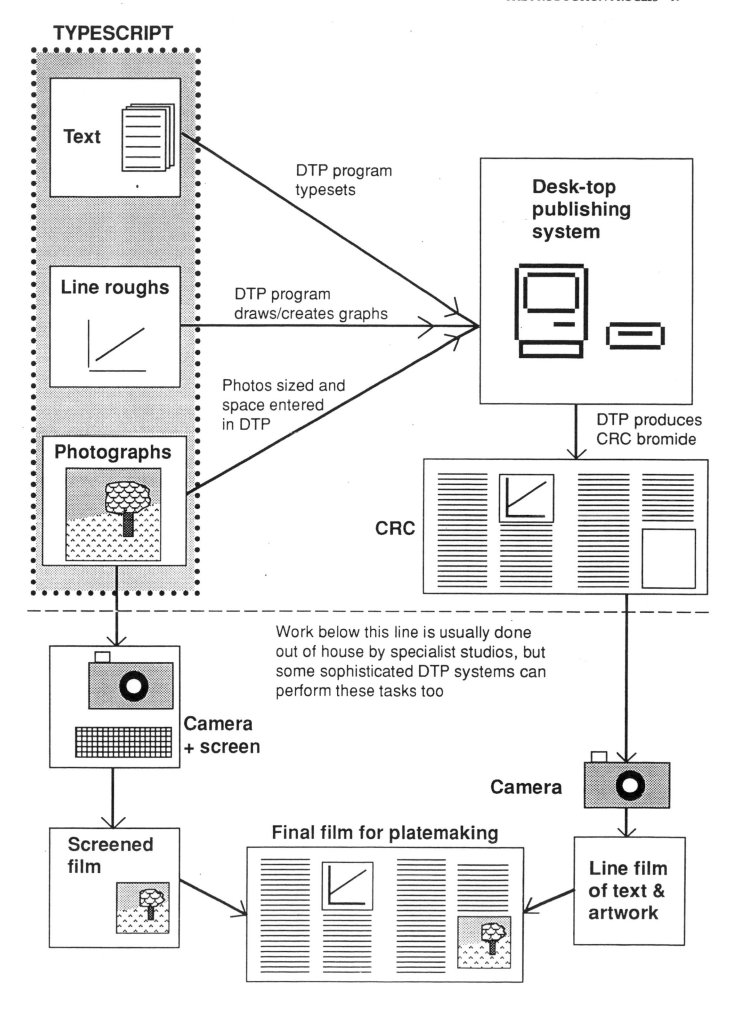

TYPESCRIPT

Text

DTP program typesets

Desk-top publishing system

Line roughs

DTP program draws/creates graphs

Photos sized and space entered in DTP

Photographs

DTP produces CRC bromide

CRC

Work below this line is usually done out of house by specialist studios, but some sophisticated DTP systems can perform these tasks too

Camera + screen

Camera

Screened film

Final film for platemaking

Line film of text & artwork

Some books, such as primary school textbooks, are planned from the beginning in double-page spreads, to divide the material neatly into sections and achieve a specific extent.

You will quickly become used to the ideal extents most frequently used in your books:

In the shorter range:	32,	64,	96,	128
In the medium range:	160,	192,	224,	256
In the longer range:	288,	320,	352,	384

Remember though that these do not apply to all book sizes or all kinds of printing machinery. (For example, some books, especially in full-colour work, print in 24-page signatures.) Do check with the design or production department or direct with the printer if there is any doubt.

Book sizes (or formats)

Each area of publishing traditionally uses different book sizes or **format**s (now all measured in millimetres, usually cited by **trimmed page** size, always specifying the *vertical* measurement first). Most books are **portrait** (that is, the vertical measurement is longer than the horizontal) but some are **landscape** (the horizontal measurement is longer than the vertical).

In academic publishing, the commonest sizes used are Demy Octavo (216 × 138 mm) and Royal Octavo (234 × 156 mm). In educational and trade-book publishing, Crown Quarto (246 × 189 mm) is frequently used. (Octavo may be abbreviated as 8vo and Quarto as 4to.) In paperback fiction, A format (178 × 111 mm) and B format (198 × 129 mm) are the most common sizes.

Apart from cost differences, there are often marketing reasons for selecting a particular format. (B format, for instance, is used for more up-market fiction; Royal Octavo is thought to look more authoritative than Demy.) On the design side, the shape of illustrations or maps may demand a particular format.

Production

Look back at the network of contacts diagram on p. 15. The production controller is usually responsible for placing and chasing typesetting, printing and binding. Again, with increasing use of DTP systems, in some firms the typesetting component may diminish and production become largely confined to the printing and binding processes (the **manufacture** of the book). In others, production is increasingly being combined with design.

The production department is concerned with estimating and controlling costs, the overall scheduling of the project and quality control of the finished product. All the other members of the team, including the editor, also participate in and contribute to each of these areas.

Promotion

The promotion or publicity department (sometimes part of a marketing department that combines sales and promotion) is usually responsible for catalogues, review copies, advertising – indeed, the whole promotional campaign for a book. The editor and commissioning editor will liaise with them and the author (in different ways, according to the company) to finalize the jacket or cover illustration and design, and the blurbs about the book and its author. (We look at these in Unit 32.)

The timing of promotion may depend on a particular **market window**: the period when bookshops stock up for the Christmas selling season; the period when lecturers are deciding which books to recommend for the next academic year. To take full advantage of this market window, the promotion department and sales representatives need adequate **lead time**, with jackets or manufactured books available, in order to launch the project successfully. Everyone in the team – editor, design and production – has to take account of these marketing needs and schedules.

Now do Exercise 3.1   **G**

Further reading

A useful glossary of terms is to be found in:

Judith Butcher, *Copy-editing* (Cambridge University Press, Cambridge, 3rd edition, forthcoming)

For an illuminating view of the different roles and functions within publishing, as well as career paths and prospects, see:

Giles N. Clark, *Inside Book Publishing: A Career Builder's Guide* (Blueprint/Book House Training Centre, London, 1988)

UNIT 4
Marking the Typescript

From this point, we concentrate on the all-important activity of editing the typescript. In this unit we look back at the editor's marking of the copy used in Unit 2 and learn to do likewise.

The term **copy** (from newspaper terminology) is used in phrases such as 'reading proofs against copy' or 'there's some copy missing from Chapter 2'. The copy usually takes the form of a typescript. Rarely today is it a manuscript (handwritten copy) in the true sense, although the term is still current as a synonym for typescript. Increasingly often the script you are working on may be a hard-copy printout from an author's computer disk that is to be **interfaced** with the typesetting machine. (For more on authors' disks and editing on screen, refer back to Unit 3; we also return to them in the Consolidation section at the end of the book.)

The typescript should come from the author typed on one side of the paper and double-spaced throughout (including any notes, references and long quotations).

The pages of a typescript are called **folios**. The term 'page' should be reserved for the typeset (printed) page of a proof or book. (Somewhat confusingly, the word 'folio' is also used for the actual page *number* on the typeset page of a book.) Folio may be abbreviated to 'fo.' (plural 'fos') as in this book or to 'f.' (plural 'ff.').

I say 'typeset' page of a proof because strictly speaking the page is not printed until multiple copies are made. Similarly, we distinguish between the typesetter, who is responsible for **origination** (up to camera-ready copy (CRC) or film) and the printer, who is responsible for manufacturing (printing and binding) the books.

Now Look at the Copy (Typescript) for Exercise 2.1 (The Morse Machine)

Find examples of the editor's marking of:

- addition of a letter
- deletion of a letter
- substitution of a letter and of whole words
- transposition of letters
- addition of a stop, a comma and an opening quote
- alteration of double to single quotes
- marking of a capital and of small caps
- marking of italic

All these symbols should look familiar: they are very similar to those used for marking proofs. What is the main difference? The difference – and it is a very important one – is that in a typescript *all marking should be between the lines*, not in the margin. Why? (Think about the person who is to follow your marking in each case.)

The marginal mark in a proof is designed to catch the eye of a busy typesetter skimming through to make corrections. He or she needn't look at any lines without problems. At the initial typesetting stage, the situation is quite different. The typesetter must read every word of the typescript, so any amendments should be written as close as possible to the sentence or word affected.

Notice that the same convention of circling a full stop, but not a comma, is followed in editing as in marking proofs. Wherever possible, squeeze the comma in on the line: if you have to use an insertion mark it can look like an apostrophe.

Just as for proofreading, only use the symbol: do not write 'ital', 'bold', 'n.p.', etc., as well. Simple underlining is all that is necessary to indicate italic, a wavy line underneath to indicate bold.

The only complication is that sometimes (in educational books for example) actual underlining is required as well as italic. In that case it is best to keep the standard underline to mean italic and use another device (a highlighter or a dashed line) to indicate true underlining. You'll need to explain your system at the beginning for the typesetter, since there is as yet no convention covering this point.

As you can see, marking a typescript is really far simpler than marking proofs. You do not, for example, need the deletion symbol ⌐ at all. It is enough to draw a clear vertical stroke through a letter, or a horizontal stroke through a word or phrase, with short verticals to show clearly where the deletion begins and ends.

Similarly, if you wish to remove underlining (that is, to have words set in roman, not italic), mark it thus:

Another rap

It might seem even easier to 'white out' the underlining, but you should not normally use correcting fluid on a typescript, except to correct your own mistakes. The author's original must remain visible under your editing in case of disagreements.

As you have seen, a change to capitals is shown in much the same way as in proofs. However, the convention for changing to lower case in a typescript is quite different:

the Reader will see   for a single letter

the READER will see   for a word or words

It is very important to make the stroke diagonal (not vertical, as a deletion would be) and to position it at the top of the letter.

Notice on l. 32 that the dash has been marked as a closed-up em rule. Check that this has been correctly interpreted in the proof. An en rule would be shown by writing 'N' on top. Some editors prefer to circle the 'M' or 'N'. Since there is little likelihood that the typesetter will think an actual capital 'M' or 'N' is wanted, I prefer to keep the sign simple. It is usual to mark the style of dash throughout a typescript. (Alternatively, a general instruction may be given.)

End-of-line hyphens

When reading a *proof*, you check that end-of-line hyphens do not divide a word in an unacceptable place. This is important because the proof shows the word-breaks as they will appear in the printed book. This is not the case in a typescript – the whole thing is yet to be typeset and word-breaks may occur in quite different places when you see the proofs.

The problem in a typescript is that the typesetter may not know whether a hyphen appearing at the end of a line is to be retained wherever the word appears in the typeset line – for example in 'pre-war' or 'non-lining' – or whether it is just the typist's word-break. (In computer parlance, is it a **hard hyphen** or a **soft hyphen**?)

It is therefore helpful if the editor marks all end-of-line hyphens:

If it should stay, wherever the word falls: one-

If it should not stay in mid-line: one

The typesetter should not have to read on in order to find out that the word is 'one-way street' (requiring a hyphen) or 'oneself' (one word).

Paragraphs

The first line of The Morse Machine is typed without an indent, and the typesetter should follow that style unless instructed otherwise. It is quite common to set the first line of a passage or chapter **full out** (that is, beginning at the left margin).

Other paragraphs (often called **paras** by editors) are marked with a square box. This denotes an **em space** (or **quad**): the typesetter is being asked to indent each new para 1 em.

If the typesetter should follow the typed style, why has the editor marked this indent each time? Provided a typescript has been typed regularly, showing paragraphs in the same way throughout, a general instruction may be given instead. In this case, however, the author has not been consistent (see l. 22). Some editors prefer always to mark paragraphs. Certainly if you begin marking them in a typescript, you must keep it up to the end.

If you don't know how paras are to be treated, it is better to use the 'new para' sign throughout (as on l. 23), rather than the 'indent' symbol. If you *do* know how paras are to be treated (for example because your firm follows a standard style), it is safer to show the desired form. The most common options are **indented** (usually indented 1 em; sometimes 2 ems), without any additional space between paras, or **blocked**, where all lines, even the first, begin full out, usually with a space (perhaps a line or half a line) between paras.

Colours to use

My preference is to use blue for editing a typescript. This is because I return the top copy to the author for checking before typesetting and red marking looks offputtingly like a schoolteacher's. Also, if you use blue for the editing, you can switch to red to distinguish instructions to the typesetter. Some editors prefer to work in red throughout. (If you send a photocopy rather than the original with queries, make sure that whatever colour you use for editing shows up clearly – there can be problems with both red and blue.)

Other editors use pencil but this is generally thought dangerous since it can too easily be rubbed out or obscured as the typescript goes through its later processes. Correcting fluid enables you to edit just as flexibly and effectively in pen.

A soft pencil can, however, be helpful for indicating queries and suggestions to the author: these can then be rubbed out to present a neat typescript to the typesetter.

Do not use black. You need to be able to check back through your own editing quickly and punctuation, etc., added in black will not show up. Green is often reserved for the designer.

Style instructions in the exercises

Various style instructions are given at the beginning of the next and most other exercises because such decisions between alternatives usually have to be made when you are editing. Often you cannot just impose your own preferences or accept the author's but have to follow a set style. Indeed, you may already have become so used to your own firm's style that you find it difficult to change. Throughout this book the style deliberately varies in order to help you to adapt to specified styles, as you may have to during your career as an editor (particularly if you work freelance).

Note that you are asked to apply **double quotes.** (For the moment you can ignore 'single inner', which is explained before Exercise 4.2.)

With a **list comma** (or **Oxford comma**), the standard example would read 'red, white, and blue'. The extra comma before the 'and' is used by Oxford University Press (and is therefore in *Hart's Rules*) but is not otherwise widely favoured in British English. (It is much more widespread in the USA.)

It is quite common to set 'AD' and 'BC' in small caps, especially when figures are to be old style (or non-lining). As you saw in Exercise 2.2 (Distinctions in Print), old-style figures merge into the text better, as do small caps, so these forms might be chosen for a book full of dates. If, on the other hand, lining figures are to be used, full-cap 'AD' and 'BC' will match up better.

Now do Exercise 4.1

Remember that you are marking a typescript, not a proof.

Review of Exercise 4.1

Check your work against the sample answer on the next page. As well as making sure that you found most of the mistakes, compare your marking technique carefully.

The additional 'l' in 'collapsed' could equally well be added before the hyphen at the end of l. 8. (Remember that this is not a proof, so we are not concerned here with acceptable and unacceptable word-division.)

Notice that if you insert a hyphen by hand there is no need to identify it as such. A hyphen is assumed *unless* you mark for an en rule or an em rule.

You may have been tempted to put a hyphen into 'highly placed' on l. 34. Resist the urge: this is not a parallel situation to 'eighteenth-century farm' (in Exercise 2.3). An adverb, by definition, modifies another word (usually a verb but often an adjective) and a word with the suffix -ly is unmistakably an adverb. So it requires no hyphen to connect it with the word it modifies.

The use of capitals may have concerned you too. The lower-case 'eastern' has been left on l. 22 because its use is general, whereas 'the East' and 'the West' (in the sense of major cultural divisions in the world) are often given capitals (ll. 12, 20) to distinguish them from points of the compass.

As the passage demonstrates, decision-making on hyphens and capitals forms a significant part of everyday editing. We examine them both in more detail in Unit 10.

Now Look at the Copy for Exercise 2.4 (Caring), fos 145 and 146

Sample answer to Exercise 4.1

Silk was at first rather shocking to the Early Romans, a rough
farming and fighting people. In a major Battle with the Parthians
at Carrhae in 53 B.C., the Romans, already at a disadvantage
against the powerful Parthian archers, were completely disrupted
when the Parthians unfurled their brilliantly dyed irridescent   5
silk banners, apparently the first silk seen ever by the roman
troops. The affect was devastating. The roman attempt to
imitate Alexander the great's triumphs in Asia quickly collapsed, and the Roman eagles — the standards of the defeated
legions — were taken up onto the Iranian plateau to decorate   10
Parthian palaces on the Silk Road.

( )

For the Romans, silk was also a symbol of Eastern decadance.
Cleopatra, queen of Egypt, may have owed some of her reput-
ation as a seductress to her love of dressing in fine silks.
This was, perhaps, a more daring attire that it might seem, for   15
many of the sliks of early times were extremely sheer gauzes
— the Indians called them "woven wind" — not the later and heavier
satins, damasks and brocades, nor even the light but more opaque
fabrics of modern times.

( )

In the first century BC, silk was still rare in the west.   20
The Chinese may have penetrated halfway across Asia to open
the eastern half of the Silk Raod but the 5,000-mile route
remained long and tortuous. With peoples all along the way
battling to control a peice of the great trans-Asian highway,
only tiny amounts of the tissuelike fabric reached the West.   25
Even the richest and most powerful ROMANS wore only small pieces
— strips, circles or squares — of silk sown on to their
otherwise all-white wool, cotton or linen togas or tunics.
if these silk fragments were then dyed purple or embroidred
with gold and silver threads, their cost might increas forty-   30
fold. It is no wonder, given its expense and rarity, that dyed
silk was used to indicate high station. So, purple edging on
a toga was the mark of a patrician, as stripes of scarlet and
and purple identified a highly placed court soothsayer.

Note first how to mark as full out a para that has been typed indented. (The symbol is the same as for proofs.) The spaces between the typed paras have also been marked to be closed up.

The style wanted for a dash here is a spaced en rule. (Check that it was in fact used in the proof.) Show the spaces, even though the words are already typed spaced, in order to distinguish clearly between a dash and an en rule between words (as discussed in Unit 2).

If you are *removing* a hyphen between words, show clearly whether you want two separate words or one word:

every⌣day   OR   every⌢day

Whether or not an editor puts an insertion mark when making a change will depend on clarity. Just changing a word of the same length ('cf.' to 'see' on l. 5) does not require it. The longer change on l. 61 is clear enough too, but an insertion mark has been used on l. 23 as an extra pointer because the typesetter has to cast his or her eye back.

We noticed earlier that the editor should have deleted the comma on l. 23 when adding the dash. One of the commonest errors in editing is to forget to delete all the relevant words or punctuation when substituting. Typesetters often save you by realizing that you can't really want an obvious duplication. But it is your job, not theirs, to get the typescript right. (If you are working on a hard-copy printout, or editing on screen, there may be no such second chance.)

Headings

You will notice that the editor has written 'B' beside both the headings on the copy for Caring. If you look at the proof, you can probably see why. These two headings marked 'B' have been treated in the same way (both in italics). On l. 1 of the proof, however, before both these B headings and typeset in a more prominent style, in bold, you will see another heading. You can guess that the editor will have marked this 'A' in the typescript.

We call such marking **coding the subheads** within a chapter. The code 'A' is used for the heading for a major section of a chapter; 'B' for the heading for a subsection within a major section; 'C' for the heading for a sub-subsection, etc. Some chapters in a book or articles in a journal may only have A heads; others may have A and B heads; others again may require several levels. The coding shows that all A heads must be treated alike (for example set in bold); all B heads must be treated alike; and so on.

How do you as editor know what level each subhead should be? Only by reading the text carefully. You cannot always rely on the author (or the author's typist) to have made distinctions correctly or to have applied a system consistently. Naturally you should be guided by the system the author seems to be following (for example, capitals for major headings and lower case for minor ones) but do also think about the logic of the hierarchy of headings as you read. We address the problems more fully in Unit 5.

In Caring, the B heads in the copy are underlined and the B heads appear in italic in the proof, but this need not be the case. With such **generic coding**, the typesetter may be given a general instruction to set coded features in any way specified. So there is no need to show in the typescript that A subheads are to be bold or B subheads are to be italic: such decisions can be made later, when the book is designed. Nor should you mark space above and below headings: the specification will give precise instructions on that too.

Above these levels of subhead within the chapter comes the **chapter head**. This may take many forms: 'Chapter 1' or 'Chapter 1   Caring for the Elderly' or '1   Caring for the Elderly'. (In textbooks such as this, chapters are often called 'units' but you can still code them as chapter heads.) Mark all these elements together as 'ch hd' like this:

```
Chapter 3
The Life History of the Frog
```

Decisions on whether to include the word 'Chapter' and whether the number should appear on a separate line from the title are sometimes the editor's, sometimes the designer's. Whether headings of any level are **centred** or **ranged left** is certainly a question of design.

To ensure consistency, standardization of the use of capitals is best seen as the editor's responsibility, at least for the subheads within the chapter. Nothing you do by way of marking capitalization should prevent a designer from specifying that a particular level of heading is to be set *entirely* in caps or small caps. Marking should, however, prevent the confusion that sometimes arises in upper- and lower-case (**u/lc**) headings.

The two alternatives within u/lc setting are capitals for significant words (or **cap sig wds**) and minimum capitals (or **min caps**). (An alternative, perhaps clearer, name for min caps is **init cap and lc** – the **initial** being the first letter.) Try to find out which style is wanted before you begin editing a typescript.

It is particularly important to indicate cap sig wds specifically because there is disagreement about which words should have a capital. In the example above, for instance, some might prefer *The Life History of The Frog.* (Some might even capitalize '*Of*' as well.) The usual system, however, is to lower-case all prepositions (such as 'of') and all articles (such as 'the'). The treatment of verbs will vary according to their significance: 'has', 'do', etc., would be lower case but 'Elects' would take a capital.

Even for min caps, in which only the initial and proper names begin with a capital, specific marking is helpful. If, for example, a heading has been typed in capitals but you don't know whether it is to be set in capitals or u/lc, mark the initial and proper names thus:

THE CLIMATE OF WESTERN AUSTRALIA

This ensures that the designer and typesetter do not have to search through the text to find out whether the heading refers to the western half of the country in general or to the particular state, Western Australia.

Note that I have not shown that the heading is *in fact* to be set u/lc: that would be done by marking as we did for 'ROMANS' in Exercise 4.1 (Silk), l. 26. The designer is still free to set the whole heading in capitals.

As always, if the typing already shows where the capitals occur, there is no need for any marking, except where changes are required for consistency.

Extracts

Look at the run-on marks in the copy of Caring, ll. 8–12. Why do you think this quotation has been run on into the normal text? It is, after all, quite common to see broken-off or set-out quotations in books. They are sometimes set indented, sometimes in smaller type, sometimes in italic, usually with a space above and below. I use the term **extracts** here for such broken-off or set-out quotations.

The reason for marking this particular quotation to be run on is that it is very short. In the typeset version it occupies only three lines, even in the same type size as the rest of the text. Most publishers have a general rule that quotations should be set as extracts if they are more than a certain length (it may be 40 or 50 or 60 words, or perhaps 5 typed lines).

In addition to marking this extract to run on, the editor has added an opening and a closing quote. These are, of course, essential when a quotation appears in the text. In an extract, however, quotes are unnecessary because it is already set off from the rest of the text by its different typographical treatment. So if you are creating an extract (because it is too long to stay in the text), you will delete the opening and closing quotes.

When you are coding generically, you show an extract like this:

Familiar as he was with the immense terraced gardens of Samarkand, Babur's contribution |.|.|.| was to establish in India fine gardens in the Persian tradition. Divided into four by water courses that represented the rivers of life, they abounded in terraces and waterfalls⊙|.|.|.| The occupants could sit on raised platforms under embroidered awnings, looking down on an intricate pattern of walks, beds, pools and ordered ranks of flowers.

It is best to use a ruler to mark an extract. Do indicate clearly where it begins and ends. The designer will then specify that all passages coded 'ext' should be set in a particular type size, whether to indent on the left and right or only on the left, how much space to leave above and below, etc. We look at extracts in more detail in Unit 11.

Ellipses

Often, as in the extract above, an author quoting another source will omit a few words, or indeed whole sentences, because they are not relevant to the present discussion. If words are omitted in the middle of a sentence, an **ellipsis** (three dots) is put in to show that something is missing.

If something is left out *between* sentences, a full stop completes the sentence and is followed by an ellipsis, making four dots altogether. (An equally valid alternative system standardizes to three dots all the time, whether a sentence has finished or not. We return to this and further variations in Unit 11.)

Some publishers like the three dots of an ellipsis close together (as they have been set in this book, for example on p. 39). Many prefer them evenly spaced thus: 'either . . . or'. The marking on the extract opposite shows how to ask for an evenly spaced ellipsis. However, the full stop, if there is one, is set close up to the word it follows. Your circling distinguishes it from the ellipsis.

Quotation marks

The style instructions for Exercise 4.1 (Silk) specified: double quotes (single inner). In that exercise there were no 'inner' quotes but there often are some:

> "Did you enjoy your visit to 'the cradle of jazz', as they call it?"

This demonstrates double quotes (single inner), that is, double for all general purposes throughout the work, but single where there are quoted words within a quote.

The same sentence in single quote (double inner) would be:

> 'Did you enjoy your visit to "the cradle of jazz", as they call it?'

The mixed system sometimes recommended in typing schools (double for quoted sentences and single for words and phrases) is frowned upon by publishers. (Some linguists and philosophers do, however, insist on a mixed system where single quotes serve a different purpose from double quotes.)

Instructions to the typesetter

These codes ('A', 'B', etc., and 'ext') are circled, or boxed, so that there should be no doubt that they are coding instructions (rather than, for example, a capital 'A' to be inserted in the text). Circling in general is used to identify matter that is not to be set.

If a name in the text is unclear, spell it out in the margin in capitals but circle it to show that the word is not wanted twice, nor in capitals. Sometimes you need to clarify a symbol in the same way – a zero or a capital 'O', a one or the letter 'l', a Greek gamma (γ) or a 'y' – especially where the context is ambiguous. Such clarification, either above the line or in the margin, should also be circled.

Because circling means 'do not set' you need to be careful how you mark the **transposition** of a paragraph or sentence. Never put a complete circle or box round the section you want to move. The marking of this paragraph demonstrates the neatest way. Alternatively, you can follow the standard proofreading symbol (see Unit 2) but it is clumsy and may occasionally be mistaken for an instruction to set in italic.

Now do Exercise 4.2

Remember to continue marking paragraphs and end-of-line hyphens as well as coding headings and extracts.

Review of Exercise 4.2

The typescript is messy and unevenly typed. So delete more positively the extra 'to' on l. 4; clarify the obscure 'w' in 'own' on l. 28; write in or strengthen several 's's (for example on l. 42). You do not, however, need to worry about the uneven margin on ll. 41 and 43, the uneven line spacing at the end, or, in this context, the slipped 'a' on l. 52 (though in mathematical work, where a subscript might be intended, you'd be wise to clarify this). These are points you would mark when correcting a proof but not when editing a typescript. (Only if this were a printout from an author's disk to be used for typesetting would you need to correct them.)

The **subheads** on ll. 3 and 16 are probably best treated as equal A heads. Those on ll. 17 and 32 are clearly subsidiary parts of 'Sartre's Solution' (l. 16) and so are B heads. (You could instead make l. 3 an A head and l. 16 a B head, with C heads after that, but this extends the hierarchy unnecessarily.) Did you hesitate over the level of the heading 'Summary' (l. 46)? I hope so: there is some ambiguity here, even if in the end you decided one way or another. (Remember that, if you cannot decide, you should note a query for the author.) 'Summary' as a B head like ll. 17 and 32 (my preference) implies that the section from l. 16 onwards is being summarized. You would then go back to A for 'Objections' (l. 52). The alternative would be to call 'Summary' an A head, on a level with 'Sartre's Solution'. The 'Objections' (l. 52) might possibly then be a B head under 'Sum-mary': you cannot really tell without being able to read on.

You will have marked the **extract** from ll. 24 to 31. An arrowhead, to show that the vertical marker in the margin continues, is helpful at the bottom of the first page. Did you also notice that an extract should be created starting towards the end of l. 37? This is best done thus:

```
He illustrates this by means of a long story:  ⌐I start out on a

     hike with friends.  At the end of several hours' walking my fatigue
```

By this method you can neatly delete the opening quote in the same stroke.

As we saw with the split infinitive in Exercise 2.4 (Caring), you should not usually change anything in a quotation. Here, however, the errors are obvious – it should be 'any way' on l. 29 and 'pleasurably' on l. 45 – and you can correct them without query (especially as the original is presumably in French). You must also change the double quotes to single round 'sissy' on l. 42 because you have eliminated the single quotes at the beginning and end of the extract.

'Chapter' on l. 6 must be lower case, though a cross-reference such as 'in Chapter 6' may take upper or lower case according to the style adopted.

On l. 23, either eliminate 'e.g.' altogether, changing the comma to a colon, or convert it into 'such as'. If you spelt it out as 'for example', you would have an ugly repetition of the word 'example'. The introduction of repetition is another common pitfall for the unwary editor.

'On the one hand' (l. 9) and 'On the other hand' (l. 12) should be made consistent, either both with commas or neither with a comma. (You would usually follow the author's prevalent style, or your own house style, on such matters.)

Starting a sentence with 'For' (ll. 7 and 35) seems to be part of the author's style and I wouldn't interfere with it. Like occasionally starting a sentence with 'And' or 'But', it does seem to serve a useful purpose here. If the use of 'which' worried you, return to this exercise when we discuss the question in Unit 7.

You will, I hope, have found plenty of other errors and opportunities for practising your marking-up technique.

Summary

The Morse Machine passage was from a literary novel, in general carefully wrought; Caring came from a competently, though not excitingly, written academic book on sociology that was typical of its genre; both Silk and Sartre on Freedom were written for the adult general reader. None of these passages should have tempted you to do much style improvement work: they are reasonably well constructed in the author's own style.

A good editor does not interfere wantonly, but only for justifiable reasons (many of which we shall discuss in the units to come), and at the level appropriate to the book's market. Look at other books in your field as much as you can to help you to judge the norm.

Units 1–4 have introduced a great many new terms and techniques. Don't worry if it has not all sunk in at once: we shall be using the same terminology and techniques throughout the book and you will soon learn them.

Do, however, make time to skim through these four units tomorrow looking for the new terms (shown in bold). Refresh your memory about their meaning and, if possible, get a friend to test you. If you have tackled the four units in one day as suggested, remember also to look again at your answer to Exercise 2.3 (The Farm).

UNIT 5

Structure and Headings

This unit is concerned with wider aspects of editorial work: the overall structure and logical presentation of material, particularly the use of headings. An introductory section addresses the organization of the project as a whole.

Initial preparation and general organization

- Brief yourself on the project. If you are working in house, talk to the commissioning editor; read the file; look at other books in the series (or previous issues of the journal); make sure you know what market it is intended for. If you are working freelance, you need to be just as fully briefed, at least on series style and market; ring for further discussion if necessary.

- Look through the typescript to ensure it is all legible (the author should supply the top copy or a good photocopy) and to assess the kinds of problem you are likely to encounter (obvious inconsistencies, poor spelling, etc.), particularly how much **style improvement** is required. Look at the author's system of headings, notes and references; look at the extent and type of illustration. If it is an edited collection, a journal issue or other multi-author work, you'll need to assess how far you can or should standardize the diverse contributions.

- Once you have made this preliminary (necessarily rapid) assessment, discuss any unexpected time (and therefore cost) implications with the commissioning editor (if you work in house) or with the person briefing you (if you are freelance).

- You may need to carry out or arrange for a cast-off (an estimate of the printed extent – the number of pages – as discussed in Unit 3); find out or contribute to budgets or estimates; work out schedules.

- Make sure the typescript is complete. Draw up a checklist of anything still to come – a foreword or illustrations perhaps. Some prelims, such as the title page and copyright page (discussed in Unit 31), will not come from the author and may be your responsibility. An index (Unit 29) is not usually compiled until proof stage but find out whether there is to be one, so that you can judge the amount of cross-referencing necessary in the text and arrange the proofing schedule. For a journal your checklist might include book reviews, abstracts, translations, biographical notes on the authors.

- Either at the beginning or during the editing, you may think of other useful items – perhaps a glossary or maps.

- Figures (diagrams, etc.) are often dealt with separately, as we saw in Unit 3. The author should supply roughs or an artwork brief on separate sheets (although photocopies in the typescript as well can be helpful). Tables (statistical information) should also be on separate sheets. You may need to do some of this organizing work if the author has not presented the material clearly. We look at these aspects in more detail in Units 21 and 26–8.

- Either at the beginning or as you edit, number the folios (or check existing numbers). The advantage of doing this at the beginning is that you will lose nothing if the whole script flutters to the floor. The danger in numbering before editing is that you may not notice a problem and may have to renumber later or add, say, fo. 30A. Look out for gaps, repetition and transposition of folios in the author's system. Numbering may be either right through the typescript or by chapter (fo. 2/1, etc.). (If you number by chapter, note on the opening folio how many folios there are altogether in that chapter.)

Chapters and parts

The chapter (or unit) heading, as we saw in Unit 4, is usually coded 'ch hd'. Above the chapter level there may be part titles (coded 'part hd') dividing the whole book into, perhaps, two or three parts. Where possible, a part title occupies a full leaf (recto with verso blank). When space is at a premium, the part heading may have to be fitted in above a chapter head or the next chapter may have to start on the verso of the part title.

Hierarchical headings

Again as we saw in Unit 4, the usual system is to code subheads within a chapter 'A', 'B', 'C', etc., according to their importance (and therefore the weight to be given to them at design stage).

Unless you know for sure what style is to be used for each level of heading, do not lower-case headings typed all in capitals, add or delete underlining, mark to range left or centre or show spaces above and below. Such specific marking could cause confusion if the designer later decided on a different treatment. Generic coding is intended to ensure flexibility.

As we saw, however, it *is* worth finding out before editing whether any subheads set in upper and lower case (u / lc) are likely to take cap sig wds or min caps (see Unit 4), so that you can ensure consistency. The designer may then simply specify 'caps', 'small caps' or 'u / lc' (which should be taken to mean upper and lower case *as marked*).

Usually each subhead will occupy a line of its own, with no full stop or colon after it. The text will start on the next line, often full out. At the lower levels of the hierarchy (perhaps 'C' or 'D'), however, you or the designer may decide instead to make the heading a **shoulder head**, that is, to run on the text that follows. In this case the heading and text may be separated by a full stop, a colon or just an em space. As with the capitalization system, it is safest if the editor decides what form of punctuation to use and makes it consistent.

Keep the number of levels in the hierarchy to a minimum. An over-elaborate system can be self-defeating, engendering confusion by its subtle distinctions. Simplification, perhaps with some rearrangement, often clarifies the structure. Before you tackle such a task, however, make sure that you have understood the distinctions intended.

Headings as flags

Sometimes a heading is not part of the overall logical hierarchy but a flag or signal that a particular kind of text follows. Examples might be: a Summary or Notes at the end of a chapter or section; Exercises or Questions interspersed with the text discussion.

Although these could be treated in the same way as, say, the A head, they are different in kind and a designer might wish to emphasize the distinction. So, in the examples above you could code 'S', 'N', 'Ex' (not 'E' as that is too close to the usual hierarchy) or 'Q'. Remember to explain your coding in your **notes on design** (which we return to in Unit 24). I write as though there was always a separate designer but (as we saw in Unit 3) this may very well be you on your second run through the book.

Similarly, **displayed** matter such as extracts, reading passages, theorems or boxes (discussed below) may require one or two levels of heading. These are often coded in a separate hierarchy as 'X', 'Y' and, if necessary, 'Z'.

Boxes, tints, different typefaces

Structure may be indicated in all sorts of ways apart from headings. Different treatment of distinct types of material can be especially helpful in textbooks. But remember that the purpose is to enable students to find their way easily around complex material. As with headings, too many fine distinctions can defeat that purpose.

Boxes distinguish certain material from the rest of the text by means of **rules** (lines), sometimes with a background tint or second colour. This treatment can be helpful either for supplementary material (background information, projects and other out-of-class activities, hints for the teacher, etc.) or to highlight the essentials (conclusions, theorems to be learned, etc.).

A different typeface may similarly help to set off a particular kind of material, for example comprehension passages. A second colour may be used to distinguish particular features, such as instructions at the beginning of an exercise. Some of these decisions will be made at design stage; many will arise out of the editor's suggestions. Collaboration between editor and designer is essential, especially where there are cost implications.

All such features may be indicated with a marginal line and code, for example 'box', 'thrm', etc., just as you learned to do for extracts ('ext') in Unit 4. For less easily categorized material you can simply code 'display'.

Alternatively, or as well, **highlighters** in different colours can be particularly useful where the distinctions are complicated. Again, explain the system of coding in your notes for the designer.

Standardization

Another key concept in successful textbook publishing is predictability (without tedium). Using the book is easier if the same heading or the same phrase introduces the same kind of information in each chapter. A familiar – and, above all, logical – framework helps the reader to absorb new material.

Now do Exercise 5.1

Look through the passage quickly before you start so that you know what topics are covered. At the end of each section or subsection, check back to the relevant heading to see that it describes the content accurately. If not, devise a better structure or wording. When you finish, recheck the logic of your system.

You'll notice that the figures (maps in this case) appear on the same page as the text. These are just photocopies to indicate the positioning (which needs to be fairly precise). The top copies of the author's roughs will be separate.

Review of Exercise 5.1

It is not essential to mark paragraphs here since they are typed in the same way as they are to be set. If you do mark them, then use the 'new para' symbol (see Unit 2) because they are not to be indented.

Just as you go back to the relevant heading when you finish each section or subsection, go back to introductory sentences and paragraphs to see that promises have been fulfilled. This introduction (ll. 2–5) covers the topics adequately but in a different order: in the discussion itself, direction (l. 3) comes before measurement of distance (l. 2) and streets and buildings (l. 5) before hills and rivers (l. 4). I'd certainly change ll. 2–3 but might leave ll. 4–5 because the sentence leads on helpfully into the next section.

Headings

Following the style instruction on the use of capitals in headings, you will have marked 'Directions' (for example) on l. 7 lower case but should only have shown the capital initial in 'READING MAPS' (the chapter head) and in the headings on ll. 6, 13, etc.

The present heading structure is unsatisfactory in several ways. For example, the subsection on 'Measuring distances' (ll. 19–24) does not fit logically within a section on 'Points of the compass' (l. 13), as the typed style of the headings would suggest. The heading on l. 33 is a strange mixture in form of the author's capitals for A heads and u/lc for B heads, so you must consider its role particularly carefully.

One way to improve the pattern is as follows. (Your own way may be equally valid but it would be confusing to attempt here to cover all possible permutations.) The sentence on ll. 4–5 and the content of the two exercises suggest a major division into discussion first of a street map (ll. 6–32) and then of a relief map (ll. 33–77).

So we can make l. 6 an A head and create an equivalent A head above l. 33. These two A heads must be parallel in wording, *either* keeping l. 6 as it is and making the A head above l. 33 'Understanding a relief map' *or* (preferably) omitting 'Understanding' on l. 6 and making the A head above l. 33 'A relief map'. (We return to 'Contours' below.)

The structure of the first half of the piece could then be:

ch hd	Reading maps
A	A street map (l. 6)
B	Giving directions (l. 7)
B	Points of the compass (l. 13)
B	Measuring distances (l. 19)

With more radical alteration to the author's scheme, this could be neatly paralleled in the second half:

A	A relief map (above l. 33)
B	Contours (at l. 33)
B	Gradient (l. 44)
B	Scale (l. 50)

Thus I have split the awkward heading on l. 33 into two: an A head followed (on a separate line) by a B head. By contrast, I have eliminated the heading 'Points to note' (l. 43). Such uninformative headings rarely serve a useful purpose. This one joined together two points without any particular logical connection: as in the street map section, we are dealing here with separate topics, each using examples drawn from the same relief map. Numbered headings (ll. 44 and 50) are also best avoided, although they can be helpful when there are frequent cross-references to other sections. You would need to ask for the author's confirmation of these more radical changes.

The two 'Exercise' headings (ll. 25 and 69) may either be coded within the normal hierarchy (as B) or flagged as different in kind by a code such as 'Ex' (or 'Q'). (The designer is still free to treat them in exactly the same way as B heads if he or she prefers.)

The material called 'Interesting facts' (ll. 64–8) is an ideal candidate for a box (provided similar features appear in other chapters of the book). Mark it with a line down the margin, as for extracts but coding it 'box'. (For clarity you would usually draw in the horizontal rule as well.) Since the present heading could reflect badly on the rest of the discussion, a better heading might be 'Facts and figures'; in another book it might be 'Did you know?' Whatever heading you settle upon will have to be general enough to be used throughout the book. (Or indeed you may decide that no general heading is needed: the box alone sets the material off from the rest of the text.) The headings in the box should, as we have seen, form a different hierarchy from the text: code 'X' for l. 64 and 'Y' for l. 65 (or 'X' here if you cut out l. 64).

'Cross-section' (l. 38) is not a heading within the text hierarchy at all but a caption relating to that part of the figure. For now just code it 'fig. caption'. (Often, as we shall see in Unit 28, you will be asked to draw up a separate list of captions.) 'The village of Isla' on the artwork for the street map is similarly the map's caption, telling you its subject matter.

Finally, the heading 'Example' on l. 56 may be coded 'C' as the lowest in this hierarchy. Remember that it is not always necessary to go through the whole hierarchy: if an example appears in the introductory part of an A section, before the first B subsection begins, you can still code that example head 'C', so that it matches similar ones elsewhere.

The lowest level, if it occurs frequently and requires no extra space above or below, is often just specifically marked for italic or bold by the editor, in which case no coding is required. I would be tempted to do this for 'Example' (l. 56) and to treat 'Question' (l. 8) in identical fashion. Whether you call this a C head or just mark it, perhaps for italic, a run-on style would then be best. If the style is run on, retain the colon; if 'Example' is to remain on a separate line, delete the colon. Treating 'Example' and 'Question' in the same way does not necessarily mean standardizing both instances to the same word – there is a slight difference that may be worth preserving.

You might code the worked example (ll. 58–61) 'display' to show that it would be best with space above and below and/or indented, to set it off from the rest of the text.

Standardization and other text editing

You should standardize the identification system in the exercise questions, preferably to numbers, as in Exercise 2a. (You will then be free to use '(a)', '(b)', etc., for subdivisions within questions if they are required in other units.) Be consistent about including or excluding a stop after the number; you'll also have noticed the repetition of '2' on ll. 27 and 28. (The exercises are called '2a' and '2b' because both are in Unit 2.)

For the questions in the text (probably to be discussed out loud in class), numbers, letters and **bullets** (large dots) seem to have been used indiscriminately. I would standardize to bullets throughout: they offer a helpful way of listing points without introducing the formality of numbering systems. (This means changing ll. 21–4 and 48–9 to bullets.) The word 'So' on l. 47 is best deleted. We look at lists in more detail in Unit 23.

Standardize to bold *or* italic for words being introduced or defined (on ll. 16, 20, 35, 54). (A distinction may have been intended but, if so, it is more confusing than helpful.) It is safest here to mark for bold (with a wavy line, as in proofs), even though the typing already shows it. In a typescript where bold had been used reasonably consistently, you could instead give a general instruction to 'follow copy for bold'.

'Relief' on l. 34 should probably be treated the same (whether bold or italic) as these other terms. 'Gradient' is used in the heading on l. 44 but is not defined: either ask the author to supply a definition or devise one yourself and ask for confirmation. Remember, however, that the best explanation of a term is sometimes through use, rather than formal definition. For this reason I would not ask for a definition of 'ratio' on l. 54.

A distinction is often, though not necessarily, made between four-digit and five-digit numbers, as indicated by the style instruction; a space, rather than a comma, is also common in scientific material. (As we shall see in Unit 15, the space is often a fixed thin space.) Delete the comma and close up on l. 67; mark a space between '1' and 'cm' on ll. 59 and 60 and before 'm' on l. 68.

Unlike a colon, the symbol for ratio (ll. 55 and 61) should have the same space before and after it. (Compare the colon on l. 52.) If a ratio sign has been typed like a colon, mark it for even spacing in the same way as an ellipsis (see Unit 4).

Always clarify ambiguous symbols. So on l. 54, above the typed 'l', write 'arabic one', circling the words so that they are not set.

Why do you think the author has put the **page cross-reference** in parentheses on ll. 32 and 77? It is a reminder that this is the relevant folio, not the final printed page number. (That cannot be known until we have page proofs.) It is safer still to delete this number (without obscuring it) and replace it with '000' (or '00'). This will show up more clearly in the proofs, as a reminder to insert the page number when known. The folio number visible underneath helps you or the author to find the place referred to. (Some typesetters use bullets, which show up better still in proof.)

These two sentences on ll. 32 and 77 are typical examples of formula sentences, which are best standardized.

A few changes were needed to clarify the questions. On l. 29, specify whether 'as the crow flies' (probably the intention) or by walking; l. 30 would be clearer as 'Say what you see, what roads you cross, etc.' On l. 41 'highest' should be 'higher' since there are only two hills. (As each hill has several slopes, ll. 48 and 73 are all right.) Convert full stops to question marks on ll. 18 and 72 (also on l. 31 if you did not alter the original).

In general, the questions are already carefully worded in similar ways, so that pupils will not be confused. On the other hand, some variety has been introduced in the facts (ll. 66–8) to avoid tedium: do not make those sentences identical.

Throughout the exercise you had to *cross-check* between the text and figures in order to make sure that the questions were sensible and could be answered by looking at the map given. No particular problems arose in this case, but it is very important to establish the habit. We return to the point in Unit 27.

Finally, delete the hyphen in 'post-office' on l. 12;

standardize 'sea level' on ll. 36 (twice) and 70, with or without a hyphen; amend to 'shown' on l. 39; the verb on ll. 57 and 58 should match ('represents' is probably more usual); mark a capital for 'hill' on l. 71. On l. 37, transpose the full stop and closing parenthesis: where a whole sentence is in parentheses, the stop must also be enclosed, as part of the sentence.

Running heads

If you look back at Exercise 2.4 (Caring) one last time, you will notice that a heading appears at the top of each page of the proof. This is not shown in any way in the corresponding copy. Such a heading, set on the same line as the page number, is called a **running head** (or **headline**).

Often the book title will appear on the verso and the chapter head on the recto. Sometimes (for example, in an edited collection or a journal) the author's name appears on the verso and the chapter head on the recto. Other options are part title on the verso and chapter head on the recto; and chapter head on the verso and A head on the recto. The part, chapter or section *number* is not usually included in the running head, although it can be helpful when there are many cross-references.

Problems arise only when a chapter head, say, is too long to fit comfortably into this single line of type. Depending on type size, the right fit may be 40 to 50 characters (including spaces).

The editor either types up a list of running heads (showing the necessary shortenings) or writes on the first folio of each chapter what the verso and recto running heads should be. (If only a few require shortening, a marked or highlighted photocopy of the contents page may be used.)

Now do Exercise 5.2 **G**

There is no need to count characters precisely – just bear in mind that five eight-letter words would be about right. You do not, of course, have to use the maximum: shorter can be clearer. Set the running heads out in two columns, one headed VERSO, one RECTO. (This helps you to see how the two relate to each other and how they will look on the double-page spread.) Their purpose is to guide the reader through the book: when you have finished, recheck that they do so.

Review of Exercise 5.2

Many academic articles in journals or contributions to books (as here) have a chapter **title and subtitle** (separated by a colon). Sometimes the title points up the wider relevance of the article and the subtitle explains the actual subject matter (as in Chapters 4 and 9); in other cases the title is specific and the subtitle expansive (as in Chapter 7). Usually in running heads you will want to pick out the specific, though sometimes you may be able to capture the flavour of both. So for Chapter 4 you have a choice of either *Chilembwe's revolt reconsidered* or *Stress and identity: Chilembwe's revolt*. In this particular book

other option, *Psychological stress and identity*, would be wrong because it is out of line with the rest of the chapters. (In a psychology book, on the other hand, it might be correct.)

For Part II the verso running head is probably best as *Resistance movements in the colonial period*; for Part III it could be *Revolutions and coups since independence*. Places where, as the style instruction puts it, 'part is inapplicable' are the prelims (including the Introduction) and the endmatter (including the Conclusion).

Dates are almost always best left out. The exception here would be in Chapter 9, where the best choice is *Fall of Nigerian Federal Government, 1966*. (Otherwise the implication would be that it fell for ever.)

Abbreviations are also usually best avoided, so Chapter 6 should probably be *The Tanganyika African National Union*, although *TANU in the Lake Province* is possible.

Whenever you have to shorten chapter headings to create suitable running heads, do check that the author or (for an edited collection such as this) the volume editor finds your wording acceptable. As in so many other areas, changes at page proof can be expensive. Finally, notice '000' again for page numbers to be added at proof.

Further reading

If you are in journal publishing, for a fuller guide to the organization of your own work, see:

Maeve O'Connor, *How to Copyedit Scientific Books and Journals* (ISI Press, Philadelphia, Pennsylvania, 1986; distributed in the UK by Williams & Wilkins, London)

UNIT 6
Spelling and Vocabulary

Although some people are certainly better at it than others, none of us can rely totally on our ability to spell. We all look words up in the dictionary from time to time. The purpose of this unit is to help you to find out your own strengths and weaknesses, so that you know what kinds of word you need to double-check.

A **dictionary** will often give you alternative spellings – and that can be illuminating if you had always thought there was only one acceptable way of spelling a word. For example, both 'focused' and 'focussed' are possible, although the first is generally preferred.

If you need a firm ruling on alternative spellings or hyphenation (for example, 'sea-level' or 'sea level' in Exercise 5.1, Reading Maps), the place to look is the *Writers' Dictionary*. This is part of the house style of Oxford University Press (OUP), so what it tells you is that firm's preferred style: don't assume that other ways are necessarily wrong because the *Writers' Dictionary* advises one particular form. To achieve consistency other publishers often ask their authors and editors to follow those preferred forms as well.

Finally, another important tool of the editing trade, *Hart's Rules*, is very useful for its lists, for example of words that double the consonant before a suffix. Not all dictionaries spell out the effects on a word of adding '-ed', '-ing', etc. *Hart's Rules* lists the commonest words in various categories and also explains the basis for differences in spelling, which can often help you to remember them.

For most spelling problems, look in an ordinary dictionary first. Where alternatives exist, the *Writers' Dictionary* will give a ruling. For troublesome endings, *Hart's Rules* will alert you to your own weak spots.

Now do Exercise 6.1

Look out for other problems as well as misspellings. Remember to check anything you are not quite sure about. From now on, assume that paras are always indented and closed up unless you are told otherwise in the style instructions.

Review of Exercise 6.1

The spelling problems often involved doubling of consonants: 'regrettable', 'occurrence' (both on l. 16). Others involved suffixes such as 'indefinable' (l. 6).

'Combating' (l. 8) may have surprised you. *Hart's Rules* spells it this way but the reason given is that it is *not* stressed on the second syllable, so it goes like 'budgeted', 'targeted', etc., not like 'allotted', 'omitted'. In fact many people *do* stress the second syllable, so the double 't' version may now be an acceptable alternative in some dictionaries.

There were plenty more. If you looked up 'maharajah' (incorrectly spelt at its second appear-ance, on l. 6) in the *Writers' Dictionary*, you will have found that OUP prefers to omit the final 'h'. (The same goes for other words of Indian origin such as 'veranda(h)'.) Check that you saw not just one but two errors in 'commercial' (l. 16). It is surprisingly easy to miss a second mistake coming close to one you've spotted, whether you are editing or proof-reading. Note too that it is not possible for something to be 'comparatively unique' (l. 12). On the other hand, 'whose logic' (l. 9), though unusual, is perfectly acceptable.

There are two additional features you should have noticed. One is **malapropism**, inappropriate vocabulary such as 'memorial' for 'memorable'

(l. 1) – always check back to the heading when you finish a section; probably 'diminished' for 'diminutive' (l. 5); 'reminder' for 'remainder' (ll. 14–15), 'aversity' for 'adversity' (l. 18) and classics like 'ingenuous' for 'ingenious' (l. 8) and 'illusive' for 'elusive' (l. 15).

The other feature is **tautology**, saying the same thing twice. Examples are 'necessary prerequisite' (l. 7) (if you kept 'necessary', note the spelling); 'continued to persevere' (l. 13); 'temporarily … for a brief … moment' (l. 14) (again, note the spellings); 'set up and established' (l. 17).

Now do Exercise 6.2

Hart's Rules has a useful section on this topic, -ize and -ise spellings.

Review of Exercise 6.2

A house style will usually specify either -ise or -ize spellings. Standardizing to -ise spellings is relatively simple: there are very few cases where 'z' must remain (in words such as 'size' or 'capsize'). If, however, the house style specifies -ize and you are editing the work of an author who naturally uses -ise, beware of words that are *always* spelt with 's'.

For example, as *Hart's Rules* explains, in 'incise' or 'revise' the -ise is not a suffix but part of the root -cise ('cut' as in 'incisor') or -vise ('see' as in 'vision'). 'Advertise' has no such reason for retaining the 's' but does so, perhaps to match 'advertisement'. Similarly, verbs such as 'exercise' (not a -cise word in derivation) and 'enfranchise' are spelt with 's' in order to match the equivalent nouns.

There is another system, largely disregarded by publishers but sometimes used by authors, that insists on 's' for words derived from Latin (usually through French) and 'z' for words derived directly from Greek.

The usual choice, however, is between -ise, widely used in Britain in the first half of the twentieth century but now in retreat, and -ize, always used in the United States and by OUP and rapidly gaining ground because of its advantage in international publishing.

However, -yse (in 'analyse', etc.) is still generally preferred to the strictly American -yze.

Two other points were demonstrated in this exercise. One concerns names in the **possessive**. *Hart's Rules* recommends Jones's (l. 16) and Thomas's (l. 21), although with certain exceptions on grounds of euphony, for example Bridges', and all classical names, such as Xerxes'. The second point is the use of italic for titles of newspapers and magazines. The question mark after *Country Life* (l. 19) should be roman, not italic, and the word *Observer* on l. 21 should be italic. (We address in Unit 16 the question of whether *The* might also be italic.)

American and British English

It is important to be aware of the differences between these two forms of English, partly because in some books or journals American contributions retain their original form and you still need to make sure that they follow consistent rules, and partly because you may sometimes be asked to convert American to British (or vice versa).

Butcher, *Copy-editing* gives a useful list of the points of difference between American and British spelling. These include not only the familiar 'color', etc., but other points such as the fact that many double consonants in British English are single in American, for example 'traveled'.

Punctuation is also different. In most modern British books, a closing quote following a word or phrase usually comes before a full stop, comma or other punctuation. So in the example given in Unit 4, we had:

'Did you enjoy your visit to "the cradle of jazz", as they call it?'

The comma follows the closing quote after the phrase, 'the cradle of jazz'.

Only when a full sentence (with subject and verb, usually starting with a capital letter) is in quotes does the closing quote come after the full stop or comma. So,

I replied, 'I had a wonderful time.'
'I hated it,' said Fred.

This system is called **logical order of punctuation** (as recommended by *Hart's Rules*).

In American English, and quite often in British novels and newspapers, the **conventional order of punctuation** is still followed. In this system the closing quote *always* comes after the full stop or comma:

'Did you enjoy your visit to "the cradle of jazz," as they call it?'

'I am,' I began, 'the wrong person to ask.'

In the second sentence, *logical* order (*Hart's Rules*) would demand:

'I am', I began, 'the wrong person to ask.'

Even in conventional order, the closing quote comes before a dash, colon or semicolon. It is full stops and commas that you need to watch out for.

When anglicizing an American piece, you often just change the spelling and punctuation. (Another punctuation difference is that double quotes are generally preferred in the United States whereas many British publishers favour single quotes.) You might also 'correct' split infinitives and other American grammatical forms. The vocabulary, however, would often still show the transatlantic origin of the piece. If you really wanted to anglicize completely, you would also have to change 'truck' to 'lorry', 'trunk' to 'boot', etc.

Now do Exercise 6.3 G

Do not make any actual changes but circle American spellings and punctuation in red, distinctive vocabulary in blue.

UNIT 7
Grammar

Just as logical overall structure (Unit 5) is an important ingredient in communicating a book's message, so is the structure of each individual sentence. Ambiguous or misleading syntax can obscure the sense; sloppiness that might go unnoticed in speech jars on the printed page.

We address specific points of grammar and usage in this unit and go on to more general issues of meaning and clarity in Unit 8.

Now do Exercise 7.1

Most, but not necessarily all, of the sentences demonstrate common grammatical errors. Without checking in reference books for now, correct anything that you think is wrong.

Review of Exercise 7.1

1 'John and me'

Always check how such sentences would read if you left out the other person. Everyone would say, 'Why not join me?' rather than 'Why not join I?' 'Me' is the object of the sentence. Similar sentences are 'Come with Jean and me' and 'Lend that to Hamid and me'; in these 'me' follows a preposition ('with', 'to'). 'I' is only used for the *subject* of a sentence: 'Benito and I are giving a party.'

2 'different from'

We say 'similar to' but 'different from' (the dis- or di- prefix always implies 'away from', as in 'dispersal', 'divergent'). American English also recognizes 'different than' but that form is not generally accepted in British English.

3 'fewer people'

One has 'fewer sheep' but 'less milk'. Essentially, the distinction is between **countable** nouns (something that can be counted, for instance sheep) and **uncountable** nouns (a quantity such as milk).

4 'to supervise closely' or, more awkwardly, 'closely to supervise'

At last we reach the **split infinitive**, widely accepted in American English but not as yet in British. The classic instance, for television addicts, is 'to boldly go'. The point is that nothing should come between 'to' and the verb, because together they make up the infinitive. Most editors still 'correct' split infinitives (as you saw in the copy for Exercise 2.4). To do so, you have to move the adverb *either* after the verb *or* before the 'to'. Sometimes one alternative will sound better, sometimes the other. I suspect this may be a losing battle and the split form will become fully accepted within your lifetime. Even now it is allowable if it is really the neatest and clearest mode of expression.

As we saw in Unit 6, 'supervise' is the correct form, whether you are adopting -ize or -ise spellings.

5 'women's ... men's'

The placing of the apostrophe is a matter of logic. It always denotes the possessive (something belongs to somebody); you have to decide whether the possessor is singular or plural. So 'the man's umbrella', 'the men's umbrellas'; 'my friend's suitcases' (one friend with an unspecified number of suitcases), 'my friends' suitcases' (more than one friend). 'Womens' jobs' is therefore *never* correct as 'women' is already the plural form. In some cases the possessor may either be a typical member or the group as a whole: 'the silversmith's skills', 'silversmiths' skills'.

As we have already seen (in Exercises 4.1 and 4.2) 'its' causes difficulty for some people too. It *is* a possessive but 'its meaning' requires no apostrophe, any more than 'his friend' or 'yours sincerely'.

6 'Both men had' or 'The two men shared'

The word 'shared' already contains the notion of *joint* feeling (similarly, 'agreed', 'concurred', 'joined', etc.), so 'both' is tautologous. This is a pet hate of mine, which I may have to give up eventually as the usage is becoming increasingly common.

7 'kinds of finch' or leave as it stands

Both the singular (traditional in British English) and the plural (standard American English) after 'kinds of', 'types of', 'sorts of' are now accepted in Britain. As editor you should, however, make sure that an author *consistently* uses one form or the other. (If you have not already noticed that I use the singular in this book, look out for it as you read on.)

8 'decide whether'

'Whether' is preferable to 'if' when a choice is being made, as here (although the use of the shorter word is becoming increasingly common). 'If' can often be ambiguous in such circumstances and is best reserved for the conditional: 'We have a problem, if the data are correct.'

'data were'

The word 'data', strictly speaking, is plural. (In Latin the singular would be 'datum'.) In computer books, however, 'data' is now often accepted as being singular. Elsewhere most of us still hold out for the plural, as for 'criteria', 'phenomena', etc. However, 'agenda' offers a respectable precedent for a Latin plural that has become singular in English (no doubt to the disgust of contemporary – remember the original meaning of that word – pedants). Similarly, people used to say, 'The news are good this morning.'

Some words that are plural in form may be used either as singular or as plural depending on the sense: most would say, 'Politics is an interesting subject to study' but 'The politics of the question are complex.'

9 'hesitated among' or leave as it stands

'Between' (because it derives from 'two') should, strictly speaking, only be used for two objects but this restriction is rapidly becoming pedantic and the alternative 'among' sounds odd. ('Alternative' is itself a contentious word for the same reason: strictly it means one of two and 'option', or some such word, should be used when there are three choices.)

'chose the last'

'Latter' should certainly be used only for the second of *two*. Similarly, in Exercise 5.1 (Reading Maps) we saw that 'higher' is used for comparing two hills, 'highest' for comparing three or more.

10 'When I had finished the shopping, the weekend was mine to enjoy' (or 'Once I had ...' or 'After I had ...'); or, changing the other half of the sentence, 'Having finished the shopping, I was free to enjoy the weekend'

Again notorious in some circles, the **dangling** (or **hanging** or **unattached**) **participle** often causes problems. The point is that the *subject of the main clause* of the sentence should also be the person or thing 'having' (or 'being', 'doing', etc.). (Such words ending in -ing are called participles.) In this case, the *weekend* is not doing the shopping, so logic requires a correction.

Other incorrect examples would be:

'Having typed the essay, my watch showed it was time for bed.' (Is the *watch* typing?)

'Dutifully using a pedestrian crossing, the car still hit him.' (Is the *car* dutifully using the crossing?)

11 'I earn money either from selling ... or from baking ...' or 'I earn money from either selling ... or baking ...'

Always check the logic of such expressions. The 'either ... or ...' (similarly 'both ... and ...') clauses or phrases must be exactly parallel. Either both should start with 'from' (the first answer given) or both should start with the activity (selling/baking), in which case the 'from' comes before the parallel passages start (as in the second answer).

12 'The game that we are playing' or 'The game we are playing'

The use of 'which' and 'that' is controversial but 'which' certainly sounds stilted here.

What are the grammatical rules involved? There are two types of **relative clause**: defining and parenthetic. This example is a **defining** (also called **identifying** or **restrictive**) clause. The main clause is 'The game ... is dominoes.' What game are we talking about? – the game 'that we are playing'. In such defining relative clauses, although many people do use 'which' (particularly in written work), the substitution of 'that' (or omission of the relative altogether) usually makes the sentence flow better. (Some would argue more strongly, following Fowler's *Modern English Usage*, that if we all applied the distinction consistently we'd avoid ambiguity. The fact is, however, that we don't: most people see 'which' and 'that' as synonymous and assess the meaning not from the word used but from the context and punctuation.)

If you do decide to apply the distinction, there is a simple test (for native speakers of English at least): if you *can* substitute 'that' for 'which', do so. If, as in the example, 'that' is not the subject of the relative clause, you can often go further and have no relative pronoun at all. Commas are never appropriate round a defining relative clause.

For a **parenthetic** (or **descriptive** or **non-defining**) relative clause, on the other hand, the test is whether you *could* leave out the whole relative clause (or put it in parentheses), because it is an aside, not the essential definition of the topic. This kind of relative clause *must* start with 'which' and is usually put between commas, which act rather like parentheses. That sentence itself was an example – the 'which' clause gives additional, incidental information, not a definition or limitation of 'commas'.

A final comparison:

The third horse that Robin rode was the winner.
(*defining*: 'that' (or nothing) preferable to 'which'; without commas)

The third horse, which Robin rode, was the winner.
(*parenthetic*: use 'which'; usually with commas)

Looking back at Exercise 4.2 (Sartre on Freedom), it is clear that the author uses 'which' for all relative clauses and you might decide to leave this as part of his or her chosen style. If, on the other hand, you were applying these rules, you would change ll. 11, 20 and 53. On ll. 13 and 22 the 'which' cannot be changed because of the 'in'; when a preposition is involved, use of 'that' is more problematic, as Fowler explains.

13 'has ... it is' or 'have ... they'

'The government' (as with similar words for institutions) is thought of sometimes as a single entity and sometimes as a group of people (or perhaps the anonymous 'they'). Although the singular is the grammatically 'correct' form, both usages are widespread. In speech we might even transfer in mid-sentence in this way (depending perhaps on whether the image of the institution, or the people involved in it, is dominant in the speaker's mind). In writing, you must certainly standardize within the sentence or paragraph, and probably within the book unless it is clear that the variation in image is deliberate.

14 'None of us has' or leave as it stands

Strictly speaking, 'none' (deriving from 'no one') is singular but to insist on this is becoming pedantic: both singular and plural are allowable (though not in the same work).

15 'This road seems to go only to a village' or (preferably in my view) leave it as it is

The **misplaced 'only'** is a preoccupation of many editors. They would insist that there is potential ambiguity in written work unless 'only' is placed as close as possible to the word or phrase it modifies (in this case 'to a village'). In speech, where 'only' normally precedes the main verb, there is no ambiguity: the stress would be quite different if the speaker actually meant 'only *seems* to go'. In my view this meaning would be so unexpected that in writing the word would have to be italicized. It seems a poor excuse for switching *all* 'only's to an unnatural, though logical, position. Fowler, in his inimitable style, roundly condemns the 'precisians' who would do this, although Partridge supports the many editors who do. (Details of the works of these influential but sometimes conflicting authorities appear at the end of the unit.)

'of which I have never heard' or (preferably) leave as it stands

Again Fowler demolishes the old-fashioned view that a sentence must *never* end with a preposition. Certainly the original form would be the natural style in the colloquial English suggested by the context. If you changed it to sound more literary, you would also have to change the abbreviation 'I've' to 'I have'. Where a final preposition can be avoided *without* sounding stilted or out of character, the change is usually worth making. There are, however, sentences in which it cannot be avoided: 'That land has been built on.' (This could not be converted to 'on which' as the 'on' is an integral part of the verb.)

Now do Exercise 7.2

Remember that we are assuming that all paras, except the first, will be indented and closed up.

Review of Exercise 7.2

As a rule, you should ask the author to explain all abbreviations. However, the drug 'LSD' (l. 1) is so much more familiar in that form that spelling it out is unnecessary here.

On ll. 1–2 'A group of people are ... their physical constitutions' conveys the image of several people rather than a homogeneous group. As for 'the government' in Exercise 7.1, common usage does waver enormously on whether such **collective nouns**, particularly what Fowler calls **words of** multitude, take a plural or singular verb. To some extent it depends on the particular word. So 'a team of athletes' or 'a herd of elephants' would take a singular verb, because 'team' and 'herd' emphasize unity, whereas 'A crowd of shoppers fill the High Street' or 'The majority of voters believe that ...' sound more natural.

You may have decided that 'are' was unacceptable on l. 1 but 'is' didn't sound right either: a possible change would be 'Each one of a group of people is ...' (which could still be followed by 'their' on l. 2). My own preference would be to leave the sentence alone.

Another word of multitude, 'number', occurred on l. 30. Modern usage certainly favours the plural for 'a number of' or, as here, 'any number of' (so change l. 31 to 'exhibit'). Another example would be: 'A number of us think that ...'. By contrast, when it follows 'the', number takes a singular verb: 'The number of errors was high.'

The first two paragraphs should have made you think hard about tenses. Probably the best solution is to retain the present tense on ll. 1 and 2 and change to 'will' on l. 3. In the second paragraph there are several options but I would go for 'may' throughout ('may experience', ll. 6–7; 'express', l. 8; 'may be flooded', l. 9; 'begin', l. 10). (You noticed too, I hope, that 'sixth' should be 'fifth': always check the arithmetic in this kind of list.)

On l. 23 it is best to delete 'which' altogether and on ll. 14 and 38 to change 'which' to 'that'. On l. 11 'of whom the' should be 'whose' (unless you changed the sentence more radically, for example, to 'A fifth individual's behaviour may show ... ').

Prepositions are often carelessly used as here: always look out for them. Change 'response of' (l. 4) to 'response to', not forgetting to add 'of' after 'experience'; change 'as' to 'like' on l. 10; 'for' to 'of' on l. 36; 'With' to 'By' on l. 38.

Look out too for a comma *intervening* between subject and verb (as on l. 15). The subject is 'perceptions and memories' and the verb is 'will remain'. However long the subject, there should never be a comma between it and the verb unless the comma is one of a pair. (We look at commas in pairs in more detail in Unit 9.) In this case the relative clause is a defining one, so it must not have commas round it.

On ll. 25–6 the commas may be left as they do form a pair, dividing an alternative subject from the first subject. Should the verb then be singular or plural? Since these are alternative primary causes, 'is' is preferable to 'are'. A simpler example of the same structure would be: 'Fred or Jean always collects the mail.'

You will have noticed an example of a wrongly placed apostrophe (l. 5) and may have changed l. 36 as well (though the better alteration is to add 'a' at the end of l. 35).

You must have 'neither ... nor' on l. 33. Similarly, 'both ... and' on l. 19 does not require 'also'.

'Nonetheless' (l. 4) is another editing classic: the *Writers' Dictionary* recommends three words ('none the less') for this but one word for 'nevertheless'. Since the two are synonymous, my own (unorthodox) view is that it's high time the distinction was laid to rest.

On l. 27 'cause–effect' should be marked for an en rule: these are separate entities brought into a relationship. Don't forget to mark the end-of-line hyphen on l. 16.

Standardize to unhyphenated 'biochemical' (ll. 3, 25), as on ll. 31 and 33; 'whatsoever' on l. 12 is redundant; on l. 14 add 'that of' before 'another'; on l. 17 'in a unique way' may be better brought forward to follow 'interprets'; on l. 18 transpose 'causes' and 'directly'; add 'the' before 'nervous' on l. 20; 'for them to be acted upon' would be better on l. 22 (though you may have preferred more radical change to this unwieldy sentence); on l. 28 change the semicolon to a colon (we return to the distinction in Unit 9); change 'it' to 'them' on l. 35 (the reference is to 'factors'); also on l. 35 'try and explore' is colloquial – prefer 'to'; on l. 39 'might' is preferable to 'could', also omit 'a'. Spelling errors occur on ll. 7, 24, 34 and 37.

(Just in case you wondered: you do not need to do anything about the short line at the top of the second folio of the exercise. This is a typescript, not a proof, so we have no need to worry about widows.)

This piece requires a middling level of intervention: problems abound but there is no need to rewrite extensively. What about the content? This is where you need to know the kind of book and its market. If it purported to be a scientific book, you might legitimately ask for further substantiation of the points. If, as seems more likely, it is a therapist's personal statement of his or her philosophy, then whether you find it convincing or not is irrelevant. If you can make helpful suggestions, especially pointing out any internal inconsistencies, that is fine, but in this kind of book readers should usually be allowed to judge for themselves the author's uncensored views.

Language change

It will be clear that many of the points of grammar discussed are contentious at the time of writing. We are talking not of hard-and-fast *rules* of syntax but of degrees of acceptability, of variations, some of which may even be common in colloquial English but are better avoided in written English.

As an editor, you need to keep your finger on the pulse. Each generation changes the language we speak and (usually at a slower pace) the language we write. It is no part of an editor's job to put a brake on natural change but inevitably all editors develop (as you can see I have) their own pet hates, their sticking points. It is certainly part of an editor's job to preserve us all, readers and writers, from sloppy and ambiguous usage. You need to tread carefully the line between pedantry and 'anything goes'. Above all, keep your ears and eyes open; be aware of the trends, both deplorable and beneficial. Every day you will need to decide where to take your stand, and every five years or so you may need to modify your judgement on a particular point.

As we have seen, American usage differs from British. Similarly, variations are developing in countries, such as India, where English is an official language much used for communication in the public sphere. In other places, such as the Caribbean, creole languages have developed that sprang originally from English (or other European languages) but now exist in their own right alongside standard English. The standard English expected in most books may be influenced in minor ways by the creole form. Editors everywhere are in a similar position: they have to decide which variations to allow and which to resist.

Further reading

Invaluable reference books on all the specific topics dealt with here, and many more besides, are:

H.W. Fowler, *A Dictionary of Modern English Usage*, revised by Ernest Gowers (Oxford University Press, Oxford, 2nd edition, 1965)

Eric Partridge, *Usage and Abusage* (Penguin, Harmondsworth, revised edition, 1973)

Both of these are in dictionary form. A more readable theme-based treatment of similar niceties is to be found in:

Ernest Gowers, *The Complete Plain Words*, revised by Sidney Greenbaum and Janet Whitcut (Her Majesty's Stationery Office, London, 3rd edition, 1986; Penguin, Harmondsworth, paperback edition, 1987)

For second-language users of English, the most helpful guide is probably:

Michael Swan, *Practical English Usage* (Oxford University Press, Oxford, 1980)

UNIT 8

Meaning and Clarity

The main purpose of checking and, if necessary, correcting the grammatical construction of a sentence is to clarify the meaning, to eliminate ambiguity. In this unit we concentrate on that aspect: communication with the reader. In this area, knowledge of the market is particularly important: you are checking whether the meaning will be clear to the likely reader of that particular book. It is not just a question of language level (which we address in Unit 12) but of whether the book will be used only for reference or read straight through; whether it is part of formal education or armchair reading. Both textbooks and leisure reading, for example, must interest the reader but the first may demand much more active participation.

Now do Exercise 8.1   **G**

---

*You are not asked to edit these passages, simply to identify the classic problem each illustrates. Often one word will sum it up. The review is on the next page so that the answers won't catch your eye too early: **turn to that review** before you go on to the discussion below.*

Principles of clear communication

For textbooks at any level, readability and clear exposition are vital. The following pointers may be helpful.

■ First things first. If you are explaining a procedure, take it step by step.

■ Think about the medium. Will the explanation be clearest as text, artist's drawing, photograph, diagram, graph or table, or a combination of two or more of these? It is certainly often true that 'A picture is worth a thousand words' (though you may need to weigh the less metaphorical costs).

■ Use simple but varied sentences. A staccato succession of sentences, each with only a main clause, is boring; on the other hand, more than two or three subordinate clauses in a sentence can impair readability. Even more important may be position: subordinate clauses *before* the main clause are more difficult to take in than ones that follow the main clause. The main clause establishes the essential message of the sentence, so if it comes early we have a hook to hang everything else on.

■ Make connections explicit. Despite the previous point, a connective phrase at the beginning of a sentence can be positively helpful. For example, 'Spread all the pieces of the jigsaw, face up, on the table. Once each piece is clearly visible, you can easily find all the straight edges and group them by colour.' The connective (although in some senses redundant) establishes the logic of the procedure or argument; it reassures the reader that he or she has understood.

Now do Exercise 8.2

Improve and clarify each example as necessary.

Review of Exercise 8.1

1 Illogic
The adjective has inadvertently been transferred – it is not the gap that is much needed but the book (we hope).

2 Cliché and mixed metaphor
They are piled up absurdly here, but do always look out for hackneyed phrases, and metaphors that, if taken literally, would conjure up impossible images.

3 Three hands
This is a surprisingly common problem in more complex passages.

4 Verbosity or circumlocution
Extraneous phrases such as 'taken to have the meaning of' and 'do actually take the opportunity to' hinder rather than aid precise definition. Legal definitions sometimes have to be lengthy but each word must make a necessary contribution.

5 Sloppy definition
Meteorites and bits of aeroplanes also fall from the sky; ice and frost form on the ground.

6 Unexplained and excessive abbreviation
The abbreviation 'CAP' certainly needs to be spelt out the first time it is used, with the abbreviation in parentheses, so that further references may use the abbreviated form. 'EC' and 'EEC' would be better just given in full. 'GNP' may be best left since it is more familiar in its abbreviated form. (Alternatively, in this context you could change it to a non-technical expression such as the 'nation's wealth'.)

Where possible, avoid an offputting build-up of initials (full caps especially will dominate the printed page). Be consistent over whether or not 'the' is used before a particular abbreviation. (The author wavers over 'the CAP'.)

You may (as here) be able to look up the short forms in the *Writers' Dictionary*. It has a wide range of useful abbreviations, including the Common Agricultural Policy. (Forthcoming editions will presumably also recognize 'EC' as the European Community.) If you cannot be sure which one of several alternatives is meant, put a query to the author. Note that the explanation may be set entirely lower case even though the abbreviation uses capitals (as for GNP – gross national product).

7 Ambiguous referent
In the last sentence 'them' presumably refers back to 'clothes' but the intervening sentence could mislead the reader into thinking 'material and style' or 'tastes' were meant.

8 Confusing word order
A lengthy explanation separates the subject of the sentence from the main verb. Changing the word order is often the simplest way to improve the readability of a sentence. So here you could start the sentence with the 'because' clause (and its dependent 'which' clause) and shift 'Janet and I' (the subject) to immediately before 'never did have' (the main verb).

Now return to the section about principles of clear communication on p. 43.

Review of Exercise 8.2

The first four examples demonstrate, respectively: an ambiguous referent; double negatives, which make the sentence hard to understand; a word-order problem ('in Pamacha' is better either at the beginning or after 'shop'); and a back-to-front procedure, which you can cure following the precept 'first things first'.

Example 5 demonstrates pompous officialese. I hope you cut and simplified it.

Example 6 may be clarified by separating the HCF and LCM into two quite independent paragraphs, explaining the HCF first and giving the example (preferably displayed on a new line); then the LCM, again with the example, using the same numbers as the original does. Only after that do you make the point that they should not be confused. (Saying it at the beginning may actually induce the problem in some readers.) You will also have noticed that, in the original, the abbreviation comes before the explanation and the order changes confusingly, from 'LCM and HCF' in the first sentence to a discussion of the HCF first. (Of course, to anyone already familiar with the concepts the original formulation is perfectly clear but you are not addressing them.)

Major style work

If you rearranged the last example in Exercise 8.2 as radically as I've suggested, you will have found it simplest to write (or type) the whole passage out again. Sometimes such rewriting is indeed the only course. If that extent of alteration is required throughout a book, you may also need to build a retyping stage into the schedule in order to produce a neat enough typescript for the typesetter. (Nowadays having everything on disk avoids that problem.)

Retyping might well have been necessary in the case of the next exercise (a genuine example) but in fact, as you will see, editing between the lines, even when it is extensive, *can* be neat enough for the typesetter to manage. When you are doing the exercise, concentrate just as much on your marking technique as on the changes you are making.

The passage comes from a manual for training primary teachers (themselves with only junior secondary qualifications) and is written by someone whose mother tongue is not English.

The schools in the country for which it is written do educate girls as well as boys, though you might not think it from the passage as it stands. We'll discuss the different ways of editing out sexism (and the reasons for doing it) in more detail in Unit 12. One way that works quite well here is to alternate between boys and girls, as there are likely to be some of each in most classes. If you take this route, however, beware of reinforcing stereotypes such as girls doing cookery and boys doing science.

When improving style, especially in a translation or a passage written by someone for whom English is a second or foreign language, you are looking out especially for incorrect use of prepositions, the article, etc., as well as for all the points such as sequence of tenses and word order that we have discussed in this and the previous unit.

In addition, poor style in English (by native speakers as much as others) can often be traced to repetitious vocabulary, and excessive reliance on the verb 'to be', instead of searching for a more apposite verb. In particular, frequent use of the passive (also entailing the verb 'to be') is at the root of much tedious writing. In instructional books, however, repetition may sometimes serve a purpose: in Unit 5 we saw the value of identical formulae as signposts to the book's structure; earlier in this unit we discussed the use of connectives. In more creative writing, variety and originality are essential to capture and hold the reader's attention.

Finally, another 'principle of communication': speak directly to your readers. Address them as 'you' wherever possible. In an educational text, give direct instructions: 'do this', rather than 'you might like to ...', or 'a good teacher should ...'.

Whenever you are doing extensive style work, always *re-read* the altered sentence. At the end of a paragraph, re-read the paragraph. It is dangerously easy to make things worse rather than better (for example by *introducing* repetition, as we saw for 'example' in Exercise 4.2, Sartre on Freedom). Look out too for places where you have forgotten to delete everything you intended to delete in the original (a pitfall mentioned in discussion of Exercise 2.4, Caring).

Now do Exercise 8.3

Remember to mark changes as neatly as you possibly can. If you cannot understand a sentence, skip it for the moment and go back to it later. To remind yourself of such points that you intend to return to, put a small pencil cross in the margin, rubbing it out again when you have dealt with the problem.

Review of Exercise 8.3

Compare your work with the sample answer on p. 48. It is included not because it shows the *only* way in which this passage should be edited – there are innumerable satisfactory options – but because it demonstrates some reasonably neat solutions, both to the language and to the technique problems. Notice that, even when the punctuation remains unchanged, it is included with the handwritten addition (for example on ll. 5, 12, 15). This keeps it close to the preceding word, which makes typesetting easier and therefore more likely to be accurate.

The sample answer takes some liberties with the rather obscure second sentence. In addition, you may have thought that a rearrangement, bringing the second paragraph in earlier, was a good idea. (The only objection to this is that reporting to the doctor might not then follow on satisfactorily.)

At least two points of terminology will have to be queried with the author: 'subnormal' and 'supernormal'. Educationalists' usage in this particular country will determine the final outcome but 'subnormal' at least is pretty derogatory and, as you are standing in for the reader who might find it offensive, you need to suggest alternatives.

Queries

I have mentioned queries to the author several times. On the next page you will see a typical list of queries that might be sent to an author *together with* the edited typescript or a good photocopy of it.

He or she then has the chance to check everything that has been done, as well as clearing up the outstanding problems. The exact position of a query may be shown, as in the sample answer to Exercise 8.3, by a discreet *pencil* question mark in the left-hand

QUERIES FOR THE AUTHOR   Book title:............................

The edited script is attached for reference. Please check that all
changes are acceptable to you as well as dealing with the specific
queries listed below.

PAGE	LINE	QUERY	RESPONSE
General		I have reduced the frequent use of italic because in print it could be distracting. Hope this is OK?	
		Because true footnotes are expensive to set, I have had to take them into the text. Plse chk pp. 30, 46, 110, 136 to make sure they are integrated in an acceptable way	
26	10	May, 1969 - or 1967 as refs?	
30	3up	'constructing ... to' - incorrect English or correct jargon?	
36	4	Koesterbaum - or Koestenbaum as refs?	
37	10-11	Plse chk my rewording	
40	6-5up	I've stumbled over this sentence - over 'since' (means 'because'?) and over 'figure into'. Plse clarify	
42	6	Confirm 1880, not 1980	
44	12	Wann, 1963 - or 1964 as pp. 49, 50 and refs?	
46	7	'a reminder ... for their subject area' - meaning?	
48	2	Graham, 1984 - not in refs; Husserl, 1931 - a or b?	
51-3	Tables	3.1-3.3 Plse give details of sources. (They appear to be photocopies of printed material.)	
51	T 3.1	Numbers in col. 1 do not add up - OK? Numbers or percentages in col. 3? Should items be ordered alphabetically as in T 3.3?	

margin on the relevant folio. You can *either* ask authors to insert their responses directly into the typescript *or* ask them to answer on the query sheet so that you may insert them yourself when the typescript comes back.

Some editors use small stickers to indicate the folios with queries, either as well as or instead of a list. Although these stickers are invaluable during the editing process, to remind yourself of lines or folios you intend to go back to, they are less appropriate for queries for the author. They may fall off *en route*, or be discarded by the author once dealt with. They also make through-feed photocopying of the typescript impossible.

Another method is to note the whole query in pencil in the margin and provide a checklist of folios to be looked at. On the whole, especially with the advent of word-processing, compiling a list of queries is the most satisfactory method. If you do not have access to a word-processor or typewriter, a neatly handwritten list may be acceptable.

If the typescript is *not* to be returned to the author with the queries, each point on the list must be explained more fully (though it should always be put as succinctly as possible). Certainly you must then give the author's *original* folio number and line number, so that he or she can refer to an unedited duplicate. (Include a column for your new folio number as well, to help you to insert the response.)

In communicating with authors, avoid jargon; for example say 'page' rather than 'fo.' A useful shorthand, however, when specifying line numbers, is to say 'line 3 up' (meaning the third line from the bottom) as in the example.

Do be tactful as well as brief. Remember the time and effort invested in any creative endeavour and authors' natural sensitivity to what may sound like criticism. Try to show that you are in tune with their purposes and are just trying to clarify, not dispute, the argument.

So much for *how* to query, but *what* should you query? This will depend on the kind of book and the amount of editorial work you have done on it (as well as on whether the typescript accompanies the queries). If you have done extensive style work, as in Exercise 8.3, you cannot possibly query every change, nor would the author want you to. You only need to query places where you are not quite sure of the sense (perhaps that second sentence) and questions of fact such as the terminology.

In a more typical book, where stylistic changes are few, you might query each one. Even there, you would probably not query the correction of a singular to a plural verb, for example.

Major deletions, rearrangements or alterations of the heading hierarchy (as in Exercise 5.1, Reading Maps) are always worth querying. If you have made a change throughout (run short quotations on into the text rather than setting them out as extracts, changed numerous capitals to lower case, eliminated excessive italic, etc.), it is certainly worth alerting the author at this stage rather than letting him or her see the result for the first time in page proof.

If there are factual or logical inconsistencies in the typescript, you almost certainly need to query them (either leaving the author to determine the solution or making your own suggestions and asking the author to confirm them).

In academic books or journals, many queries are likely to concern references (as we shall see in Units 17–19).

Throughout I have talked about 'the author' in the singular but often there will be several people involved. You may have to write separate query lists for the different contributors, another for the academic editor of the volume or journal, and (if you are working freelance) perhaps another for the publisher's in-house editor.

Further reading

A brilliant course of exercises on this aspect of editing (although written for the American market) is to be found in:

H. Wendell Smith, *Readable Writing: Revising for Style* (Wadsworth, Belmont, California, 1985; distributed in the UK by Routledge, Chapman & Hall)

You will find a great deal of sensible advice, and entertainment as well, in:

Leslie Sellers, *The Simple Subs Book* (Pergamon, Oxford, 2nd edition, 1985)

For a more austere but helpful treatment of practical language editing in schoolbooks see:

Ray Williams, *Readable Writing: A Manual for Authors and Editors of Educational Textbooks* (Longman, Harlow, 1985)

Finally, some useful practice may be found in a correspondence course (also available as a normal book), which offers a brisk introduction to various aspects of editing and handling proofs, based on the example of a newsletter:

Celia Hall, *Editing for Everyone* (National Extension College, Cambridge, 1983)

Sample answer to Exercise 8.3

(A)

Proper Attention to the Individuality of ~~the~~ Pupils

~~The~~ encouraging ~~of the~~ [personal] development and the expression of ~~the~~ individuality does not mean letting ~~him~~ [a child] 'run wild. [It] ~~Individuality~~ means ~~the~~ [encouraging self-c] expression of in~~ing~~ [the interests] some ~~others~~ and ~~the~~ re-direct~~ion~~ of others. The idea ~~here~~ is that the teacher should make allowances for a pupil's individual~~ity different from others~~ [needs and concerns.] If a ~~child~~ [boy] is deaf, ~~he should be~~ seated [him] near the front. If ~~he~~ [a girl] is near-sighted, ~~he should be~~ seated [her where she] ~~in the place at which he~~ can see to the best advantage. In ~~such and in other~~ [these and similar] cases the parents, ~~we~~ [as] well as the school doctor, should be notified. [Likewise,]

~~If~~ a ~~child~~ [boy] is exceedingly nervous, ~~the teacher~~ [you] should avoid situations that unduly excite ~~the child~~ [him.]

[As far as lessons are concerned,] ~~In the matter of subjects,~~ whil~~st~~ [e] most c[h]ildren can ~~do~~ [cope] fairly well [with] ~~the~~ work prescribed, ~~there are~~ some c~~h~~ildren in every class ~~who~~ [will] have difficulty in keeping up. There ~~are~~ [will be] also a few who a~~re~~ able to do a great deal more than the other children~~, in the room.~~ The first ~~class is called subnormal,~~ [group are said to have special needs,] the [second to have special talents.] ~~other supernormal,~~ [Genuine] ~~True, kindly~~ sympathy should be shown to ~~the children~~ [those with special needs.] ~~of the first class.~~ Extra work ~~needs to~~ [should] be given to ~~the second class, the~~ [those with special talents,] ~~members of which~~ [who] need little more than plenty of work and some direction~~, and~~ [;] t~~h~~ey will do the rest.

[People have] ~~There is an~~ individual ~~liking for subject.~~ [preferences.] When a child ~~is found with~~ [shows] a strong liking for a given subject, ~~that child should be~~ [offer] encouraged. [ment.] There was [once] a poor child in America who was regarded [as] dull and hopeless in most ~~of the~~ subjects. However, he did well in drawing. When his teacher found that out, he let him draw everything ~~in~~ connect~~ion~~ [ed] with the lessons ~~which~~ [that] lent itself to drawing. That proved to be the boy's salvation[.] To~~-~~day he is one of the greatest architects in the country.

If ~~a scholar~~ [one pupil] is strong in arithmetic, ~~he may~~ [let her] join the ~~work~~ [lessons] of the next class in addition to ~~his~~ [her] own. If ~~he~~ [another] is s~~t~~rong in history, ~~he may be~~ encourage~~d~~ [him] to read supplementary books on ~~history.~~ [the subject.] If ~~he~~ [another pupil] likes geography, ~~he may be~~ encouraged [her] to read ~~some~~ [extra] geograph~~ical readers~~ [y books] or to subscribe to a Geographical Magazine.

UNIT 9

Punctuation

Just as improvement of grammatical structures can help to clarify an author's meaning, so can attention to punctuation. We turn to that mundane but important subject in this unit.

Commas

Commas often travel in pairs. An example would be: 'The painter, as far as we know, never left Italy.' There were instances of this pairing in Exercise 7.2 (Effects of LSD).

In Exercise 4.2 (Sartre on Freedom), we saw that commas should consistently be inserted *or* be omitted after parallel phrases such as 'on the one hand', 'on the other hand'. (If these occur in mid-sentence, there will be a comma before as well as after the phrase.) Be consistent too about whether or not there are commas round (or after) 'however' (in its 'but' sense), 'similarly', 'alternatively', 'thirdly', etc.

The tide is running against the comma. So, if you find that an author rarely uses one, you should hesitate to sprinkle them through his or her work. On the other hand, the lack of commas may only strike that same author in proof and you'll be blamed for failing to edit helpfully. You can't always win, but awareness of what you are doing and why can help.

Do not allow a comma where a colon or semicolon is meant. (Their functions are discussed in more detail below.) Nor should a comma divide the subject, however long, from its verb (as we saw in Exercise 7.2, Effects of LSD), unless it is one of a pair separating off a subordinate clause.

Look back at all the commas used in the preceding paragraphs to make sure you understand the function of each one. As you can see, I am no comma-hater, although there are some places where you might put them in and I don't.

There are two schools of thought, for example, about a comma before 'and' or 'but' joining two (or more) main clauses into one sentence. According to the rule applied here, 'and' or 'but' on its own is normally sufficient indication (for example in 'and you'll be blamed') that a second main clause follows. A comma is only used to clarify a complicated sentence or to emphasize that the second half is a separate point. The example of this above is 'but awareness ...': the sense is almost a dash rather than a comma (although it is unwise to add dashes in a work that generally avoids them). To this school of thought, commas before 'and' or 'but' in any other circumstances are anathema. The alternative system (favoured by *Hart's Rules* and standard in American English) consistently inserts a comma before 'and' or 'but' joining two main clauses.

Allied to this is the **list comma** (or Oxford comma) mentioned in discussion of Exercise 4.1 (Silk). This is also in *Hart's Rules* and is standard American practice, although less common in British English than the comma before 'and' or 'but'. (You *can* use a comma before 'and' or 'but' without adopting the list comma, although they often go together.) The classic instance of the list comma, as we have seen, is 'red, white, and blue', where others would write 'red, white and blue'. Note that there have to be at least three items in the list. Even if the list comma is not adopted as a general rule, an extra comma can occasionally be essential for clarification, for example, 'red, red and amber, and green'.

I have *not* stressed my own usage here in order to urge you to follow my system: it simply provides a handy example. Editing for punctuation is not, for the most part, about applying a particular house style (or indeed your own preferences) but about analysing the author's style and making sure it is both logical and consistent. Practise taking notice of style (in all senses) in everything you read.

Now do Exercise 9.1

Review of Exercise 9.1

Remember that when you are inserting a comma it is best to squeeze it in *on the line* if you possibly can (marking a space after it if this brings it very close to the next word). Always circle any full stop you insert (as for 'B.C.' on ll. 9 and 34). Again, squeeze the full stops in below the line rather than using insertion signs. There is no need to mark 'B.C.' specifically for capitals – they are assumed *unless* you mark for small caps.

This author is undoubtedly a comma-user so, if one comma of a pair is missing, you need have no hesitation about putting an extra comma in, rather than taking out the existing one. Add a comma on ll. 3 (if you haven't adopted the better course of moving 'this' to precede 'had'), 8, 12, 15 (after 'that') and 32. An additional pair might even be helpful for 'down to the fourth millennium'. (I hope you looked up the spelling of this, though it is in fact correct.)

Whether the author uses a comma before 'and' and 'but' as a general rule or just for occasional extra separation is less easy to gauge from this short piece. On l. 18 a comma after 'jungle' would be needed anyway to avoid confusion; on l. 34 the comma before 'but' is one of a pair. On l. 28 a comma before 'and' would help in any case, as this is almost a dash. The remaining two instances (ll. 6 and 13) should be made consistent, one way or the other. In real life it helps to put pencil crosses in the margin (as for any other places you intend to go back to) and continue watching out for the point until the style becomes clear. The same technique applies for alternative spellings, use of capitals, etc.

Decisions on the list comma (or rather the omission of it) came on ll. 20–1, 23–4 and 33. The comma after 'marsh' on l. 18 would never be correct. A comma is not required after 'including' or 'such as' (l. 22; see also l. 32).

I hope you also noticed that the list on l. 24 suddenly went into the plural, with no real justification. Of course, the list on ll. 20–1 was *all* plural but I don't think it is necessary to bring this one (and l. 33) into line: you can go overboard on consistency and forget that variety makes more interesting reading. I *would*, nevertheless, change l. 24 to 'ostrich and lion'.

An additional comma is helpful on l. 7; delete one on l. 13. The commas on ll. 24–5 are quite wrong, separating off an essential section as though it were parenthetic. On l. 35, the 'which' is parenthetic (check by testing whether the whole phrase could be omitted or put in parentheses), so it must have a comma before it.

Other punctuation problems were: the colon on l. 5 is probably better as a semicolon or perhaps a full stop and new sentence; the semicolon on l. 16 should be a colon. (We'll return to these in Exercise 9.3.)

Finally, on l. 5 the verb should be 'began'; 'anywhere' is one word (l. 9); Near East takes capitals (l. 11, see l. 4); 'this' would be preferable to 'it' on l. 35. You will have noticed some misspellings (ll. 1, 17 and 18) as well as the 's' on l. 15. The clearest way to correct 'vegetation' on l. 17 is to delete all three letters and write them correctly above the line, rather than indicating a complicated transposition.

Quotation marks and dialogue

The alternative systems of double or single quotes (using the opposite form for 'inner' quotes) was explained in Unit 4. The single-quote system (with double inner) is most commonly used in adult non-fiction in Britain and is gaining ground in fiction and children's books. The double-quote system is still quite often used for those, however, and (as we saw in Unit 6) is widespread at all levels in the United States.

In dialogue, for example in a novel, a new para starts every time a different person begins to speak. Look back at the editor's marking in Exercise 2.1 (The Morse Machine), copy l. 23. A new para has been marked, to show that we are switching from 'the man', at this end of the wire, to the answerer, Obuasi. This separation enables the reader to change his or her mental image quickly, even before reaching indicators like 'Jane said'. It often means that such indicators only need to be used occasionally, rather than every time a different person speaks.

If a single speech goes on over several paras, the opening quote is repeated at the beginning of each para but there is no matching closing quote until the very end of the speech.

Now do Exercise 9.2

If you don't understand something at the first reading, put a pencil cross in the margin and go back to it later. Do not change any of the words: just add punctuation where it is needed.

Review of Exercise 9.2

Compare your work with the sample answer on the next two pages. Again, this is by no means the only answer but is included partly so that you may check your marking technique and partly because the pattern of a speech within a speech can only be explained visually.

Note that the ellipsis on l. 25 is a three-point one. It denotes a sentence that tails off (and so is by definition unfinished), not the omission of part of the passage.

Colons and semicolons

We cannot explore every kind of stop here. *Hart's Rules* has useful advice on many of them; see also the Further Reading section below. One problem that troubles many people, however, is the distinction between colons and semicolons.

The most straightforward use of a colon is to introduce a list. Often the items in the list are phrases (rather than single words) and they are divided from each other by semicolons. So, using examples from Exercise 9.1 (Egypt),

rich fauna, including the elephant, rhinoceros, …

only requires commas but

fauna thrived in the hot climate: hippopotamuses and crocodiles in the swamps; elephants and giraffes in the jungle; …

becomes clearer through the introductory colon and the semicolons between items. Incidentally, there is never any need for the old-fashioned ':–' introducing a list.

The other main uses of the colon are similarly introductory. It is helpful where the first half of the sentence leads to the second half:

The uncontrolled inundation of the Nile left pools and swamps: in these conditions fauna thrived.

Similarly, a colon may introduce an example of the point made in the first half of the sentence. Either way, there has to be a logical connection: premise and conclusion, or statement and example.

A semicolon, on the other hand, indicates two (or more) parallel parts of the sentence:

The Neolithic Revolution had its origin in the Near East; it began soon after the end of the last ice age.

The first half is concerned with place, the second with time. Because of this connection, they are placed within the same sentence; unlike my last sentence (which requires only commas), each half of the displayed sentence has its own subject and verb.

So, when you want to make more than the usual connection between two statements that could easily stand as separate sentences (with their own subjects and verbs), use a colon if one leads to the other, a semicolon if they are parallel.

Parentheses and brackets

Look at the use of parentheses and commas in the previous two sentences. Commas are never required both before *and* after parentheses but one comma, as in these sentences, helpfully shows the end of the phrase beginning 'unlike' or the subordinate clause beginning 'when'.

The order of a closing parenthesis and full stop (mentioned in Unit 5) also sometimes causes confusion. The following examples demonstrate the correct order:

These could easily stand as separate sentences (because they have their own verbs).

These could easily stand as separate sentences. (This is because they have their own verbs.)

I use the term **parenthesis** because in technical usage (and in the United States) 'bracket' means a *square* bracket. These, as we shall see in Unit 11, have a specific application in quotations. They may also occur for a second order of bracketing *within* parentheses (just as double quotes are used within single quotes). This style is, however, becoming less common: instead you can simply have two sets of parentheses. (Note that parentheses are also sometimes known as **parens**.)

Now do Exercise 9.3

---

*In addition to looking at punctuation, pay attention to the use of capitals. Remember to refer to the **Writers' Dictionary** when you need to make decisions between inconsistent forms of all sorts.*

Sample answer to Exercise 9.2

boss, i saw mehitabel

the cat yesterday she is

back in town after

spending a couple

of weeks   5

in the country

"archy," she says to me,

"i will never leave the

city again, no

matter what the weather   10

may be me for the

cobble-stones and the

asphalt and the friendly

alleys the great open

spaces are all right but   15

they are too open; i have been

living on a diet of

open spaces the country is

all right if you have a trained

human family to rustle   20

up the eats for you, or know

a cow who has the

gift of milking herself for

your benefit but, archy,

i am a city lady   25

hell, archy, i am always

a lady and always gay"

she says it is her

romantic disposition

```
        that keeps her young                    30

        and yet i think, if some
               =
        cheerful musical family

        in good circumstances were to

        offer mehitabel a home
               =
        where she would be treated in          35

        all ways as one of the family,

        she has reached the point where

        she might consent to give up

        living her own life.
        ' " only three legs left, archy," she says,   40
            =                              =
        " but wot the hell archy,
                         )  =
        there's dance in the old
              )
        dame yet." " )
```

Review of Exercise 9.3

The *Writers' Dictionary* will have answered most of the minor points of inconsistency here. As well as giving practice on colons and semicolons, the exercise leads on to one of the topics of the next unit. On ll. 1–3, no capital is required for 'southern', 'coast' or 'the' but the Northern Province is the name of that part of Ghana. (You would need to check this point in an atlas.) Some institutions now insist that 'The' is an integral part of their name and so takes a capital but I find it hard to see any justification for this usage. The wet and dry seasons (ll. 4–5), like spring and autumn, require no capitals; nor does the earth (l. 8), unless it is contrasted with other planets. Again, the Gulf of Guinea (l. 15) is a proper name. South and north on ll. 3–4 and 21–3 must be consistent (probably, though not necessarily, lower case).

As far as the punctuation is concerned, ll. 10, 13, 24 should be colons and ll. 4, 9, 25 semicolons. Do mark incorrect spacing after punctuation (as, for example, on ll. 4 and 9). The typesetter *shouldn't* reproduce such errors but in some circumstances (particularly in reference systems, as we'll see in Unit 19), publishers' preferences do differ. It is best to develop the habit of noticing and correcting.

There must be no comma on l. 2 (it intervenes between subject and verb); the style should match for commas round 'in the south' and 'in the north' (ll. 3–4). Clearly the author's style is to put in a comma before 'and' or 'but'.

The author's italics for 'winds' on l. 7 serve little purpose (even though this is strictly the first mention of the word). A better place for a distinction (if needed) is l. 8, where the word is defined. (We found the same convention in Exercise 5.1, Reading Maps.)

Finally, though these are by no means the only other problems, on l. 5 'which' is better as 'that'; on ll. 5–6 the 'amount of rainfall' and the 'way in which it is spread' are *joint*, not alternative subjects, and so require a plural verb, 'depend'.

Further reading

The main authorities (both published some time ago) are:

G.V. Carey, *Mind the Stop: A Brief Guide to Punctuation* (Cambridge University Press, Cambridge, revised edition, 1958; Penguin, Harmondsworth, paperback edition, 1971)

Eric Partridge, *You Have a Point There* (Routledge, London, 1978)

UNIT 10

Capitals and Hyphens

Some of the thorniest problems of everyday editorial work involve decisions over capitals and hyphens. The words affected will be different in each book and it is helpful to keep a record of your decisions on a **style sheet** of the kind discussed in Unit 14 below.

Capitals

As with punctuation, you need to be able to assess the author's own system. Many feel very strongly about fine distinctions of meaning according to whether a word begins with a capital or a lower-case letter within the same work. Be sure you understand the existing system before you make adjustments to it.

Your firm, or the journal or series you are working on, may also have general preferences, for or against capitals, or indeed may impose specific rules on words that occur regularly. Current fashion favours lower case wherever possible because a forest of capitals is thought distracting.

Now do Exercise 10.1 **G**

You are not asked to edit the passages but to look carefully at places where a capital initial is used and similar places in the same passage where a lower-case initial occurs. Try to work out the logic of the distinctions being drawn.

Review of Exercise 10.1

1 Here a capital is used for a recognized party affiliation ('he is a Democrat') but lower case for general orientations ('liberal', 'communist'). No one is suggesting the Democratic candidate is also a card-carrying member of the Communist Party. This distinction is a widespread convention. 'Presidential Election', on the other hand, like 'general election' (as recommended by the *Writers' Dictionary*), would often be set lower case.

2 In this passage, by contrast with the first, 'party' is lower-cased, even when attached to the name of the organization. This is a not uncommon style (limiting the use of capitals as far as possible). It may look odd in the case of the SDP but to use a capital 'P' for that one, just because of its initials, would look equally inconsistent in relation to 'the Labour party'. The reference to 'social democrats in other countries' again indicates their *general* orientation (although in practice many of them will be in parties called, for example, the Social Democrats).

If the system in this passage is to lower-case 'party', even when it comes into a title, why is its equivalent, the 'Alliance', capitalized? This is because, as the final sentence shows, that was to be the abbreviation used in the continuing discussion. Similarly, in a one-party state, 'the Party' might be the usual term for the organization and as such it might be accorded a capital. (It doesn't *have* to take a capital, however, any more than 'government': see 5 below.) The phrase 'one or other party' would *always* be set lower case because this is a general, not specific, use of the term.

3 Here the system is to use a capital for all the artistic movements discussed, even when, as in the case of Duchamp, the artist might not have recognized the designation himself. (Another author might have differentiated on a similar basis to party membership versus general orientation, as discussed above, though it is not such an easy distinction to apply to artistic movements.) The extensive use of capitals demonstrated here now looks rather old-fashioned: a modern book might lower-case both 'surrealist' and 'cubist'. What decision did you make in the similar instance in Exercise 4.2 (Sartre on Freedom) over 'existentialist', 'libertarian', and 'determinist'? I would lower-case all these; some might say 'Existentialists' should have a capital as a specific school of thought.

Most people would retain the capital for 'Dadaist', even when lower-casing 'surrealism', etc. The reason would be its origin in a proper name (albeit in this case a pseudonym). Similarly, Marxist usually retains its capital, although many authors now like to make distinctions between 'Marxists' and 'marxist tendencies', on the same basis as 'Liberal' and 'liberal' in 1 and 2. It is usual to write 'Cartesian philosophy' (from Descartes) but 'cartesian coordinates' (the x, y designation of position on a graph, which he invented).

In the last line of 3, 'exhibition' is set lower case, suggesting that the event was not actually called 'a Surrealist Exhibition' (or even 'the First Surrealist Exhibition'), as, for example, the Impressionist Exhibitions were.

4 This passage, by contrast, demonstrates the modern preference for lower case wherever possible. Even the pope is lower-cased when just mentioned as is the khan (king), a grand duke, sultan and caliph, whereas Friar John has a capital because the title is attached to his name. The pope would, similarly, be called Pope Innocent IV when his full name was given but simply 'the pope' in any other context.

5 This system is less extreme: the Minister of Agriculture has capitals, where in 4 the high constable of Armenia did not. However, 'parliament', 'cabinet' and 'government' are lower-cased (as was 'the empire' in 4). Compare 1, where 'Presidential Election' had capitals, which would be seen as unnecessary in the style of 5. The *Writers' Dictionary* recommends using a capital for 'Parliament' and 'Government'. Even then, lower case is used for an adjective derived from the word, for example 'parliamentary privilege' or a related noun, for example 'parliamentarian'. Similarly, even if 'Empire' has a capital, 'imperial' does not (except in a specific title, such 'His Imperial Majesty').

The reasons for the capitals for 'White Paper' in 5 is the possible confusion between the official document and just any piece of white paper. Similarly, an Act (of Parliament) always takes a capital. Several recommendations in the *Writers' Dictionary*, however, are less necessary: a capital is recommended for 'the Press' (presumably to distinguish them from a printing or clothes press), which looks odd alongside 'the media'; 'Civil Servants' hardly seems essential in order to distinguish them from polite domestics. The more dominant one particular usage of a term becomes, the more likely we are to drop the capital. The decision may, of course, also depend on context. In Exercise 6.1 did you opt for 'bridge' or 'Bridge'? Although the lower-case version *could* be ambiguous, it is much the more common.

The topic addressed by the White Paper is described as part of the normal text and so has no capitals. If the actual title had been given, it would be in italic, probably with capitalization of significant words.

6 The final example demonstrates the standard **botanical classification** system: **genus** in italic with a capital; **species** in italic, lower case; **variety** roman in quotes with a capital. The genus name is often abbreviated, for example to '*E.*', after the first mention. Classifications of animals (such as *Homo sapiens*) follow a similar pattern. The name of the **family**, above the genus level, is again roman but without quotes: for example Mammalia. The English word for a plant may often be similar to the Latin or Greek classification, as in 'eucalypt' here, or even identical, as in 'rhododendron'. Plant and animal names in English, however, do not usually take a capital unless a proper name is involved, for example 'Thomson's gazelle'.

Hyphens

Whereas an author's system of capital and lower case is often highly conscious and tenaciously held, few care passionately about hyphens. Whether a word such as 'proofreading' is one word, two words or hyphenated will often vary through a typescript – sometimes starting as two, becoming hyphenated and ending up as one. Similarly, words with prefixes, such as 'postmodern', may start hyphenated and end as one word. No difference in meaning is intended; the variation is the unconscious result of the author's increasing familiarity with the word. Nor can you expect hyphenation of such words to follow a logical system: this is a transitional feature in the language today and is governed by changing convention rather than logic. Follow the *Writers' Dictionary* or the author's prevalent style; list your decisions as you go along and ensure that the final typescript is consistent, both on particular words and on the treatment of related words. Even on this, as you will have noticed when doing Exercise 9.3

(Ghana), the recommendations can seem illogical: 'south-west' but 'southwester(ly)' for the wind.

As with capitals, there are several circumstances in which you should *not* make every instance consistent.

- Noun and verb are treated differently: 'The map has to be a pull-out' but 'Don't pull out the map'. Equally different but the opposite way round are: 'He was court-martialled' but 'He faced a court martial.' (In both cases there is a strong tendency for the hyphenated version to become one word.)

Treatment of **compound adjectives** before a noun (introduced in Unit 2) follows one of two systems.

- In the simplest, no compound adjectives are hyphenated, so you would write: 'eighteenth century farm', 'long lost relative' or sometimes (especially in American usage) 'the panicstricken waiter', 'the decisionmaking process'. This hyphen-avoiding style is most common in newspapers, magazines and advertisements but is perfectly acceptable in more formal contexts too.

- Advocates of the hyphen would say that the two-word forms above were ambiguous. (We *could* be talking about the eighteenth farm or the length of the relative, though neither seems very likely.) In these circumstances they would therefore use a hyphen: 'good-looking child', 'six-seater saloon'.

However, few people actually admit to being hyphen-lovers and so even in this second system there are several circumstances in which no hyphen is necessary.

- When the first half of the compound adjective is unmistakably an adverb, as I mentioned in Unit 4, there is no hyphen. The cause of the possible ambiguity in the examples above was the fact that 'long', 'good', etc., are equally often used as adjectives. The suffix -ly regularly converts an adjective into an adverb. So, 'the superbly cooked dish' or 'the frankly inedible pie' require no hyphens.

- No hyphen is used in, for example, 'a White House official'. Where the modifier is a compound proper name, the name is usually familiar enough to cause no confusion.

- Compound adjectives only require a hyphen when they are used **attributively** (that is, when they come *before* the noun they modify, as in all the examples given so far). If, on the other hand, they are used **predicatively** (after the verb), they rarely require a hyphen. So, 'The meal was well cooked.'

Finally, a reminder about **en rules**. In Exercise 10.1, 'the SDP–Liberal Alliance' would have an en rule (not a hyphen) because two separate parties were joining forces. If you were editing the piece, you would need to mark the en rule. Other examples we have come across are 'cause–effect relationship' (Exercise 7.2, Effects of LSD), 'cost–benefit analysis' and the archetypal 'London–Brighton railway'.

Now do Exercise 10.2

*Remember to look the words up, first in the **Writers' Dictionary**, then, if that is no help, in an ordinary dictionary. **Hart's Rules** also has a section on the topic. When you delete a hyphen, remember to show clearly by your marking whether the result is to be two words or one (see Unit 4). Look out, as usual, for other points besides hyphens.*

Review of Exercise 10.2

As we have seen elsewhere, there is sometimes a difference in meaning between an expression in two words and in one. 'Everything' (l. 17) has a different emphasis from 'every thing'. Even a hyphen can make a semantic difference: 'recover' (l. 10) is used for retrieval and 're-cover' for upholstery. Less obviously, 'up on the cliff' (l. 12) is quite different from 'upon the table'. Some people make a similar distinction for 'onto' (l. 16) (as for 'into') but the *Writers' Dictionary* recommends that it should always be two words.

Just as 'the eighteenth-century farm' becomes 'a farm built in the eighteenth century', a 'middle-aged person' would return 'in middle age' (l. 3). Similarly, you would write 'high-ceilinged rooms' (ll. 19–20) and 'air-conditioned coaches' (l. 22) but 'the sea is fast encroaching' (l. 18) and 'became well known' (l. 23).

It would be 'an overhead cable' but 'seagulls call … over head' (l. 1; similarly, 'under foot' on l. 11). On l. 15 delete the hyphens, although 'a stone-by-stone reconstruction' would retain them. 'Target practice' (l. 8) is best as two words. 'Worth while' is two words when used predicatively (as on l. 27) and one word when used attributively.

Possible mispronunciation often makes one-word solutions inadvisable. There is no problem over 'landmark' (l. 29), or even 'lighthouse' (l. 12) (though in other combinations the 'th' could be confusing, for example, 'moothall'). There is a strong tendency to retain the hyphen when identical vowels come together, as in 're-erected' (l. 26). On these grounds, the *Writers' Dictionary* prefers 'co-operative' (l. 4) and 'co-ordinate' but to many these are now so familiar without the hyphen that there is no longer a pronunciation problem.

On the same principle as 'cartesian coordinates' (mentioned above), 'french windows' and 'venetian blinds' have lost their original capitals: the association with France or Venice is now remote. On the other hand, 'War' (on l. 6) for a specific, named war would usually have a capital. Whereas 'the Downs', a particular range of hills, usually has a capital, 'downland' does not.

There are other hyphenation problems not mentioned. An en rule is needed on l. 22; note spelling errors on ll. 3 and 21; on l. 27 'that' is preferable to 'which' and on l. 24 'has' must be 'had'.

UNIT 11

Dialogue and Extracts

In this unit we look first at dialogue in fiction, consolidating what you have learned about outer and inner quotes and order of punctuation; we then tackle quotations (both long and short) of what other people have said or written, as they would appear in non-fiction works.

Dialogue

In Unit 9 you saw that each new speaker begins a new paragraph. This helps the reader to follow the conversation, reducing the need for indicators such as 'Costas said'. If the same person speaks for several paragraphs, a fresh opening quote begins each new para but no closing quote is needed until the speech ends. (We look at drama-style layout, which is rather different, in Unit 22.)

House style usually determines which system of quotes you apply. The clearest specification is, for example, 'single quotes (double inner)' but this system is often referred to simply as 'single quotes'. You are still expected to use the other kind of quote for inner quotes.

As we saw in Unit 6, there are also two distinct systems for **order of punctuation** when a closing quote coincides with a stop. (A **stop** is any form of punctuation.) In **logical** order, the closing quote comes before the stop when a word or phrase is in quotes; it comes after the stop when a sentence is in quotes. In the other system, **conventional** order, no distinction is made between words/phrases and sentences: the closing quote always comes after the full stop, comma, etc. Even in this system, there are certain stops that always follow the closing quote: dash, colon and semicolon.

You rarely need two stops:

'I said, "How do you know?" and he snapped back, "What do you mean?"'

Both question marks belong within the double quotes (whichever system of ordering you are following). The overall sentence extends from 'I' to 'mean' and is a statement, not a question. In theory this could imply that there should be an extra full stop at the end, but there never is. (In just the same way, if 'etc.' ends a sentence, you *don't* have a double full stop, one for the abbreviation and one to end the sentence.) Equally, it is unnecessary to add a comma before the 'and' here, even when your punctuation style is always to insert a comma before 'and' and 'but'. The question mark is sufficient indication of a pause.

Now do Exercise 11.1

Review of Exercise 11.1

Indent l. 3 as a new paragraph; end Dempsey's speech (with double quotes, since we are in that system) following the full stop after 'terms' on l. 7, starting a new para there for Persse's speech; and run on l. 9. The last of these assumes that Persse is still speaking on l. 9. An alternative *might* be that this is Angelica's interpolation (though, if so, it's surprising that no indication is given). It may be worth noting a query for the author: 'Please confirm Persse still speaking.' A new para is needed too towards the end of l. 16.

On l. 2 a comma rather than a full stop should follow 'urgency' (before the closing quote, since this is a full sentence). It is conventional to have some form of punctuation in this position (so on l. 17 add a comma after 'else'). The question mark on l. 3 is sufficient on its own without the comma; on l. 16 the question mark should follow 'animals', with a full stop after 'Persse'.

The 'woof, woof' passages (ll. 12 and 23–5) have

to be treated the same, probably lower case with a comma. There must certainly be no full stop after 'woof' on l. 12 and the full stop should follow the closing quote after 'miaou'; on l. 24 the commas (both the existing one and the list comma you add before 'and') similarly follow the closing quotes. (I suppose these expressions could be interpreted as sentences, in which case the stop would come first, but that seems somewhat anthropomorphic.)

Is it always necessary to have a comma before an opening quote? There often *is* one:

Jo asked, 'Where is the lorry?'

It is not needed, however, in such cases as

I say 'lorry', you say 'truck'.

Similarly, it is best here to standardize without a comma after 'goes'/'go' (ll. 12, 23–4). On ll. 15 and 25 the verb is understood rather than stated; in one case a comma has been used to show this. They should be treated the same, preferably without the comma.

The foreign terms for 'dog', etc., are italicized as they usually are – we look at this in more detail in Unit 16. Capital *Hund* and *Katze* are correct because in German all nouns begin with a capital. So only *gatto* (l. 21) has to change to lower case, to match *cane*. (Don't forget to delete the underlining under the commas: the punctuation is part of the overall English sentence and an italic comma is marginally different from a roman one.)

Although foreign terms are usually italicized, what someone *says* in a foreign language is not necessarily put in italics (as we shall see in Unit 16). Roman is certainly preferable here since 'woof' and 'miaou' would have to stay that way, as the English forms, and the distinction would look inconsistent.

I hope you noticed 'arbitrariness', 'expertise' (not an s/z spelling problem because pronounced quite differently from 'recognize', etc.) and 'quadruped'.

Embedded quotations

Looking back at Exercise 2.4 (Caring), you will see that (unlike dialogue in fiction) an author quoting someone else's opinion does not need to start a new paragraph to indicate a different speaker. The quotation is simply run on (**embedded**) in the text:

Ungerson does not discuss the motivations of wives … 'on the grounds that …'

In such a work, logical order of punctuation would normally be applied, so you need to check whether the quoted material is merely a phrase or a whole sentence. Different criteria are used for this judge-ment: certainly there must be a subject and verb if the quotation is to count as a sentence; many would say it should also begin with a capital. (This normally indicates that it was a complete sentence in the original.)

Extracts

In Caring, this quotation had originally been typed as a displayed extract but the editor ran it on as text because it was short. Conversely, in Exercise 4.2 (Sartre on Freedom) you converted an embedded quotation (ll. 37–45) into a displayed extract because it was long. As explained in Unit 4, it is usual to specify a particular length (commonly 40, 50 or 60 words) above which quotations should be displayed as extracts.

Never apply the word limit too rigidly, however: it is more important to treat parallel passages the same. So, for example, interviewees' responses might sometimes be short, sometimes long, but would need to be given equal weight. The same goes for display of all kinds. Example sentences or theorems, for instance, may all have to be displayed, whatever their length.

Rules for handling quotations

Whether quotations are embedded in the text or displayed as extracts, there are certain ways in which you treat them differently from ordinary text.

- Quotations are normally sacrosanct: do not edit or change them. If part of a quotation doesn't make sense, query it with the author (or look up the original yourself, if you can do so easily). Even when the solution seems obvious (for example, 'in' would make sense but 'is' has been typed), it is worth noting a query for the author to make sure.

- Exceptions, as we've seen, might be errors such as those in Exercise 4.2 (Sartre on Freedom) – 'any way/anyway'; 'pleasureably/pleasurably' – especially, as there, in translated material. Even if mistakes like these did appear in the original, it is often best to correct them without comment when they are irrelevant to the present discussion. If the author wants an error to stand because it *is* relevant, then '[*sic*]' should be added. (*Sic* is Latin for 'thus', meaning it was printed thus in the original; it is usually, though not necessarily, set in italic as a foreign word.)

- How far should you standardize quotations on matters of style? It is acceptable to apply the same quote system (single or double) as in the rest of the book; and to standardize the style of a dash (en or em, spaced or closed up). On all other matters (alternative spellings, use of capitals and italic, words or numerals for numbers, etc.), you should usually retain the original style.

- However, do *use your judgement* about this. If, for example, an author has -ise spellings in the text and all quotations also appear with -ise spellings, but your house style requires -ize, you have two choices. You can make the author recheck every quotation against the original; or (often more practicable) you can standardize the quotations to -ize to match the text. What you must not do is to apply the usual rule (that is, to change the text to -ize and leave all the quotations as -ise).

- Most authors will punctiliously follow the original, both for points like -ise/-ize and for capital or lower case at the beginning of the quotation (reflecting whether or not a new sentence began in the original). Preserve such distinctions.

- If a change in the original is necessary to help the reader to understand, you can add or substitute words in square brackets. These always denote an addition or substitution or an editorial comment on the original. If you suspect an author has used parentheses where there should be square brackets (perhaps for an explanation or change of his or her own within the quote), check by noting a query.

- Similarly, it is often necessary to put a query about the use of italic in a quotation. Was a particular phrase printed in italic in the original? Or is the italic used by your author to draw the reader's attention to a particular aspect of the quotation? The latter is perfectly legitimate but should be noted. So it is usual to state, after any quotation that includes italic, whose emphasis the italic reflects.

- An ellipsis is by nature normally your author's addition. (It shows that something has been omitted from the original.) It is therefore not usually thought necessary to put the ellipsis into square brackets. The three points of the ellipsis are usually marked for space by the editor, as you learned in Unit 4.

Sometimes an additional full stop appears before the ellipsis to show that the original sentence ended before the omitted words. Purists demand a third option, an ellipsis followed by a full stop. (This would *look* quite different because the first dot would not be closed up to the word

before it.) This seems an unnecessary refinement since normally the use of a capital or lower case after the three points adequately indicates whether or not a new sentence is starting.

If you are not convinced that the author has applied the distinction between three- and four-point ellipses consistently, you can simply standardize throughout to three points. This is a perfectly acceptable alternative method.

Extract layout and punctuation

Extracts will be set in a different way from the rest of the text (perhaps in smaller type or italic and/or indented and spaced), so you *either* remove quotes and code the extracts generically (as you learned in Unit 4) *or* mark them up specifically (as discussed in Unit 25). For now, simply code them.

To indicate that the original starts in mid-sentence, some authors begin an extract thus:

… the problem with this solution was

or

[T]he problem with this solution was

but neither the ellipsis nor the square brackets are necessary. You can simply begin some extracts with a lower-case letter, following the original, just as you do for quotations embedded in the text.

Although it's often useful for a reader to know that a quotation starts in mid-sentence, whether or not it begins a new paragraph in the original is normally irrelevant. If an author has made a distinction, starting some extracts indented and some full out, I would not preserve the system.

Do not, however, standardize the style of the *line following an extract*. Sometimes the sense will demand a new para because a new topic is starting; often the extract is logically in mid-para and the following line should start full out. (If the typescript has block paragraphing, rather than indents, it is not always easy to tell which is intended: you may need to query some instances.)

The punctuation before an extract will also vary according to the structure of the introductory sentence. There may be a colon (if the introduction leads directly on to the quotation) or a full stop (if they are more separate) or no punctuation (for example after 'that' or 'is').

Sources of quotations

The precision of source information will vary according to the type of book. In a book for children, you do not want an overwhelming apparatus of notes or references. So, for example, the text might simply say 'According to Marco Polo ... ' or 'In Einstein's words ...'. In non-fiction for the general reader, there might be an amalgamated list of major sources at the end, either for the whole book or for each chapter.

In more scholarly books or articles, exact citation of the source of each quotation is a standard requirement (as we shall see in more detail in Units 17–19). The author should certainly show which of someone's works the quotation comes from. Normally the page number will be given as well, although some authors only cite the exact page number in a book, not in a shorter work such as an article in a journal.

In addition to citing the source of an actual quotation, the author of an academic work will often show the source of an idea or results of an investigation by a reference (again either to a work as a whole or to the exact page).

The subject of different reference systems is addressed more fully in Units 17–19. For now, you only need to recognize that a surname and date (with or without a page number), in parentheses, constitute a reference in the author–date system. We saw examples of this in Exercise 2.4 (Caring). The

punctuation of such author–date references will often be specified as a matter of style.

If the author's name is already in the sentence, there is no need to repeat it inside the parentheses. If different pages of the same work are cited throughout a passage, you don't even have to repeat the date each time a reference is given.

When an author–date reference follows an embedded quotation, 'it usually comes before the final stop of the sentence like this' (Harris, 1991, p. 61).

The position of a reference in relation to an extract will also often be specified as a matter of style. In Exercise 11.2, the style instruction means that the source should appear like this:

> The reference will be in parentheses (*not* usually in square brackets even though, strictly speaking, it is an interpolation), following the final stop of the extract, with no additional punctuation of its own. (Harris, 1991, p. 61; her italics)

Remember that permission is usually sought for extensive quotation, even under the 'fair dealing' convention. A whole chapter, say, based on another person's work may even run the risk of plagiarism. (We look at both points in greater detail in Unit 30.)

Now do Exercise 11.2

---

*You need a separate sheet of paper (preferably lined) to make a **query list** as you go along. First, rule columns on it with the headings: Page, Line, Query, Response (see the sample query list at the end of Unit 8). (As this is only practice, the Response column will, of course, remain blank.) In a query list for the author always write 'page' rather than the technical term 'folio'. The folio number (60, 61, etc.) appears in a circle on the exercise. (Such circling when you number the folios is not essential, though it can be helpful.) For queries in the lower half of a folio, count up from the bottom and refer to line '3 up', say, as you learned in Unit 8. (The line numbers shown on the exercise would not, of course, be there in real life, so ignore them.) Write your queries as briefly as possible, assuming that the whole typescript (or a photocopy) will be sent to the author with the query list.*

Review of Exercise 11.2

Do encourage an author (assuming there is only one) to say 'I' (as on l. 1), rather than using the authorial 'we' (an old-fashioned convention) or the passive ('it was found that ...').

This author quotes extensively from a single source (Game and Pringle, 1984). If this reliance on the same work continues, you might have to ask for confirmation that permission had been obtained. (As you'll see in Unit 30, this is often, though by no means always, the author's responsibility.)

There is no special need for the definition on ll. 16–19 to be displayed as an extract: it is best run on (so change the double quotes to single, rather than deleting them). The following sentence probably runs on too. On ll. 55–63 you should have created an extract, this time deleting the opening and closing quotes. To turn text into an extract, follow the marking style you learned in Unit 4. You may notice that this doesn't show unequivocally whether the first line of the extract is to be aligned with the rest (as you want) or indented (as a new para). Unless you know for sure whether extracts are to be set full out or indented, there is unfortunately no way of showing this (and even when you do know, it is difficult). (Most typesetters, however, will know that extracts rarely start with an extra indent and your marking on l. 75 will confirm that.)

On ll. 33, 36–8, 51–3 double quotes become single and the inner quotes on l. 53 consequently change to double. Transpose the closing quote and full stop on l. 72. In a sentence in parentheses (ll. 4–5 and 25), as we have seen before, the full stop similarly comes before the closing parenthesis.

Don't mark a *transposition* of the full stop and reference on ll. 34–5, 62–3 and 86: just delete the full stop where it is typed and write it in where it should be. On l. 34 the closing quote is missing too, a common error that sometimes goes unnoticed until proof stage: *always check where quotations and parentheses end*. On l. 86 the square brackets should be parentheses.

You will have noticed minor inconsistencies in the reference style: mark a space after 'p.' on l. 38; insert a comma before the date on l. 49 as well as 'pp.' not 'p.' (the plural form because two pages are mentioned); insert a stop and space on l. 67.

References to 'p. 00' indicate that an exact page number is to be added in proof, as we saw in Unit 5. Clearly, the 'associated reader' (readings from original texts) referred to on l. 5 has not yet been typeset. You therefore need to alter 'p. 160' on l. 25 to 'p. 000', as well as standardizing to either 'associated' or 'companion'. The reference to 'p. x' on l. 35 is not the same as 'p. 0' – this is a roman numeral in the prelim pages of a book.

Although not particularly easy to read, the style is reasonably appropriate for the undergraduates it addresses: I wouldn't make major changes. There were, however, some singular/plural problems: on l. 21 change 'analysis' to 'analyses'; on l. 29 'take' to 'takes'. (As we saw in Unit 7, 'a number of studies' in l. 1 does take a plural verb, despite its grammatical form.) Add a comma before 'however' on l. 9 to pair up with the one following it.

In the sacrosanct quotations you cannot improve the style in any case, for example word order on l. 52; nor should you standardize 'recognise' on l. 78 to the overall -ize style.

You will have to query whether a word is missing on l. 56 (though it may just be that 'the' should be 'this'). You can silently correct to 'assumption' on l. 82. A change to square brackets round 'There is' on the same line is highly likely but probably worth querying for confirmation.

On l. 63 query both the page number (this is the only place where none is given) and whose italics they are in this extract (l. 58). ('My italics' and 'my emphasis' are both acceptable, although you should be consistent throughout a book.)

An ellipsis at the beginning of a quote (l. 68) is unnecessary but the square brackets for '[B]y' on l. 77 *are* helpful here since lower case would mislead us into reading 'biased by'. Don't forget to mark all ellipses for spacing, as well as marking dashes as spaced en rules. On l. 22, the end-of-line hyphen in 'pre-dates' should be 'stetted'. (This would be misleading as a single word.)

At the end of fo. 61, mark a run on so that the typesetter does not think a break is wanted (or wonder whether copy is missing).

There were misspellings on ll. 2, 22, 24, 30, 66, 73 (as well as the one mentioned on l. 82) and a 'z' is required on l. 67.

Coding different kinds of extract

We have dealt solely with prose extracts here. In many books you may be able to help the designer by coding 'verse ext', 'letter ext', 'drama ext' (for example for an interview set out like a play), etc. We return to the layout of poetry as well as drama in Unit 22.

Either prose or verse extracts may be epigraphs at the beginning of a chapter or section. An **epigraph** summarizes the message of the whole chapter (or section), rather than being just the first long quotation. They are quite often designed in a different way from other extracts, so again may be separately coded 'epigraph'. Like an epigraph to the whole book (as we'll see in Unit 31), they often give less detailed source information, because the quotation or author is normally well known.

UNIT 12

Perspective and Level

This unit addresses circumstances in which you might need to intervene in a more substantive way than merely improving style or clarifying meaning. This might be in the interests of widening, or even altering, the work's perspective or of making it more appropriate to the readership level.

Perspective

You may or may not have agreed with the various points of view expressed in Exercise 11.2 (Gender at Work), or in other exercises you have done so far, but it is not your task as editor to gag or censor authors. You may legitimately mention in your query list places where an argument seems unsubstantiated or facts misrepresented, but ultimately such matters are between author and reader, part of the cut and thrust of debate.

Sometimes, however, an author's (often unconscious) prejudices or assumptions may quite unnecessarily offend a proportion of the readers and/or limit the market. Even more seriously, they may infringe the law of countries in which they are to be marketed: incitement to racial hatred, blasphemy, libel and so forth. On the publisher's behalf you have to be on the lookout for any such problems, whether legal or marketing.

Now do Exercise 12.1   **G**

This is a draft typescript in the development stage, intended for a non-specialist series on successful management. Identify the perspective problems you would bring to the author's attention.

Review of Exercise 12.1

You will, no doubt have noticed a number of causes for concern (sexism, racism, class prejudice, etc.). Most modern books, particularly in the management field, take care to avoid using 'he' throughout. Here matters are made worse by the assumption that the secretary will be female (so that 'he' for the potential manager becomes more than a literary convention). The patronizing tone seems to apply to both, so it may or may not count as sexism, but would certainly put off many readers. The thin disguise put on the racism almost makes it worse than flagrant rejection.

I hope you also noticed the **parochialism** of 'in this country'. Most books have to sell internationally and you should always make such expressions – indicative of a narrow perspective – more explicit, for example by substituting 'in Britain'. Where attracting readers in many countries is crucial, you may need to ask for, or find, wider examples.

Similarly, although no instances appeared in this exercise, you should look out for expressions of time such as 'last year' or 'until recently'. The book may be read several years hence and, again, you do not want to limit its applicability. The answer is usually to substitute something more specific, for example 'in 1990' or 'until the late 1980s'.

Editing out sexism

A disclaimer in the preface that '"he" should be taken to include "she"' is not now generally regarded as acceptable. The use of 'he' throughout is offputting to a considerable number of readers and will limit a book's market, particularly in the United States.

How you edit out such usage is more of a problem.

Ideally we need a new unisex pronoun. At the time of writing, there is sadly no sign of movement in this direction, so we have to work with the language we have.

Even within these limits, there are several options – the main ones are listed below. Whatever you do, avoid replacing elegant expressions with cumbersome ones: authors have every right to object to mutilation of their prose. Be careful too if you are dealing, for example, with research studies or historical events where the participants *were* in fact all men, so 'he' has been used deliberately and accurately. Frequently, however, the author's usage is quite unintentionally sexist and he or she will be glad that you have spotted the problem in typescript.

The main options are:

- Use 'he or she' or 'he/she' or 's/he' throughout. Some would prefer to alternate between 'he or she' and 'she or he'. The abbreviation 's/he' is certainly useful in contracts, forms, etc., but not very satisfactory in ordinary text since there is no speech equivalent. All these options become awkward if used frequently (especially in sentences requiring 'him or her', 'his or her', etc., as well), but are fine when needed only occasionally.

- Change to the plural wherever possible, using 'they'. This can work well in many circumstances and can be combined with 'he or she' to vary and lighten. It does not help, however, when you have to convey the image of a one-to-one situation, such as a discussion between lawyer and client.

- Combine 'he or she' as the subject with 'them' (object) and 'their' (possessive). This solution (followed in Exercise 2.4, Caring), although frowned upon by many as ungrammatical, does have the advantage of making the sentence less heavy. An example would be: 'He or she takes the racket in their right hand and the ball in their left.' This usage is common in speech and becoming increasingly so in writing. I wouldn't impose it but nor would I 'correct' it if that was the author's chosen style.

- Use 'the' rather than the possessive wherever possible. For example, 'the' would do perfectly well instead of 'their' in the example above.

- Speak directly to the reader, using 'you', as we saw in Exercise 8.3 (Individuality of Pupils). So, the same example could read: 'Take the racket in your right hand …'.

- As we also saw in Exercise 8.3, you can alternate, talking now about a male, now about a female. This is frequently done in educational books and particularly in management books, where the situation is often necessarily one-to-one. So in one chapter the boss would be a man and the underling a woman, and vice versa in the next chapter. Do, however, look out for the danger of reinforcing stereotypes mentioned in Unit 8. Giving protagonists names can often help, so that the reader can identify with them as individuals, not as gender types.

Look out too for vocabulary that discriminates – again, more often than not, unthinkingly. Write 'people' rather than 'men', 'executive' rather than 'businessman', 'chair' rather than 'chairman', etc. Similarly, keep your eyes open for expressions that are offensive to particular ethnic groups or reflect prejudice.

Now do Exercise 12.2

Edit the paragraph into a less cumbersome style by whichever combination of the means discussed seems most appropriate. When you have finished, re-read the edited passage to make sure it runs smoothly.

Legal responsibility

If you suspect that anything might be libellous or violate any other laws, bring the relevant passages to the attention of the commissioning editor so that legal advice may be sought. (We look at such problems in Unit 30.)

Readership level

Such checking for sexism, racism, parochialism, libel and so forth is part of reading the typescript on behalf of the potential reader, forestalling unnecessary criticism and widening the market as far as practicable. We turn now to *targeting* that market more precisely. If you are involved in general non-fiction, children's or educational books, the language and content level are of prime importance. All the points about clarity and readability discussed in Unit 8 apply. Some additions and reminders follow.

- The first or **lead para** of a section should catch the reader's interest, echo and reinforce the heading, point up the connection with what has gone before, or relate it to knowledge the reader is likely to have already.

- Use personal examples, accompanied by dialogue where possible, to make the material live. Arousing interest is the key and most people respond best when there is a human angle.

- In this kind of book the integration of illustration and text is a major consideration (as we shall see in Units 26–8). Choose the best means of putting across each particular point.

- In writing for children in particular, keep sentences short but not staccato. One main clause after another can become tedious but there should rarely be more than three clauses in a sentence. As we saw in Unit 8, it is easier to understand a sentence in which the main clause comes early.

- As well as keeping the grammatical structure appropriate, editing for level involves making sure that vocabulary is kept simple. This does not mean that there will be no technical terms but that they should be clearly explained, in monosyllables wherever possible. Explanation of terms does not have to be by definition. As Persse reminded us in Exercise 11.1 (Structuralism), understanding is often best reached through use and examples.

Now do Exercise 12.3   G

Although here you are asked not to edit but to write, all the same considerations apply. You may need two or three sheets of paper. Indicate in the margin where an illustration is wanted. If possible, 'test' the result on a child of the right age.

Further reading

A useful guide to avoiding gender bias is:

Casey Miller and Kate Swift, *The Handbook of Non-Sexist Writing for Writers, Editors and Speakers* (Women's Press, London, 2nd British edition, 1989)

For practice in adapting to the appropriate language level, see:

Ray Williams, *Readable Writing: A Manual for Authors and Editors of Educational Textbooks* (Longman, Harlow, 1985)

UNIT 13

The Author's Voice

In the previous unit you had a taste of being an author. Much of this book emphasizes helping the reader, through attention to structure, clarity and so on, but harmony with the author's purposes is equally important. In this unit we look at two areas – creative writing and specialist terminology – in the light of the maxim: 'Let the author's voice come through.'

Your role is that of a midwife (male or female) – assisting the process of communication, not initiating it. In most (though by no means all) areas of publishing, the book is ultimately the author's. Each project should retain its individuality, not be rendered bland or anonymous by the editorial process.

At some point in your career (but not, I hope, too early on) you will no doubt handle a project where the relationship becomes adversarial. Don't let that colour your general attitude: far more can be achieved through mutual understanding.

Creative writing

Quality varies as much in fiction as in any other field. Some authors concentrate on plot or description with little regard for grammar or punctuation; others employ wildly unusual forms but have thought out each word and comma as carefully as a poet. As for any other editing, the skill lies in recognizing such distinctions and helping only where help will be welcome. In any good writing, whether fiction or non-fiction, take special care not to disrupt the rhythm of sentences by insensitive changes.

In any novel or short story, one of your major roles may be likened to 'continuity' in film-making: red hair must not turn to blonde halfway through; the murder must not switch from Tuesday to Wednesday; someone flying to Calcutta must not return from Bombay.

Now do Exercise 13.1

Read the sample first to give yourself the feel of the author's style. It can only give a quick taste: normally you'd have the whole typescript and so would be able to make a better assessment of the author's range and concerns. When you have finished, turn to p. 68 for the review of this exercise.

Academic or technical writing

Sometimes an editor is asked to convert technical writing into a text that will be accessible to the non-specialist. If you are doing that, you will naturally make extensive revisions. All the points discussed in Units 8 and 12 will come into play.

When editing work written by professionals for others within their field, you are in a very different position. Clarity is still important but the author's individual mode of expression and use of technical terms should not be changed without good reason. Sometimes the overall argument will be complicated and, as a non-specialist, you may not fully appreciate it. Nevertheless, it is important to try to understand each individual sentence.

Now do Exercise 13.2

Have a query sheet beside you.

Review of Exercise 13.2

There are several infelicities I would change without noting them as queries: on l. 4 delete the last of the three 'to's; on l. 20 delete 'as to' (but probably not the similar 'of' on l. 38, which is less clumsy); on l. 25 bring 'also' forward, either before 'goes' or before 'for'; on l. 38 delete 'exert' and insert it instead after 'way' on l. 39 (again, deletion and insertion is clearer than transposition); on l. 41 delete the second 'with'; on l. 51 change 'it is' to 'we do so'.

I'd query whether we might change: l. 7 'takes it' to 'assumes' (to avoid the two 'it's); l. 48 'is' to 'seems' (like l. 27). In both these cases the author might see subtle differences in meaning and should be given the chance to object.

All the minor word changes mentioned so far are optional – other editors might have a different list, leaving some or all of these and picking up others. The point is that you should not be making massive changes; nor should you feel that you cannot make any.

There are three obligatory changes in the passage (none of which need be queried unless you are doubtful about them yourself). First, on l. 29 change the full stop to a comma and lower-case 'we': the subordinate clause beginning 'although' on l. 25 does not end until 'kind', so we are still waiting for the main clause. The result is, of course, a very long sentence but that is not unusual in this sort of text. (An alternative would be rewording to create two sentences.) Second, on l. 36 the author's hand-written change has created a problem. Since he or she evidently intended to change *away from* 'we', the best option is to insert 'be' after 'to' and add 'd' to 'concede'. Finally, on l. 44 'it' should be 'in'.

The punctuation needed some attention too: for example, delete the comma after 'because' on l. 3; on l. 9 either (preferably) delete the existing comma or add its pair after 'If'; probably add a comma before 'like' on l. 28; certainly after 'inner' on l. 36; probably after 'well-formed' on l. 43; and on l. 54 either add one before 'and' or delete the existing one after 'sustain'. In addition to changing the double to single quotes on ll. 34–5, transpose the closing quote and full stop since a complete sentence is quoted. There should be a dash, not a hyphen, at the end of l. 47.

Some would dislike the frequent use of dashes; personally I would leave them all. Equally, I'd leave the sentences beginning 'For' (l. 25) and 'Or' (l. 34), as discussed in Exercise 4.2 (Sartre on Freedom).

Many would think that the author's use of italic is excessive and would remove at least some of it.

As demonstrated in Unit 4 (Marking the Typescript), this is done by cancelling the underlining, not by 'whiting out'.

There were problems with the hyphenation of compound adjectives on ll. 16–17, 37 (compare l. 43) and general standardization on ll. 16 and 30. You also had to decide whether to keep 'noncognitive' (l. 2) as one word. (In American usage this is standard but British practice is still generally to hyphenate 'non-'.) You may have a house style ruling on 'judgment' (l. 43). ('Judgement' is more common but, oddly, 'judgment' *has* to be used for a court decision – not the case here.)

In addition there are misspellings (ll. 14, 19, 31, 35) and a repeated word (ll. 38–9). When you are finding the sense difficult at all, it is easy to miss more mundane problems. If the book is being typeset conventionally the typesetter might pick these up but today such books are often set direct from the author's disk (as we saw in Unit 3). You could be the last one to check the book in any detail.

Don't forget to code the heading 'A' and lower-case 'O' in 'Social'.

Specialist terminology

When editing academic or technical work, especially in an unfamiliar field, you may come across new words and strange expressions. The distinction between 'social' and 'societal', for example, in this exercise (l. 6) is not familiar in everyday life but is meaningful to sociologists. Whenever you can, look words up (in specialist dictionaries if necessary) to check that they are being applied in the accepted sense – but remember that dictionaries rarely keep pace with evolving usage.

Without specialist terminology it is hardly possible to communicate the details of a complex field of knowledge or a skill. You saw, for example, how many new terms were picked out in bold in the early part of this book. Understanding the language is half the battle when you are learning something new.

So there is nothing wrong with special terms (provided they are explained where appropriate). Sometimes, however, jargon and abbreviations are poured in for their own sake rather than to aid communication; technicality can spill over into verbosity and obfuscation. In dealing with technical texts, watch out for this danger but take care not to obscure an author's fine and deliberate distinctions by wantonly changing terminology you may not fully understand. If you have any doubts, raise a query.

Review of Exercise 13.1

I hope you were not tempted to sprinkle commas or standardize the English. The power of the passage lies in its success in taking us right inside Auntie Mary's breathless expectancy. All you have to do is correct details such as 'Marty' on l. 17 and 'arch-deacon' without its capital on ll. 10 and 26.

You should not, for example, change 'save' to 'saved' on l. 9 or the first 'a' to 'an' on l. 27 – these accurately reflect Caribbean pronunciation. Of course, you may be unfamiliar with the particular variant of English you are editing in such passages. Raise a query about anything that looks as though it could simply be a mistake.

The omission of apostrophes in 'can't', and 'don't', 'Mothers' Union', etc., is clearly deliberate (presumably on the grounds that their appearance might disrupt the flow by distracting the eye). Nevertheless I'd be tempted at least to ask the author whether we might put them in: unlike commas (which reflect pauses) they are solely part of the written language and we are not here converting to phonetic spelling.

Apostrophes in words such as 'don't' indicate a vowel or consonant that is dropped in speech. Note that it is always an apostrophe, never an opening quote, even when it begins a word: 'ere, 'cos, etc.

Now return to the section on academic or technical writing on p. 66.

UNIT 14

Consistency and House Style

Inconsistencies that went unnoticed in a typescript will leap out at you (and the author and reader) in print. Most editors begin as proofreaders – a good discipline for alerting you to a variety of problems. Continuing involvement with the proofs of projects you have edited, if only in collating them, can deliver a salutary reminder of your aim: to catch everything at typescript stage.

Now do Exercise 14.1

No style instructions are provided: make your own decisions as you go along and note them down on a separate sheet of paper. In addition, you will need the usual query sheet. It is a great help (both here and in real life) to have different colours of paper for your style sheet and query sheets, so that you can easily distinguish them from the typescript and each other. (Nothing is missing at the end of the exercise – this is just one folio of a continuing typescript.)

Review of Exercise 14.1

Again remember to code the headings (both as 'A'). The first one at present uses cap sig wds. On l. 17 the lower-case 'b' may intentionally follow French style (which rarely uses capitals, as we'll see in Unit 16) but you cannot be sure about that without the rest of the typescript. You may in any case prefer to standardize to min caps. On l. 17 a grave accent is needed over 'a'.

You have to make all sorts of consistency decisions. Will you allow shorthand or always spell out 'the mushrooms' (l. 10), 'put them' (l. 13)? Do mushrooms have 'stems' (l. 10) or 'stalks' (l. 23)?

Should numbers be given as figures or words? Certainly in the lists of ingredients figures will be more readily understood. 'Serves four' (l. 18), on the other hand, is probably best as words. Might it be a good idea also to put the number of minutes in words (ll. 12 and 14) to distinguish them from the cooking temperature given in the same sentence (a feature likely to recur)? This is presumably a gas mark (electricity is measured in degrees) but we need to say so; most recipe books give both gas and electricity all the way through. Often the cooking temperature and time receive special prominence, perhaps at the beginning of the recipe, to alert the

reader to pre-heat the oven. In Unit 15 we look in more detail at the perennial problem of when to use words and when to use figures for numbers.

What about abbreviations? 'Teaspoon' and 'tablespoon' (ll. 4, 7, 19) must either both be written out in full or both be abbreviated. (The standard abbreviations are 'tsp' and 'tbsp', without an extra 's' for the plural.) In either case 'of' is unnecessary, as it is for the garlic (ll. 9 and 21) and butter (l. 18).

All units, whether they are metric (the 'cm', 'm', etc., you came across in Exercise 5.1, Reading Maps) or imperial ('oz' here), are better without a stop and without an 's'. Again, most recipe books give both metric and imperial units throughout; if you opt for one, a conversion table is helpful.

Always check each list of ingredients against the instructions in the recipe to ensure that everything mentioned is listed and nothing is listed that remains unused. The list conventionally follows the order in which the ingredients are needed. So 'lemon juice' should be moved to second position in the first list (water is never counted as an ingredient). Since the rest are all mixed together (l. 13), the order in this first recipe can simply be a logical one, placing the major items first and the garlic, salt and pepper together at the end. (We cannot check the correct ordering of the second list.)

Whether the list of ingredients is in one column or two will depend on the design and format but will have to be made consistent one way or the other. Clearly 'Serves four' (l. 18) needs special treatment. It might occupy a line of its own under the title or perhaps come at the end; often it would be in italic. How many does the first recipe serve? A query is indicated.

On l. 13 'combine the remaining ingredients' is very vague: note a query asking the author to expand. (Do we cut the anchovy fillets into chunks or mash them, for example?) The chopping of the garlic might be better mentioned down here too, rather than on l. 9.

In the second list *sauce espagnole* (l. 19) may need a cross-reference (though it could be that the book relies on the index or an introductory section on basic techniques). On l. 20 Sauterne is more likely to be measured in fl. oz (fluid ounces). The exact amount of parsley (l. 20) evidently can't be given because it depends on the weight of the mushrooms (see ll. 23–4) but we probably need some indication

of the weight of breadcrumbs (l. 22). Although 'salt, pepper, nutmeg' (l. 21) could be 'to taste', more precise quantities were specified in the first recipe.

On l. 22 would it not be simpler to weigh the mushrooms before chopping (though after removing the stalks)? The sentence on ll. 23–4 is very unclearly expressed (even apart from the obvious error).

In addition to consistency problems, numerous queries will thus have emerged from your examination of these two simple-looking recipes. Clear, unambiguous instructions are self-evidently essential in any book with practical implications. Don't forget the even more important **safety aspect** of working on such books, whether they are on cookery or chemistry. Both author and publisher are responsible for taking reasonable precautions lest readers poison themselves or blow themselves up by following the advice or instructions in a book. As with other legal responsibilities, if you have any suspicions on safety grounds, alert the commissioning editor so that he or she may seek professional advice.

Now do Exercise 14.2   G

Review of Exercise 14.2

Many publishers distinguish between **abbreviations** (words shortened by omitting the end) and **contractions** (words shortened by omitting the middle) and treat them differently. Thus, a house style may require a full point for 'Fig.', 'ed.', 'vol.' (abbreviations) but not for 'Mr', 'St', 'Ltd' (contractions). From this point of view the unmatched pairs here are 'Prof.' (l. 1) and 'Col' (l. 2) (abbreviations) and 'Dr' and 'Mr.' (both l. 2) (contractions). All abbreviations and contractions could be followed by a stop or by nothing: the distinction is simply one of style. *Hart's Rules* and the *Writers' Dictionary* do not make this distinction: in general OUP prefers to include the stop, allowing certain exceptions such as 'Mr' and 'Dr' (but not 'Ltd.') and all SI (Système International) units (such as 'mm', 'kg').

There would be no need to standardize to full names for all, or initials for all, in the list of names on ll. 1–2 – these *could* be those people's preferred form of address (though the variations may, in this case, just result from an age and/or class distinction).

You will have noticed discrepancies in the treatment of dates (ll. 1 and 13), numbers ('one' on l. 3 and '2' on l. 16; '6' on l. 3 and 'three' on l. 4 are the mismatched pairs in *precisely* the same circumstances) and percentages (ll. 13 and 20). We return to numbers and percentages in Unit 15.

The system of cross-reference varies too: 'p. 6' on l. 3 and 'page 2' on l. 24. Such a distinction can be legitimate if 'page' is always used in ordinary text and 'p.' in parenthetical references or in notes, but the two instances here are exactly parallel. (Such references to page *always* use figures, not words, for the page number itself.)

The other discrepancies in these parenthetic cross-references on ll. 3 and 24 are *not* mismatched pairs: 'see' is different from 'see also'; 'Letters' has a capital (while 'photos' does not) as the title of a column.

Other pairs are 'recognized' (l. 5) and 'vandalisation' (l. 18); single and double quotes (ll. 19–22); 'well-known' (l. 16) and 'long suffering' (l. 17) (both compound adjectives used attributively); no list comma before the 'and' on l. 2 but a list comma on l. 12; spaced and closed up initials (ll. 1 and 2). All these are points commonly covered in house-style instructions.

Inconsistencies less likely to appear in house style but equally in need of attention here are punctuation (no comma after 'undergraduates' on l. 4 for 'In one party' but a comma on l. 6 for 'In another party'), hyphens ('rate-payer', ll. 17 and 23) and the use of capitals ('Ball', ll. 1 and 10; 'College', twice on l. 19 – although the second instance is a quotation, it is *not* sacrosanct in terms of spelling because it was almost certainly a spoken comment). Note that 'undergraduate' and 'under-lying' (better without a hyphen) do not strictly count as a pair: hyphenation can vary even with the same prefix, although you should create a logical pattern as far as possible. Finally, 'city' (l. 18) and 'town' (l. 20) must be a factual contradiction.

House style

As I said in Unit 1, a house style can help you to maintain consistency, particularly if you work for one publisher for some time. Some publishers' house styles run to many pages; others are relatively brief. They will often refer you on to *Hart's Rules* or the *Writers' Dictionary*, on certain points or in general. If a house style is too complicated or rigid, it can defeat its purpose and involve you in making extensive minor changes that absorb time and energy better spent understanding the text. An example of a succinct and generally sensible house style forms part of the next exercise.

Now do Exercise 14.3

First read carefully through the instructions on house style. Most of the points should be familiar to you by now but some may be new. Then edit the passage on Canadian architecture to conform with this particular style.

Review of Exercise 14.3

The house style specifies that chapters of the book should be referred to in the text as 'Chapter 1', etc., but also (under abbreviations) mentions the short form 'ch.' We can take this to mean that in notes referring to other works there is no objection to the shortened form, but in the text even parenthetic references to other chapters and to figures should be spelt out in full.

It specifies too that 'ed.' ('editor') has 'eds' as its plural (following the usual rule for a contraction since 's' is the last letter of 'editors'). So in n. 1 of the passage you should have deleted the full stop after 'figs'. An alternative system favoured by Butcher, *Copy-editing* has 'eds.', 'figs.', etc., to keep singular and plural consistent. Since the abbreviation 'ed.' can already mean either 'editor' or 'edited', it is best to use 'edn' for 'edition'.

In view of the general instruction to avoid capitals, resolve the inconsistency on ll. 27 and 29 of the exercise by making 'Wing' lower case, as well as 'Halls' on l. 30. ('River' on ll. 7 and 12 and possibly 'Buildings' on l. 12 will become lower case too, although the latter *might* be an official name, like Parliament Hill on l. 4.)

You will, I hope, have noticed that 'Art' (l. 4) is not part of the National Gallery's title on the photo (in the English version at least). In the National Museum's title the -ize spelling should be retained since names, like quotations, must not be changed to conform with house style.

As we've seen before, when spelling out abbreviations such as 'e.g.' and 'etc.' you have to check that the sentence still reads smoothly. On l. 28, for instance, I'd also change the existing 'and' to 'as well as'. Note the parenthetic (or as the house style calls it 'commenting') relative clause on ll. 8–9.

The instruction about decades under dates means that *either* 'the seventies' *or* 'the 1970s' may be used, although you would usually standardize to one or other of these forms in a particular passage. Sometimes the century *has* to be stated because in the context 'the nineties', for example, could mean the 1890s. In that case, figures are much more usual: certainly here you should change l. 31 to 'the 1980s'. No style guidance is given on centuries but house styles often do specify that they should be spelt out in full, as on l. 31. An apostrophe in '1970's', 'MP's' and similar instances would now look old-fashioned. It *is* usually still thought necessary in lower-case plurals such as 'p's and q's'.

One surprising feature of this house style is that '3ft' is set closed up (although no specific instruction confirms that that style is wanted). I'd query this with the publisher before applying it to the passage (on l. 25; and on l. 27, if you changed this to '23 m' rather than '23 metres'). Symbols for money, as we saw in Unit 2, *are* usually closed up, as the dollar signs are here.

To show that a decimal point that has been typed as a raised point should be set on the line, mark thus:

9ʌ6   or   9ⲅ6

If it has already been typed as you want it to be set, there is no need for any marking.

It is customary, however, to mark each **superscript** (or **subscript**) number, even if it has already been typed as such. Marking all the **note indicators** in the text as superscripts is particularly helpful because this enables you to identify them quickly if you need to check the numbering sequence or renumber them. The usual marking is:

```
Safdie.⩗ Standing on land that
```

If the note is to be set as a true footnote (at the foot of the relevant page) it too will have a superscript number. We return in Unit 18 to note indicators and the notes they refer to.

Notice that the figures (photos of the buildings) have already been **keyed into the text**, that is, someone (perhaps the author) has written a note in the margin to show where the figure is discussed. As editor, you will usually be doing this yourself as you go through the typescript, and again if the project has a galley proof stage. The purpose is to show the typesetter (or the designer) where to position the illustrations in the page proofs.

This exercise also demonstrates a common problem in typescripts with block paragraphing. The typesetter has no way of knowing whether the second page should begin with a new paragraph or run on unless you give an instruction. (From the sense, a run-on is probably intended.)

Style sheets

Although the core coverage of different publishers' house styles may be similar, they vary greatly in clarity and organization and may not always apply *in toto* to your particular project.

In these circumstances, a style sheet such as the one shown on the next two pages, specific to a book or journal, is an invaluable aid. If you are expected to follow the author's prevalent style, such a style sheet becomes essential.

The style sheet consists of two pages backed up, preferably, as we've seen, on coloured paper, so that you can easily lay your hands on it among the various heaps on your desk (typescript, tables, references, illustrations, query sheets).

The headings used in the example are suitable for high-level arts and social sciences of the kind covered in the house style you used in the last exercise. You may need to adapt it in different ways to suit your own field. The sheet is intended as a shorthand reminder of the points discussed in more detail in a house style. If you work freelance, being able to transfer a publisher's house-style requirements or author's preferences on to a handy sheet in a format that has become familiar to you can be particularly helpful.

The back of the sheet allows you to record the main capitalization, hyphenation and spelling decisions you make as you go along. If you are working in house with an established house style, this second sheet may be all you require.

For both freelance and in-house editors, additional style guides (or examples taken from a similar book) are helpful to show you **reference** style and **table** style. Examples of these are given in Units 17–19 for references and 21 for tables.

Further reading

There is a very useful chapter on house style in Butcher, *Copy-editing*.

For a short but helpful guide to the main concerns of house style and to the preparation of academic typescripts generally, see:

Basil Blackwell Guide for Authors (Basil Blackwell, Oxford, 1985)

At the other end of the scale is the massive tome that sets standards on all aspects of editing in the United States and is widely used elsewhere as well:

The Chicago Manual of Style (Chicago University Press, Chicago, 13th edition, 1982; distributed in the UK by International Book Distribution, Hemel Hempstead)

STYLE SHEET   Title:
_____

Spellings (gen.)

Hyphenation (gen.)

Quotes

Order of punctuation

Commas

Possessives

Ellipsis

Dash

Abbreviations/contractions

Spacing (units, initials)

Numbers (words/figs)

Elision of numbers

Thousands

Decimal point

Variables/vectors

Dates

Cross-refs

Caps in headings

Lists

Special sorts

A – D	E – H

I – L	M – P

Q – T	U – Z

UNIT 15

Numbers and Mathematics

This unit first explores in greater detail the problems of handling numbers and percentages that were touched upon in the discussion of consistency and house style. It then introduces some of the basic techniques for editing mathematical material.

Handling numbers and percentages in text

A house style, or specific style sheet for a project, is likely to address some or all of the following points.

- Small numbers – either below 10 (in scientific books) or below 100 (in more general books) – are normally spelt out in words, rather than given as figures, when used in a general way: 'two views', 'six students', 'thirty-one cows'. Whichever limit is chosen, this general rule is always subject to certain exceptions as listed below, even if this is not specifically stated in the house style.

- Figures are normally used for exact measurements and series of quantities (even when they are small numbers). Percentages and age groups are usually (but not always) treated likewise. It is particularly necessary to use figures where units are given as abbreviations, for example '20 km' (not 'twenty km'), or where some of the numbers in the series are fractions or decimals, for example '3.6 per cent'. 'Per cent' is often (though not always) spelt out in text but the symbol ('%') is usually allowed in tables.

- Round numbers or approximations may be spelt out in words even when they are beyond the limit for general use – 'a thousand fountains', 'over three hundred species'. The word (rather than a row of zeros) is normal for 'million', although the accompanying number is often a figure, for example '£5 million'. If abbreviated,

the unit is closed up ('40m'), which helps to distinguish it from '40 metres' ('40 m').

- Equally, where a measurement is not particularly exact, or statistics occur only occasionally in the book, it is common to write 'twenty kilometres', 'fifty per cent', etc. What is general use and what is exact measurement depends largely on the kind of book: general books will favour words whenever possible; technical books will favour figures whenever possible. So in a novel you would write 'quarter past one', 'two kilos of sugar'; in a schoolbook you'd put '1.15 p.m.', '2 kg of sugar'.

- Sometimes, even in a series of quantities, *two sets* of numbers are involved. Putting one set in words and one in figures can help to distinguish them: 'In six months the growth rate was 7 per cent; in twelve months it exceeded 10 per cent.'

- Similarly, if numbers span the spelling out limit (say, 10) they are best treated the same (usually in figures): 'There were 19 satisfied clients; 9 others expressed minor complaints.'

- As we saw in Exercise 14.2 (Picking the Pairs), cross-references to other pages or to tables, etc., are always given in figures.

- Finally, as far as the question of words versus figures is concerned, a sentence must not begin with a figure: either turn the sentence round or spell out the number in words.

- A **range of numbers** can *either* be given in full (167–168) *or* be **elided** (shortened) except for the last two digits (167–68) *or* be elided as much as possible (167–8). Some publishers and authors prefer to treat dates differently from other numbers, for example '1962–66' but 'pp. 162-6'. In headings ranges are often (though not necessarily) given in full, even when they are elided in the text.

The 'teens' in each hundred should never be fully elided because they are pronounced quite differently: so, 21–3 but 11–13; 125–9 but 115–19. Some also make an exception for numbers ending in 0 (20–23), again because of the pronunciation, but this is less common.

Where the numbering sequence goes backwards, a range cannot be elided, for example '69–67 BC'. (Nor should numbers be elided if there is any danger of misinterpretation, where, that is, '21–3' *could* be taken to mean '21 to 3'.)

As we saw in Unit 2, an en rule is normally used in a range of numbers, although a hyphen is possible.

The shortening 1967/8 can have a different meaning from 1967–8: the oblique stroke (or **solidus**) usually implies a financial year (April to March in the UK) or academic year, etc., as opposed to the calendar year. Check that such a distinction has been consistently applied but don't obliterate it.

■ A decimal point, as we've seen, will be either on the line or raised (median). (In much of Europe a comma is used instead of a point: 2,5 g.) There should normally be a zero before a decimal point: 0.25 m (not .25 m). Do not be tempted to remove a final zero from a decimal: 2.50 means that the number has been rounded to two decimal places.

■ Thousands may be shown by a comma (2,000) or, in more scientific works (to avoid possible confusion with the decimal comma), by a space (2 000). Often (but by no means always) four-digit numbers are closed up (2000) and the comma or space only inserted in five-digit numbers (and more), as specified in the house style used for Exercise 14.3 (Canadian Architecture).

Now do Exercise 15.1

*Decide on the most appropriate style as you go. Look at the examples in **Hart's Rules** as well as the notes above for guidance.*

Review of Exercise 15.1

Years (l. 1) are rarely spelt out in words. Throughout, I would keep the units ('miles per hour', 'feet', 'degrees') in words (changing '%' on l. 24 to 'per cent' to match) but would standardize the numbers to figures on ll. 12–13 (to match l. 19). However, unlike l. 19, these examples should not have en rules: we say ' between … and …' (not 'to'), so retain 'and' on l. 12. I'd add 'between' and follow the same style on l. 13.

Some editors mark each en rule; others only mark them when they come between words (London–Brighton railway, etc.), giving a general instruction that en rules are to be used throughout for a range of numbers. An intermediate route is to mark all of them in running text but give a general instruction at the first occurrence in each list of references and in the index, the places where ranges of numbers occur most frequently. (We look at this again in Units 17 and 29.)

'Fifty per cent' (l. 24) is best spelt out since this is general use (as is 'two-thirds' on l. 15); 'twenty minutes' on l. 25 is probably best kept as words too. On ll. 8–9 and again on l. 28 all the numbers should be in figures because they span even the 100 limit.

Remember that ll. 26–7 are a quotation, so your overall style will not apply. For **degrees of temperature**, if we *were* abbreviating, *Hart's Rules* (and Royal Society, *Quantities*) requires the spacing, '35 °F'; whereas the degree sign on its own (as for angles on l. 19) is closed up, '30–35°'. Preferred styles differ on the spacing for temperatures: the *Chicago Manual of Style* even recommends '35° F'; others avoid the issue by closing up, '35°F'. Similarly, either closed-up or spaced style is possible for longitude and latitude ('35°N' or '35° N'). We return to all this below.

Now do Exercise 15.2

Again decide appropriate styles as you go.

Review of Exercise 15.2

All the percentages here should be given as figures, probably spelling out 'per cent'. Make sure that the units are unmistakable, for example by adding 'per cent' after '1.2' on l. 20.

The fraction on l. 6 has to be a decimal, to match ll. 7, 18 and 20. (In a different passage, on its own, the $\frac{1}{2}$ would be fine; occasionally too the equivalent decimal would give a misleadingly precise impression – just as conversion to a figure, '50 per cent', would have done on l. 24 of Exercise 15.1.) You will have noticed that '0' has to be added on l. 7 and that some decimal points are low and some raised.

On l. 8, in contrast to the previous exercise, 'between' is best omitted: 'by 2–3 per cent' is sufficient. The en rule here almost has the sense of an oblique stroke ('2 or 3'). On ll. 13–14, however, 'from 3 to 7 million tonnes' is best left as it stands, to maintain the balance between 'from' and 'to'.

On ll. 14–15 'eleven thousand' *could* be left in words, as a round number. If it is (preferably) changed to figures, the form must be '11,000' (not '11 thousand'). On l. 21 'a hundred and fifty years' is probably best left in words, as a round number.

On l. 17, where a date begins the sentence, change the words round, for example to 'The eventful and difficult year 1962 ...'. The date on l. 1 must, of course, also be in figures.

Convert to '10 million' on l. 22 to avoid the string of zeros. 'Eleven', as the first word in the next sentence, will remain spelt out, unless (preferably) you change the preceding full stop to a semicolon (with a colon after 'problem' on l. 21). This alteration assumes that the author means that 10 million hectares are badly damaged and a further 11 million completely useless – if so, it could be worth adding 'a further' to clarify – but note a query to confirm that this interpretation is correct. (The problem might be a mix-up in the figures.)

Finally, the preferred spelling is 'Khrushchev' (l. 10); see the *Writers' Dictionary*, which usefully includes many proper names as well as ordinary words.

Marking up mathematics

Variables, for example in algebra, are set in italic. So an equation might read:

$$4y = 2x + 10$$

Usually you have to mark the typescript for italic by hand. Authors are discouraged from following the normal underlining convention when typing maths because italic would then be indistinguishable from a bar under a letter, or the rules (division lines) in **two-line formulae**:

$$\frac{2x}{y} = 10$$

Nowadays authors are often able to type in true italic or bold (used for vectors, as we shall see below). If these have, on the whole, been applied correctly, you can give the typesetter a general instruction to follow copy for italic (and/or bold). (The same goes for editing *any* material containing true italic or bold.)

Where Greek appears in maths, identify each letter by putting a small cross underneath: α (preferably in a different colour, such as green), to distinguish it from similar Roman-alphabet letters. For example, 'ρ' (rho) can look like 'p'; 'ω' (omega) like 'w'. (This identification is worth while whether the Greek is typed or handwritten.) On the first appearance of each letter write, for example, 'Gk alpha' (circled) either above the line or (preferably) in the margin.

As we have seen, in any typescript you should identify symbols that are unusual or could, in the context, be ambiguous (for example, where a subscript could be either cap O or zero). Similarly, identify a minus sign (not quite the same as an en rule in print) if it could be mistaken for a hyphen or en rule, and a multiplication sign (using the abbreviation 'mult', circled) if it is typed as an 'x'. (Again, in print, the sign is different: ×.)

As we saw in Unit 14, all superscripts and subscripts also have to be marked in maths setting. (In more complex material a subscript may itself have a subscript, etc.)

Units, for example '40 kg', are often set with **variable spacing**, that is, justified like the other words on a line. There is no need for any marking unless they are typed close up, in which case you instruct for variable spacing by marking:

$$40\,kg$$

Alternatively, you can ask the typesetter for a **fixed space** of a particular size. (The closed-up option we looked at in Unit 2 is not common in books or journals.)

The gap in 14 000, etc. (when no comma is wanted) is usually a **thin** space. The recent British Standard on maths symbols recommends:

ɤ for a 'normal' space and ɤ for a 'small' space

Both of these may be defined as the publisher wishes (though 30 and 15 per cent of an em, respectively, are recommended). The normal space is probably the most appropriate for a fixed space in units, if that style is wanted. Unfortunately the small-space symbol, which might be appropriate for the thin space in thousands, is ambiguous when used between numbers. (It can look as though you wish to insert a 0.) Safer options are:

14ꞁ000   or   14ꞁ000   or   14ꞁ000

However, as they are not officially recognized symbols, you need to explain in the margin the first time you use them that you mean a thin space.

A thin space can also neatly solve the problems of degrees of temperature and longitude/latitude discussed earlier in this unit: '60 °C' and '60° N'.

Equals signs, multiplication signs, 'greater than' (>) or 'less than' (<) signs, etc., normally have some space around them but you *don't* need to mark this each time. If the typing is irregular, mark for even

spacing (in much the same way as for the dots in an ellipsis):

$x = 10$

In Exercise 5.1 (Reading Maps) you came across a worked example, which we saw could be coded 'display', leaving the designer free to decide how to treat it. **Displayed maths** in general may be centred on the longest line (not necessarily the first), or indented a specified amount, with or without extra space above and below; it is usually set in the *same* type size as the text. (Sometimes you will be expected to mark such features specifically, as we shall see in Unit 25. In specialist mathematical setting, displayed formulae are often so frequent and readily identifiable that no coding is required.)

Now do Exercise 15.3

Mark up the maths in the way explained above. In addition, key in the figures (diagrams), following the method demonstrated in Exercise 14.3 (Canadian Architecture).

Review of Exercise 15.3

Check your work against the sample answer on pp. 80–1. The only marking required on the figures themselves was italic 'd' in Figure 1 and a space in '5cm' in Figure 2.

The paras are marked with the 'new para' sign because we do not know whether they are to be indented or to start full out. Remember that when you are coding headings generically, there is no need to delete or add italic: the design instruction overrides the typed style.

As you see on l. 10, thin spaces are often put into numbers *after* the decimal point for clarity, just as in thousands.

On l. 12 notice the instruction 'frac' (for fraction). Most typefaces will contain $\frac{1}{2}, \frac{2}{3}, \frac{3}{4}$, etc., as a matter of course. Any other *numerical* fraction can also usually be made up so that it fits within the normal printed line but you need to indicate that this is what you want. (Do also mark the '7' to be centred under the '22'.)

In general, however, avoid two-line formulae in text. You can often convert into a one-line formula, by using a solidus, with parentheses if necessary. So a formula in the text $\frac{a + b}{c - d}$ could be marked thus

$\frac{(a + b)}{(c - d)}$ to show that it should be typeset as: $(a + b)/(c - d)$. Alternatively, to show that the

text should be broken off and the formula displayed, mark: $\frac{a + b}{c - d}$

It is essential to state the units in the answer, so add 'cm^2' on l. 33, and also wherever units change, so add 'cm^2' (note: not 'mm^2') on l. 40. On the other hand, it would be wrong to add 'cm' or 'cm^2' on ll. 27 or 30 because a formula has no specific value in units until you substitute a number for *r*.

Show that equals signs should line up under each other, if they have not been typed that way (ll. 30–3 and 40). Make sure too that punctuation is *either* consistently included in and around displayed formulae *or* (as here) consistently omitted. An **equation number** is often needed in higher-level maths for cross-reference – perhaps in parentheses or square brackets and ranged right.

You often do have to mark the italic throughout, as you did in this exercise. However, if a densely mathematical text is going to a specialist typesetter, it may be possible (as the British Standard expects) to give a general instruction to set all maths in italic except where roman is indicated. In that case, the simplest way to indicate which subscripts, etc., are to remain roman is to use a highlighter, explaining its meaning the first time it appears in the typescript, (A highlighter is useful too for showing what should remain roman if the author has typed true italic.)

Operators, such as 'd' in differential calculus, are

often (though not necessarily) set in roman to distinguish them (dx, dy, etc.). Words such as 'log' and 'tan' are always roman. Geometrical points ('the line AB') may be either roman or (increasingly often) italic, as long as you are consistent. Vectors are typeset either in bold roman or in bold italic.

Make a list of any special sorts, that is, unusual symbols. These would include maths symbols, Greek, accents, etc. For the more complicated symbols such as summation signs with limits, supply a printed sample of the style required (or at least find out in advance what the typesetter usually provides).

If phonetics or logic symbols are required, similarly supply printed versions where possible, perhaps numbering them and identifying each with that number in the margin of the typescript, at least the first time it appears. Butcher, *Copy-editing* has helpful appendices on such symbols.

Further reading

The British Standard on proofreading mathematics is BS 5261: Part 3: 1989. Useful examples of mathematics setting and editing are to be found in:

The Chicago Manual of Style (Chicago University Press, Chicago, 13th edition, 1982; distributed in the UK by International Book Distribution, Hemel Hempstead)

On science editing generally, see

Maeve O'Connor, *How to Copyedit Scientific Books and Journals* (ISI Press, Philadelphia, Pennsylvania, 1986; distributed in the UK by Williams & Wilkins, London)

At school level, helpful guidance on scientific conventions generally is to be found in:

Association for Science Education, *SI Units, Signs, Symbols and Abbreviations* (ASE, Hatfield, Herts, 1981)

Equivalents at a higher level are:

Symbols Committee of the Royal Society, *Quantities, Units and Symbols* (Royal Society, London, 2nd edition, 1975)

Royal Society of Medicine, *Units, Symbols and Abbreviations: A Guide for Biological and Medical Editors and Authors* (Royal Society of Medicine, London, 4th edition, 1988)

Finally, the forthcoming edition of Butcher, *Copy-editing* spells out in greater detail than previous editions the major concerns of editors in particular scientific disciplines.

Sample answer to Exercise 15.3

Ⓐ   The circle

Follow copy for bold

Fig.1
near
here

Look at the circle, **diameter** d, shown in Fig. 1. Estimate the length of the **circumference**. Is it twice as long as d? Three times? Three and a half? Four?

The ancient Egyptians discovered the intriguing fact that,   5
however large or small a circle may be, the circumference is
always a little over three times the diameter. The Greeks measured

Ⓖk
pi

this **constant** more accurately and named it π (**pi**).

display

Circumference = π x diameter
(mult)

throughout
t = thin
space

The decimal value of π would go on for ever: 3·141¦592¦653¦.¦.¦.¦   10
So you have to use an approximation: 3·14 (to 2 d.p.) or 3.142
(to 3 d.p.) The fraction equivalent is 3 $\frac{1}{7}$ or $\frac{22}{7}$.
(frac)

The formula for the **circumference of a circle** is commonly
expressed in terms of the **radius**, rather than the diameter.
Since d = 2r (the diameter is twice the radius),   15

display

Circumference = π x 2r
(mult)

= 2 π r

The **area of a circle** is also found by using π , in a
different formula: 20

display

Area = π r²

The only difference between the two formulae is the position of the 2. It is easy to remember which is which because areas are always measured in cm^2, km^2, etc.

Ⓑ Example 1

Find (a) the circumference and (b) the area of the circle shown in Fig. 2. For π use 3·14.

Fig. 2 near here

display

$$\text{Circumference} = 2\,\pi\,r$$
$$= 2 \times 3\cdot14 \times 5 \text{ cm}$$
$$= 31\cdot4 \text{ cm}$$

$$\text{Area} = \pi\,r^2$$
$$= 3\cdot14 \times 5^2 \text{ cm}^2$$
$$= 3\cdot14 \times 25 \text{ cm}^2$$
$$= 78\cdot5 \text{ cm}^2$$

Ⓑ Example 2

If a circle has diameter 1 200 mm, what is its area? For π use 3·14.

display

If diameter is 1 200 mm, radius is 600 mm.
$$\text{Area} = \pi\,r^2$$
$$= 3\cdot14 \times 600^2 \text{ mm}^2$$
$$= 3\cdot14 \times 3600 \text{ cm}^2$$
$$= 11 304 \text{ cm}^2$$

UNIT 16

Use of Italic

I have already mentioned that excessive use of italic for emphasis can be distracting. There are many occasions, however, where convention demands italic, for example for titles of books or journals and foreign words used in an ordinary English sentence. A helpful summary of many of these uses may be found in *Hart's Rules*. In addition to the select list of words found there, rulings on whether a particular word has been sufficiently absorbed into English to be set in roman rather than italic are to be found in the *Writers' Dictionary*. As we have seen, there are also many technical uses of italic, for example in botanical terms (Unit 10) and mathematics (Unit 15).

Now do Exercise 16.1

Use the reference books: do not just guess or make your own decisions.

Review of Exercise 16.1

The reference books make some interesting choices on specific words – ones that naturally may have to change as language evolves. (By picking out some and not others in italic, we have, of course, spoiled the effect but this is only an exercise.)

If a word is to appear in italics, it must have all the correct accents (*ingénues* on l. 10). If it is set in roman, it *may* still retain accents but often does not. So 'role' (usually) and 'hotel' (always) lose the circumflex they would have in French. Many publishers would also omit the grave accent on 'première' and the acute on 'élite' as, to an English-speaker, they make little difference to the pronunciation. A final 'e' usually keeps its accent (for example 'blasé'), to show that it is to be separately pronounced. (Note too that, since words such as 'hotel' and 'historian' are now normally pronounced with an aspirated 'h', they are better preceded by 'a', not 'an'.)

Other languages have different conventions for the use of capitals. In German, for example, nouns always begin with a capital, so we have *Zeitgeist* on l. 4. If, on the other hand, a German word is to be set in roman (as you might decide to do, for example, in a whole book about 'Gestalt counselling'), the capital could be dropped.

Even though 'hotel', as an English word, has no circumflex, you should *add* one on l. 5 because the Hôtel du Lac is a proper name. As such, although in French, it remains roman. Similarly, a company name such as Le Clerc et Frères would be roman, as would an academic institution such as the Centre National des Recherches Scientifiques.

The title of a book or journal (including a magazine or newspaper) is set in italic; a chapter in a book, or an article in a journal, is set in roman with quotes. Films, TV programmes and names of ships are italicized like book titles. Remember that the italic and the quotes are *alternative* ways of setting the title off from the normal text: it is seldom necessary to use both, whether for titles or for foreign words and phrases.

Sometimes, capitals alone make a sufficient distinction. In *Hart's Rules'* separate section on musical works, we find that Largo (l. 12), as a movement, remains roman (although an Italian word), with a capital but no quotes; on l. 13, the quotes should end after 'Pastoral' (a nickname).

The French convention on the use of capitals in titles is different from the English system; see *Hart's Rules* on setting French (capital and lower case). According to this system *La Jeunesse dorée* is correct. This convention may be followed for French titles (whether in text or in a bibliography); a common alternative is just to apply min caps to French (and Italian and Spanish) titles, even when cap sig wds is applied to titles in English. For German titles, it is essential to follow the original (never attempting to standardize either to min caps or cap sig wds) because, as we've seen, only the initial word and all nouns may (and must) have capitals.

On l. 15, it should be *Le Monde*, because 'Le' is part of the French title, but the *Tatler* ('the' lower case and roman). *Hart's Rules* suggests roman 'the' with a few rather arbitrary exceptions. (Many other periodicals that use 'The' in their mast-head might prefer to have it regarded as part of the title.) Besides the *Hart's Rules* compromise, there are two other valid options: *either* always set 'the' in roman; *or* follow the current mast-head of that particular periodical.

Specialist works

- As you will have read in *Hart's Rules*, abbreviations such as 'e.g.', 'i.e.' and 'etc.', although originally from Latin, are now regularly set in roman. As we shall see in Units 17–19, many such abbreviations that crop up throughout reference systems are usually set in roman.

- Similarly, in specialist works foreign terms may occur frequently as part of the English text and you will need to make your own decisions on whether or not to italicize them, since they are not all likely to appear in the *Writers' Dictionary*. In addition, the author may sometimes have used the foreign word and sometimes the translated equivalent: you need to make sure that there are logical reasons for the variation.

- In a novel, an occasional sentence spoken in French might be italicized, just as a single word or a phrase would be. In a non-fiction work, however, for example one about French history or literature, quotations in the original language should not be italicized.

- Names of institutions are always difficult. You (or the author) may have decided, for example, to italicize *parlement*. (The word cannot be translated as 'parliament' because it was a very different institution, essentially a body of lawyers.) The Paris Parlement or the Rennes Parlement, however, as proper names, should be in roman with capitals.

- A similar distinction is made for people's titles: 'a *maréchal* is the equivalent of a marshal' but 'Maréchal Joseph was put in charge.'

- These examples are taken from French as the best-known foreign language for many of us. The same principles apply to Chinese or Zulu. The problems are compounded for languages not using the Latin alphabet, as you also have to make sure that the same **transliteration** system has been followed throughout. For example, in a book on India you would not mechanically apply the *Writers' Dictionary*'s ruling on 'maharaja' (which we came across in Exercise 6.1, Bridge) if other similar terms had been transliterated with '–ah'.

Now do Exercise 16.2

Look out for the use of capitals as well as italics.

Review of Exercise 16.2

The terms *ancien régime* (ll. 1, 35 and 38) and 'bourgeois' (l. 14) are not usually translated; apply the *Writers' Dictionary*'s preferred forms. Other terms used here are more specialist. In general, the author has translated where there is an acceptable equivalent, for example 'Constituent Assembly' (l. 3) and 'Legislative Assembly' (add the capital, l. 28). However, *constituants* (ll. 9 and 21) is better in italic (lower case), since these constitutional legislators bear no relation to English 'constituents'. Similarly, *corporations* (l. 34) should remain italic since the meaning is 'professional bodies', not English 'corporations'.

The Loi Le Chapelier has, however, consistently been given in French here (although it is sometimes translated as the Le Chapelier Law – 'Le' is part of its originator's name). As a proper name, it is best in roman with capitals (ll. 9 and 23), even though in French *loi* would be set lower case.

The French word for 'journeymen' (*compagnons*) is given at their first appearance on l. 4 (helpfully, especially as *compagnonnage*, l. 44, derives from it). Their societies should be referred to in a consistent way throughout (ll. 11, 18 and 36), probably as 'journeymen's societies'. Similarly, on l. 49 there seems no reason for the switch to *compagnons* rather than 'journeymen'.

Cancel the italic for the institutions mentioned on ll. 8 and 28 (matching l. 30). If we had been talking about *écoles polytechnique*s in general, they would indeed be treated like the *écoles de santé* (l. 31). (Compare 'the curriculum for secondary schools' and 'the Elms Road Secondary School'.) The *officiers de santé* (l. 31) should similarly be in italic, without quotes, with an accent. Note that a capital 'E', as in 'Ecole', does not usually retain its accent (see *Hart's Rules*).

As we have seen, quotes and italic together are rarely necessary. Italic alone is preferable for *libre* (l. 25), *mères* (l. 48) and *rouleurs* (l. 49). On l. 54, *marchandeurs* should also be italic.

Finally on italic versus roman, the quotation on ll. 13–14 remains roman in quotes.

You will notice that you have added a good deal of italic. That is fine here since the author has translated into English wherever possible ('journeymen', etc.). In other books you may find that particular foreign words occur so often that they become very familiar. In such cases it is quite legitimate to set them in roman throughout to avoid a welter of italic. We return to the question in Exercise 23.2.

The *Writers' Dictionary* recommends a capital for the 'Revolution' (l. 15) although, once the specific revolution had been established (l. 2), many would lower-case this. (Similar decisions may have to be made in other books for 'after Independence', 'before the War', etc.) Even when the capital is retained for the noun, the adjective 'revolutionary' (ll. 17 and 32) is always lower case, as we saw for 'parliamentary' in Unit 10.

In addition to the necessary changes to -ize forms on ll. 24 and 37, there are spelling errors on ll. 3, 19, 20 (two), 25, 28 and 45. On ll. 33 and 52 spellings

should be 'license' and 'practise' because these are verbs. On l. 8 the date had to be put into style; I hope you didn't forget to delete 'the'. On l. 51 change to 'shared an interest' or 'had a common interest' (as discussed in Unit 7); on l. 53 'like' should be 'such as'. If you are hyphenating compound adjectives, add hyphens on ll. 16 and 54.

Commas are needed after 'matter' on l. 22 (alternatively, delete the comma after 'or') and 'however' on l. 32 (as ll. 8 and 26). They are also helpful to mark off the parenthetic 'who' clauses (ll. 48, 49, 53 and 54) and round 'or subcontractors' (no hyphen) on ll. 54–5. As the sample house style you used for Exercise 14.3 (Canadian Architecture) stressed, 'who' clauses (like 'which' clauses) may be either defining or parenthetic but it is much less common to substitute 'that' for 'who' to mark the distinction. If there is any danger of ambiguity, commas will clarify.

How far does an editor take responsibility for **factual accuracy**? As we saw in Unit 14, you have to be specially careful where safety is concerned. In certain areas of publishing the editor (or a specialist researcher) is explicitly employed as a fact-checker and will do library research to ensure that everything is correct. In most specialist publishing, however, it is neither necessary nor possible to do this in any systematic way – academic advisers will report on the soundness of the work more competently than you can and the author takes responsibility for the original research. Even so, do bring your general knowledge to bear whenever it is relevant, and cross-check internally wherever possible.

In this passage, I hope you spotted that 1794 must be meant on l. 30 and that Louis XIV (the seventeenth-century Sun King) cannot be relevant on l. 43 – it could be Louis XVIII but you would have to put a query. (Such roman numerals in kings' names are usually set in full caps, rather than small caps, so no marking is required.)

UNIT 17

Styling a Bibliography

In non-fiction publishing, whether for the general reader or the specialist, an editor spends a good deal of time and energy dealing with bibliographies, notes, sources and references. In this unit and the two that follow, we look at the problems, and pleasures (for me and I hope for you too), arising from such features. The discussion is necessarily confined to the two most widely used reference systems, the **short-title** system and the **author–date** system. The other main option is a **number only** system (such as **Vancouver style**, which is widely used in medicine). Once you have grasped the basics of the two major systems, you should find it easy enough to adapt to any given style with the aid of the relevant reference books.

The bibliography or list of references

The term 'bibliography' is applied to a list of works, usually arranged alphabetically but sometimes divided up by subject matter or by type of work (for example, with primary sources separated from secondary sources). The list may include all works referred to elsewhere in the typescript (as the source of a quotation, the explanation of a theory, etc.) or, if it is a select bibliography, to a selection of the works used. It may also include works that are not referred to in the text but are relevant to the subject or recommended for further reading.

A list entitled 'references' (rather than 'bibliography') normally *only* contains works referred to during the course of the discussion.

Any of these lists (bibliography, select bibliography, further reading, references) may appear at the end of the whole book, or at the end of each chapter or article.

Content of bibliographical entries

Each **entry** in a bibliography or list of references must give the reader enough information to trace it easily. The information included depends on the kind of work referred to. This can vary hugely and, as your experience of different subject matter grows, you will become familiar with conventions for dealing with archival material, theses, government reports, etc.

In this course, we confine our attention to the three kinds of work most frequently referred to: a book, a journal (periodical) article and a chapter in a book (often an edited collection).

Now do Exercise 17.1　　　　　　　　　　　　**G**

Review of Exercise 17.1

You will have discovered that for books (Chamberlin, McKay) the information required is: author(s), title (including subtitle, if any), edition (*not* needed in the case of a first edition – that is assumed unless otherwise stated), place (of publication, as we shall see below), publisher, date. Sometimes an entry will also contain information such as the name of a translator or, if it is a multi-volume work, the total number of volumes.

For a journal article (Bradley, Francis and James) the information required is: author(s), title of article (including subtitle, if any), journal, volume (discussed below), date, pages. You will notice that no place or publisher is given. This is because most journals are included in international listings. A place (never publisher) would only have to be specified if two journals had the same name or if a journal was too obscure to be listed.

For a chapter in a book (Dalton, Pingree) the information required is: author(s), title of chapter (including subtitle, if any), editor(s) of book, title of book, place, publisher, date, pages.

Let's examine a few points of detail.

■ Because the list is in alphabetical order, names are inverted: the surname comes first, followed by the initials or first name. You will have noticed that sometimes initials are used, sometimes a full first name. It is quite normal to have a mixture like this: it *should* mean that your author is following the title page of the original book or the heading of the original article. Some people publish under their full name; others (for example D.H. Lawrence) are always known by their initials. The list reflects this legitimate diversity, so you should not normally interfere. However, in certain books (such as edited collections or multi-author reference books where contributors' usage varies) or in journals, you may prefer to standardize for the sake of uniformity. The only practical way to standardize is to shorten to initials throughout.

■ In this list (for a book using the short-title system), the title follows immediately after the author's name. (We shall see in Unit 19 that in the author–date system, as the name suggests, the date is promoted to second position.)

■ You will have noticed several subtitles as well as titles. As we saw in Unit 5, any work may have a subtitle (usually a further explanation of the title). In a bibliographical entry the subtitle is always divided from the title by a colon (though *no* colon will have been used on the original title page in the case of a book).

■ Book titles and names of journals, as we saw in Unit 16, are conventionally set in italic; article and chapter titles roman, in quotes. (In Unit 19 we look at a different convention for the latter.)

■ Most journals use the term **volume** for all the issues published in a year. If the journal appears quarterly, say, the different issues may be called **numbers** 1, 2, 3 and 4. The pagination is often continuous throughout the volume and at the end of the year libraries will bind the issues into one volume. For this reason, volume, date and pages are usually sufficient information to identify the article unambiguously. However, some reference styles, as we shall see, demand the issue number as well. Often (but by no means always) reference styles will specify a standard numbering convention for journal volumes: some prefer to change them all to arabic; others to change them all to roman numerals. (The original journals will vary.)

■ The place must be a *town*, not just the country or state. Most publishers now operate in many countries but the convention is to list the first town given (on the title page or on the copyright page, as we shall see in Unit 31). The place of publication is helpful information to a reader using a library. Any book published in the UK, for example, should definitely be found in one of the copyright libraries; those published, say, in Paris may or may not be obtainable in the UK. The publisher's name is useful information to someone wanting to buy the book. Often both are given but it is perfectly acceptable to opt for giving either place throughout or publisher throughout.

■ Publishers' names appear in numerous guises. So here it would not be wrong to put 'George Allen & Unwin' or simply 'Blackwell' (though including 'Basil' does help to distinguish it from Blackwell Scientific) but you should be consistent, at least for each individual publisher within the bibliography. Do *not*, however, impose consistency by updating, for example changing 'Routledge & Kegan Paul' to 'Routledge': the publisher's name should be as given on the title page of that edition, not as the firm is known today. The ampersand (&) is often (but by no means necessarily) used for publishers' names in bibliographies, as it was in this exercise. Always omit uninformative details such as '& Co.'

■ Look out for the occasional inexperienced author who gives the *printer's* place or name instead of the publisher's or gives the date of a *reprint* rather than the date of an edition. A reprint (as we shall see in Unit 31) should have the same pagination as the original and will contain only minor corrections. In a new edition, page numbers may well be different and facts and opinions may have been updated.

Style for bibliographical entries

Several of the points already discussed touch on reference *style*, for example whether the title of a journal article appears in quotes. The specific book, series or journal you are editing will follow a particular reference style, which can be specified by showing (at minimum) how the entry should look for a book, for a journal article and for a chapter in a book.

The style shows:

■ what information is required for each entry (as discussed)
■ the order in which that information should appear
■ the use of capitals and punctuation in the entry

When you are **styling a bibliography**, pay close attention to each of these points. A consistent system enables the reader to identify information easily and quickly.

If you look again at Exercise 17.1 you will see that a consistent order was followed, for example place, then publisher, then date, both in the entry for a book and in that for a chapter in a book.

A rapid pointer distinguishing a chapter in a book from a journal article is the word 'in'.

Notice too that the use of capitals varies according to a regular pattern. In this particular style, book titles and journals take cap sig wds; book subtitles, article titles (and subtitles), chapter titles (and subtitles) all take min caps.

Unlike authors' names, there is no justification for following the original title page on capitalization: the style there often reflects the designer's preference, not the author's (and title page and jacket frequently don't tally). It is better to impose a style to make the bibliography uniform. It is usual to treat article titles and chapter titles the same, as here. Book titles and subtitles are also often treated the same, rather than differentiated as they are here.

The punctuation system imposed in Exercise 17.1 also follows a standard pattern. Notice particularly how commas bring together the journal volume and date, separating these two closely related items from the journal name before and the page numbers after.

For the page numbers, a standard style has to be followed on **elision**. For example, if the style specifies maximum elision, you will shorten to 133–7 but still keep 113–17, as we saw in Unit 15.

Finally, always observe the spacing when you are absorbing the details of a reference style. Are authors' initials to be spaced? Is 'p.' (and the plural form, 'pp.') to be followed by a space? (See Unit 2 for proof examples of these distinctions.) You will need to mark any places in the typescript where the specified style has not been followed.

Occasionally a general instruction may be best, for example if initials have been typed closed up throughout and you want them spaced. (Showing spacing each time can look dangerously like deleting the full stops.) Similarly, as we saw in Unit 15, the en rule that is often used in a range of numbers may be specified as a general instruction (for the book as a whole and/or, as a reminder, at the beginning of the bibliography).

The **turnover lines** of each entry (that is, the continuation on to a second or third line) are usually indented, as typed in Exercise 17.1. (The indent will often be 1 em, sometimes 2 ems.) Again, a general instruction may be given at the beginning of the bibliography although, if only a few entries have been typed wrongly, it is also worth marking them to be indented. (Occasionally, a small extra space is left between entries as well.)

Now do Exercise 17.2

Draw up the usual query sheet before you start. Write each of the numerous queries you will find as briefly as possible, assuming that the edited folio (or a photocopy of it) will be sent to the author with your queries. In a bibliography it is best to identify a query not by the line number (as you did in Unit 11) but by the entry: so just give the surname (or surname and abbreviated title if there are two works by the same person). You can use the terminology of the discussion above, since it is familiar to most authors. So, for example, you may simply write 'Smith – date?' or 'Franco – place?' Examine the specified reference style carefully and apply that system throughout.

Review of Exercise 17.2

Check your work against the answer and the typed query sheet on the next two pages. For once this is a definitive, rather than sample, answer because we are applying agreed rules – that's probably the appeal (for me) of this aspect of editorial work, although some find it too fiddly to be enjoyable.

As we have seen before, a comma is always best squeezed in on the line. This is especially important in bibliographies or references where it may not be immediately obvious to the typesetter whether a comma or a quote is wanted. Show unambiguously too (for example in Clower and Leijo(h)nhufvud) whether the closing quote comes before or after the comma. Mark the wavy lines indicating bold (a fairly common style for journal volume) firmly.

When you insert or transpose material, recheck the punctuation round the change. You will have remembered that it is usually better to delete and insert, rather than transpose, from one line to the next (as in Becker).

Answer to Exercise 17.2

(ch hd) Bibliography

[Indent turnover lines 1 em throughout]

Agassi, J., 'Methodological Individualism', British Journal of Sociology, vol 11 pp. 244-70 [en for range throughout]

Agassi, J., Towards a Rational Philosophical Anthropology, 3rd ed, The Hague, Nijhoff, 1981

Arrow, K., The Limits of Organisation, Norton, New York, 1974

Becker, G., 'A theory of the allocation of time', in Economic Journal, 75 (1980), 75, pp. 493-417

Boland, L., 'A Critique of Freidman's critics', Journal of Economic Literature, vol 17 (1975), pp. 503-22

Böhm-Bawerk, E., Positive Theory of Capital, trans. W. Smart, New York, Stechert,

Buchanan, J. and Tulloch, G., The Calculus of Consent, Ann Arbor, University of Michigan Press, 1962

Coase, R., 'Problem of Social Costs', Journal of Law and Economics, vols 3 pp. 1-44

Clower, R. and Leijohnhufvud, A., 'Say's Principle', Economic Review, 14 (1960), vol. 14 pp. 25-27

Coddington, A., 'Friedman's Contribution to Methodological Controversy', in G. Becker and G. Tulloch (eds), Great economists of our time, pp. 1-13

Eddington, A., The nature of the Physical World, Oxford Cambridge, Clarendon Press, 1977

Friedman, M., 'In Search of Facts', Journal of Econ Lit, omic erature, (OUP); vol 7 (1965), p. 17

Haavelmo, T., The Probability Approach in Econometrics, trans. G. Wood, The Hague, Martinus Nijhoff,

Hollis, and Nell, E., Rational Economic Man, Cambridge, Cambridge University Press,

Kamin, L. G., 'Catching out Caose: a Review of "The Problem of Social Costings"', Quaterly Journal of Economics, vol 51 (1980), pp. 209-24

Leijonhufvud, A., 'Schools, "revolutions" and Research programmes', in Latsis, S. (ed), Methodology and Appraisal in Economics, Oxford, 1972, pp. ( ),

Latsis, S., 'Rational expectations', Journal of Economic Literature, vol 17 pp. 111-

Queries for Exercise 17.2

PAGE	LINE	QUERY	RESPONSE

<u>Bibliog.</u>

Agassi, 'Meth. indiv.' - date?

Becker - some mistake in p. nos?

Boland - confirm sp Friedman as below
            (twice)

Böhm-Bawerk - date?

Coase - or Caose as in Kamin ref?
        (If Coase correct, transpose with
        Clower)
        - also shd art. title be same as
        one quoted in Kamin?
        - date?

Clower - sp Leijohnhufvud or Lei<u>jon</u>hufvud
            as in own entry?

Coddington - place?
                - publisher?
                - date?

Eddington - place change OK or diff.
        publisher?

Friedman - plse confirm one page only

Haavelmo - date?

Hollis & Nell - initial(s) for Hollis?
                    - date?

Kamin - sp of Caose?
        - title of wk reviewed?

Leijonhufvud - sp of name?
                - publisher?
                - confirm date change
                - pp.?

Latsis   - date?

You will see that I have put (pencil) insertion marks (for example after Hollis), and even empty parentheses (in Coase/Caose), waiting for the answers to queries. This helps you to insert the information quickly in the correct place and style. As for other queries, the question mark in the margin both draws the author's attention to the problem and reminds you that a problem has to be solved before the typescript can go for typesetting. Certainly if there are this many queries they should be dealt with at editing stage; if there are only a few, you may be able to insert responses at proof.

The heading is marked as a chapter head on the assumption that this bibliography comes at the end of the book, rather than the end of a chapter.

'Ann Arbor' (in Buchanan and Tulloch) may have puzzled you: it is a town in Michigan. Obscure places where publishers just happen to be will become familiar to you after a while. Less obscure, perhaps, is the fact (in Eddington) that the Clarendon Press is in Oxford, though the point is queried just in case the *place* was correct but the publisher wrong.

Similarly, you cannot just assume a transposition (rather an unlikely mistake to make) of the pages in Becker. The problem is more likely to be a single typing error: perhaps it should be '393–417' or '493–517'.

It would be equally acceptable to standardize to 'Martinus Nijhoff' in both instances (the second Agassi entry and Haavelmo). In Hollis and Nell the typed form of place and publisher is certainly wrong; an acceptable alternative to the answer shown would be just to delete the comma (provided you then followed that style consistently).

In Arrow the 's' is changed to 'z' *not* to match our own house style (as for extracts and names of institutions, the spelling in titles is sacrosanct) but because any book published in New York almost certainly uses 'z' spellings. You *could* query it rather than making the change yourself; don't just leave it as typed. Again it could be worth asking for confirmation that 'Principle' may be lower-cased in Clower and Leijo(h)nhufvud.

You may have queried the journal's name in this entry, rather than just amending it. The other abbreviated journal titles appear often enough in this list not to need querying. In Friedman (almost certainly the economist, Milton Friedman) a one-page article is just possible, since he is so well known, although it is unlikely.

I hope you did *check alphabetical order* and that you marked the transpositions neatly in the way you learned in Unit 4. The order for the two works by Agassi is alphabetical by title.

Further reading

This section serves Units 17–19 together as they all deal with reference systems.

Butcher, *Copy-editing* offers excellent, more detailed coverage of the major reference systems.

Also helpful on the scientific side is:

Maeve O'Connor, *How to Copyedit Scientific Books and Journals* (ISI Press, Philadelphia, Pennsylvania, 1986; distributed in the UK by Williams & Wilkins, London)

UNIT 18

Notes and Short-title References

Since any kind of book may have notes – additional information, explanation of specialist terminology and the like – techniques for handling them are relevant to all editors. In general non-fiction, and academic books or journals in the humanities, notes often also contain the references. One of the most satisfactory methods of referencing in notes is the short-title system. Books using the system may also have a bibliography but this is optional.

Position and numbering of notes

- In the printed book or journal, notes may appear at the end of the chapter (or article) *or* at the end of the book *or* at the foot of the page (once very expensive but likely to make a comeback with modern technology since it offers great advantages to the reader).

- Even if the notes are **true footnotes** (rather than **endnotes**), they are usually best numbered consecutively through the chapter.

- Wherever they are to appear in the final product, discourage authors from *typing* notes at the foot of the typescript folios (word-processors can now do this all too readily): it is much easier to standardize the reference style if all the notes are together.

Matching up notes and text

- As you edit the text, have the relevant folio of notes beside you and cross-check, as you come to each **note indicator** (number) in the text, that the note seems appropriate. If, for example, the text sentence discusses Henry James and the note indicator refers you to a note about Charlotte Brontë, your antennae will quiver. During revision a note may have been dropped or added, throwing out the rest of the sequence.

- Check that the numbering sequence does not skip or repeat, either in the text or in the notes themselves. This is all part of the same matching-up process but is worth double-checking at the end of each chapter or section. A note number should not be repeated, even when the reference is to exactly the same work.

- Similarly, a note '30a' between 30 and 31 can be tolerated only if an essential change has to be made at the last stage of proof. When editing the typescript, you *must* renumber if the sequence is wrong, although this cannot always be done definitively until queries have been answered.

- So that you can rapidly double-check or renumber, mark each note indicator firmly as a superscript (as demonstrated in Unit 14). Some editors use a distinctive colour, or add highlighter, to make them stand out even better.

- Check the appropriateness of each note indicator's position. It is generally best *after* the relevant text, at the end of a sentence or the end of a quotation. Occasionally, however, it must occur in mid-sentence, for instance where the note refers only to a particular word or only to the first half of the sentence. Ensure that it follows any punctuation (full stop, colon, comma, etc.); the only exception to this rule is a dash.

- Thus, as you go along, you will be editing the content of the note and matching up text and note. These techniques apply whether you are dealing with substantive notes (ones adding information) or reference notes or, as is often the case, notes that contain both additional information and references.

    Only at the end does the technique differ. Any notes containing references also have to be styled and this is best done as a separate operation. Do make any changes that are obviously needed in the references as you read them the first time, but always go through them again afterwards, looking specifically for consistency of style. The style applied in notes is *different* from the bibliography style we looked at in Unit 17, but only in minor ways (and for reasons explained in the next section).

Now do Exercise 18.1

As you edit the text, look out particularly for both embedded quotations and extracts, as well as matching up notes and text. When you come to styling the notes, don't refer back to the bibliography style of Unit 17 but try to understand the system in operation here. Just make any necessary minor adjustments to ensure that it is consistent.

As usual you will need to make a short query list. Here, and in all future exercises, assume that the typescript (or a photocopy) will go back to the author, unless you are told otherwise.

Review of Exercise 18.1

The text and extracts

As well as coding the extracts, you had to show that l. 21 was not to be indented as a new paragraph. As we saw in Unit 11, if you *know* that the typeset style will be to indent extracts, then you can mark ll. 22–5 indented; if you do not know, it may be safer to mark l. 21 full out. You also had to delete the quotes on ll. 21 and 25. The continuation of the same para after the first extract (l. 14) and **indention** for a new para after the second (l. 26) are both fine as typed. Remember that three dots are enough for the ellipsis on l. 11 (it already has a question mark before it) and that you must not standardize any of the spelling in the quotations to modern forms or to the surrounding text.

Even on l. 19, where it is part of the text, I would keep 'Mughal', rather than changing to the *Writers' Dictionary*'s 'Mogul', since the author will probably have strong feelings on the transliteration (see Unit 16).

It is important not to reduce 'James Mill' on l. 3 to a surname to conform with the rest. As the *Writers' Dictionary* will have told you, there are two economic/social theorists called Mill: this one is the father of the more famous John Stuart Mill. Among other minor changes, l. 33 should be 'principal causal'.

The note indicators

The indicator for n. 1 should be on l. 13 (instead of l. 8), at the end of the extract; the second n. 3 (on l. 30) has to become n. 4 and, because the embedded quotation is a full sentence, the order must be corrected:

kinship⁀. ›4/

You'll need to query what this new n. 4 should be. Almost certainly it will read 'Ibid.' (that is, the same Lyall reference), followed by a volume and page number (if, as is likely, the page is different from n. 3 on l. 25). As the *Writers' Dictionary* will have told you, this useful abbreviation, '**ibid.**' means 'in the same place', that is, in the work mentioned immediately above. (It is effectively a 'ditto'.) It is often, though not necessarily, set in roman, rather than italic, and usually has a capital when it begins a sentence.

The next note (old n. 4) becomes n. 5 (both in the text and in the notes). Again the order in the text must change:

base4;\5/and

(You should have considered, but quickly rejected, the other explanation of the second n. 3 on l. 30 – that it refers to the existing n. 4; the Avineri reference is unlikely to apply there but fits this half-sentence on ll. 32–4 well.)

Before the new n. 6 (on l. 37), the full stop and closing quote must be transposed because this is only a phrase, though a long one, and we are applying logical order.

The other major problem was that the note indicators on ll. 37 and 40 (new nn. 6 and 7) ought both to refer to a work by Weber, so there is clearly something amiss with old n. 5 (new n. 6). (It is common for 'ibid.' references to go astray when a note is omitted or text rearranged during revision, destroying the link between the 'ibid.' reference and its predecessor.) So put a query:

new n. 6 (old n. 5): Ibid. means Avineri but text suggests Weber? Plse chk which wk meant. Also pp?

(If the answer is that this note should be Weber, *The Religion of India*, the final note (new n. 7) must be simplified to 'Ibid., p. 111.' You would not be able to make this change, however, until you had the author's responses.)

The notes

Some standardization was needed in the notes themselves. In n. 1 the colon should be followed by a space. In n. 2 you had to underline the book title for italic and add a stop after 'p.' You will have found that '**cf.**' means 'compare'; it is always roman and may start a new sentence as it does here.

In n. 3, place ought to precede publisher (as in nn. 1 and 2) and a space should be marked after 'p.' Also 'expatiated at length' is tautologous. (Possibly spaced initials may be wanted too but we have no way of knowing.) **Book volume** numbers are often (though not necessarily) given as roman numerals (as typed here) in the books themselves. Just as for journal volume, a reference style may consistently convert to roman or to arabic, or follow the original.

On l. 49 the final stop is missing. (Because notes are often full sentences, they usually end with a stop, whereas a bibliography entry, being an item in a list, often does not.) On l. 50 add a second 'p' for the plural of pages. On l. 51 mark the 'r' as a capital and add a comma before 'p.'

Assuming these notes will be typeset at the end of the chapter, the heading 'Notes' (l. 41) must be coded. You can code it 'N' as a flag (see Unit 5), to indicate that it is different in kind from other subheads in the chapter. Often, however, it is just treated as an A head. (If the notes were to be true footnotes, you would circle the heading as it should not be set.)

In endnotes, the note number is usually set full size. Whether or not it is followed by a full stop is a matter of style preference. In true footnotes, the number is normally a superscript and is often indented.

The short-title reference system

As you will have realized, the reference system used in Exercise 18.1 was the short-title system. In this system all the references are in notes (whether endnotes or footnotes). There is no need for a bibliography as well, although if you do have one you may be able to omit some of the bibliographical details from the notes.

As we saw, full details are given the first time each work is mentioned. This may be the first time in the whole book or the first time in a chapter. (The latter is much better for the reader if there is no separate bibliography.)

Where a reference is unambiguously to the same work of the same author, you simply put 'Ibid.', followed by the page. In *other* **subsequent mentions** (anywhere that 'ibid.' is not possible), the reference is pared down to a standard short form. As we saw in Exercise 18.1 (old nn. 4 and 6), this consists of the essential information:

- author's surname (there is no need for initials *unless* there are two authors of the same name; nor do we have to state 'ed.' after Avineri)

- title or, if it is a long one (as in Avineri), short title (the distinctive feature of the system)

- page(s) where required (for example, for a direct quotation); if the reference is to the whole work, no page number is needed; if it is a multi-volume edition, like Lyall's, you have to state volume as well as page

Looking at the form of the full details in Exercise 18.1, we see some significant (standard) variations between the bibliography style used in Unit 17 and this reference style for notes.

- A bibliography inverts the author's name, so that the surname comes first. Since notes are not alphabetical listings, there is no advantage in doing that: the first name or initials always come *before* the surname.

- In notes referring to books (as all the ones in the exercise do), the minor bibliographical details are almost always tucked away inside parentheses so that they do not distract the reader from the substance of this particular note. Because the details are within parentheses, no comma is needed to separate them from the title; the comma *after* the closing parenthesis separates the page (or volume and page) from all the other details. (You'll remember that a pair of commas is never needed *as well as* a pair of parentheses.)

These are standard differences in treatment between entries in a bibliography and references in notes. We go on to look at a specific reference style for notes, and how to apply it.

Now Study the Style Sheet accompanying Exercise 18.2

In addition to the standard differences, you will see other small variations between this particular style and the one used for the bibliography in Unit 17. It is important to learn to spot such differences quickly and be able to adapt readily to any given style. So what exactly are the differences?

- Cap sig wds are wanted for book subtitles as well as titles. Note too that there is an initial cap in the book subtitle (even when it is 'A' or 'The') and no cap following a hyphen: both of these are style points that can vary but should be consistent within a particular work.

- Place only is required, not publisher.

- In journal articles this style asks not only for volume but also for issue number, with a comma between them and no bold.

- In chapters in books, the editor's initials precede the surname. (This style is often followed in bibliographies and reference lists too, since inversion has no great advantage here.)

- No overall page range is required, either for a journal article or for a chapter in a book. As we saw in Exercise 18.1, the 'p. 164' is the particular page number relevant to that note. (Some reference styles *do* require the whole range as well, often in the form: 'pp. 160–72, esp. p. 164'.)

- Plural abbreviations have stops if their singulars have stops. (As we saw in Unit 14 this is a fairly common alternative.)

Notice that, in the specified style, the **short forms of journal articles and chapters** derive from the title in just the same way as books. The only difference is that they are, naturally, roman in quotes.

An *alternative* style within the short-title system would use:

Gerhardt, *Journal of Ancient Mythology* (1962), p. 165

Gerhardt and Franks, in Perrier, *Ancient Mythology*, p. 165

Although longer, these give the reader more useful information.

The short-title system is a clearer (and therefore preferable) alternative to the traditional **op. cit. system**. 'Op. cit.' means 'the work cited', so the abbreviation follows the author's surname (rather than standing on its own as 'ibid.' does). If you are applying the short-title system but occasionally come across

Gerhardt, op. cit., p. 60

check back to the original citation and replace 'op. cit.' with the title or a shortened version of it.

The advantages of the short-title system over 'op. cit.' are that it is unambiguous and saves a reader who is reasonably familiar with the literature from having to look back to the first citation.

Technique for styling notes

As we have seen, you will read and edit the notes as you cross-check that they match up with the text. You then have to go through them a second time to make sure that the style is consistent. You will be looking for all the same points as in styling a bibliography. Is the information complete? Does the order follow the given style? Does the use of capitals and punctuation conform to the style? This is the stage you are practising in Exercise 18.2.

At first sight, notes – with their run-on style and sentences between references – look more confusing than a bibliography. Keep your head and, whenever you are checking a full citation, look across at the relevant item on the style sheet (book, journal article or chapter) to make sure all the required information is given and in the right order.

In addition, you are checking the correct application of the short-title system: full details at first mention only; subsequent mentions in accordance with the style; correct use of 'ibid.' Each time you come to a short form, check back to see that a full form has indeed already been given and that spellings, etc., match up.

Use a *consistent short form* for each work. Whenever possible follow the author's shortening, just looking out for places where he or she has been inconsistent. A rule about 'A'/'The' (either always retaining it or always omitting it) is helpful for maintaining consistency.

When you are editing a whole book or journal article, you need a way of keeping track of short forms. If there is no bibliography, you just have to make a list as you go, at least of the references that crop up most frequently and/or most inconsistently. (Divide both sides of a distinctively coloured leaf of paper into alphabetical blocks, A–D, E–F, etc. As you come to short forms, jot down in the appropriate section the author's surname, the short title and the folio where it is first used.)

If there is a bibliography, a better way is to encircle on it, *using a soft pencil*, the words used for short forms in the notes. Then each time you come to a note with that reference in it, you can easily check that the correct short form has been used. Be sure to rub the pencilling out before the typescript goes for setting.

Now do Exercise 18.2

*The accompanying text is not provided this time: you are just styling the notes. Remember that you will inevitably require a query sheet. Just as in a bibliography the **name** is the best hook to hang queries on, in short notes you can simply use the **note numbers**.*

Review of Exercise 18.2

Check your work against the answer and typed query sheet on the next two pages.

Because you must not standardize titles to your general house style, in n. 2 leave the Latin word *triclinia* in roman. You can and should, however, impose the convention that a colon is used to separate title and subtitle. Authors quite often use a full stop instead, as here, but there is no difference in meaning. (Occasionally a stop is needed as well, to avoid having two colons, for example *To the Ends of the Earth: My Voyage to China. An Account of Nineteenth-Century Travel.*)

Because references contained in notes are often part of a sentence, 'Estey's' in n. 4 is fine (nor should a comma be inserted).

Since there are relatively few ranges of numbers here, I have marked the en rule specifically (nn. 6 and 13). (As you may have noticed earlier, 'nn.' is the plural of 'n.', just as 'pp.' and 'll.' are the plurals of 'p.' and 'l.')

I hope you remembered (from Unit 16) that German titles (n. 10) must not follow your overall style on capitalization. In French, *either* follow *Hart's Rules* (essentially, apart from the proper names, using a capital for the first word and the first noun, even following an apostrophe, as in n. 10) *or* apply min caps. Arguably the 'L' might be better omitted from the short form in n. 12 but keeping it makes the reference more immediately recognizable to those less familiar with French. You would need to be consistent about this for all French titles.

Where you have to transpose a full reference and short reference, as in nn. 9 and 15, double-check that the reference to *page* ends up as the author intended. In this case, n. 9 was a general reference and n. 15 referred to p. 40.

If you are squeezing in a handwritten name, or if a handwritten name or word is unusual, do spell it out in capitals in the margin (as in n. 14), circling or boxing it to show that it is not to be set twice, or in capitals.

In n. 15 the reprehensible separation on to two lines of the initials 'C.E.' is something you would mark if it happened *in proof* but not in the typescript.

Answer to Exercise 18.2

1 On the other hand, St Albans may have been built under Carolingian
Influence. Cf. P. Kidson and P. Murray, A History of English
Architecture (London, 1962), p. 28; E. A. Fisher, The Greater
Anglo-Saxon Churches (London, 1962).

2 I. Lavin, 'The house of the lord: Aspects of the role of palace
triclinia in the architecture of late Antiquity and the early
Middle Ages, Art Bulletin, 44, 1 (1962), p. 15.

3 ibid., p. 16.

? 4 As described in Estey's 'Charlemagne's Silver Celestial Table',
Speculum, 18, XVIII (2) (1943), p. 112.

5 See Fisher, Greater Anglo-Saxon Churches, p. 60. His views are
? disputed by Kitson and Murray, op. cit. History of English Architecture.

6 Further details may be found in Lavin, 'The 'house of the lord',
pp. 21-7.

7 Lavin ibid., p. 32.

8 Estey, Speculum 'Charlemagne's silver celestial table', p. 118.

9 E. Panofsky and F. Saxl, Classical Mythology in Medieval Art:
? the continuing tradition, p. 235. Cf. Knowles, 'Preservation of
the Classics'.

? 10 ibid. See E. Lehmann, Der frühe deutsche Kirchenbau (1938 Berlin)
for a summary of the German position. On the French view see J.
? Formigé, L'Abbaye royale de Saint-Denis: recherches nouvelles (Paris).

11 Estey, 'Charlemagne's silver celestial table', p. 120.

? 12 Formigé, L'abbaye royale, p. 160.

13 Fisher, Greater Anglo-Saxon Churches, pp. 55-7.

14 Kidson MURRAY and Murray, A history of English architecture, p. 160.

15 M. D. Knowles, 'The Preservation of the Classics', in F. and C.
E. Wright (eds.), The English Library before 1700 (London, 1958).

15 Knowles, 'Preservation of the classics', p. 40.

Queries for Exercise 18.2

PAGE	LINE	QUERY	RESPONSE

Notes

    n. 4   Estey - initials?

    n. 5   Kitson as here or Kidson as nn.
             1 & 14?
             Also plse confirm addition of Murray
             in n. 14

    n. 9   Panofsky & Saxl - place?
                      - date?

    n. 10   ibid. - which ref? (Panovsky & Saxl
             or Knowles?)
             - also Formigé - date?

    n. 12   Confirm accent on Formigé (as
             n. 10)

UNIT 19

Author–Date References

The other major reference system, widely used in the sciences and social sciences, and still spreading, is the author–date system (also called the **Harvard system**). In some ways it is less complicated than the arts-oriented system we have looked at so far, but it has its own different problems and appropriate techniques for handling them. We address these in this final unit on reference systems. (Warning: don't skip to tackle this chapter first because you deal mainly with science books – you too need the skills introduced in the earlier units; the discussion and exercises here assume they have already been learned.)

The author–date system

In this system a list of references appears at the end of the book or at the end of the chapter or article. This must contain all the works referred to in the text. Occasionally it will include many other works as well, in which case it is better called a bibliography. (If it includes just a *few* other works, as we shall see, this is likely to be the unintentional result of revision.)

The list is given in alphabetical order. The most obvious difference from the title-based system we have looked at so far is that the date comes immediately after the author's name.

This is because (as we saw in Unit 11) the **short form** of the reference consists of the author's surname and the date (and, where necessary, page); it appears not in a note, but within the text itself. So, for instance, a work may be referred to as Patel (1990).

Because authors often write numerous articles (if not books) in any one year, the reference list may contain two or more works by the same author published in the same year. In that case they are called Patel (1990a) and Patel (1990b), etc. (The alternative of calling the first 1990 and the second 1990a is simpler for the author but less commonly approved by editors because *undetectable* errors can creep in.)

Occasionally, two different Patels may be listed in the references. In that case it is best to use the *initial* as well as the surname for all references in the text to those authors' works, so that the reader immediately turns to the appropriate section of the reference list. (Alternatively, you must at least include the initial in the text reference where the year is also the same.)

Matching up references and text

Just as in the short-title system you cross-check that each note indicator in the text seems to match its note, in this system you cross-check each reference in the text against the list.

Now do Exercise 19.1   G

*Look through the reference list **first** for any obvious problems such as mistakes in the order. Then, as you edit the text, check that each reference mentioned in the text does appear in the list and that the details of spelling, date, etc. match up. If they do, **tick** the reference lightly in the text (above the line) and also in the reference list (in the margin). If they do not match, add the problem to your query list.*

Finally, edit the reference list, working out what style is being followed and making it consistent. Add any further queries that arise because information is missing.

Review of Exercise 19.1

Check your work against the answer and typed query sheet on pp. 100–2.

The exercise illustrates the importance of that **initial check** of the reference list. If you were editing the text without having checked through the list first, you could easily just look for Kuethe (1962), for example, find it, tick and move on. If the list was a longer one, you might think that a reference was missing when it was only out of alphabetical or date order.

Did you find the problem about the date of Cartwright and Jones at that first stage? Spotting this kind of problem, especially in a longer list, is more a matter of chance but if, as you skim through, you do see the same edited collection coming up several times, always cross-check the dates. There may be other discrepancies too (as here in the editors' initials) but the date is the crucial one to discover early because it affects the text references.

It is not usually worth while editing the reference list *fully* before you start work on the text because further problems may emerge during editing that affect the content of the entries. But this quick initial check saves much frustration.

As we shall see, it is quite common to use 'et al.' (which means 'and others') in the text (l. 11), where a work has several authors, but to give their names in full in the reference list.

You can never be sure whether a problem stems from a date error or a missing reference. It could be, for example, that a Sommer (1965) is needed as well as Sommer (1966); Little (1969) could be a typing error for Little (1965). (The same references may, of course, be mentioned several times, not just once.) So your query list will always contain an element of guesswork.

There is no apparent reason for quotes round 'bubble' on l. 17 but they are helpful (though not essential) on l. 5. On l. 24, 'into' would do, although 'on' matches l. 25 better ('of' would be fine after 'violation' but sounds odd after 'intrusion').

Like the 'Notes' heading in Exercise 18.1 (India), the 'References' heading (probably at the end of the chapter) may either be flagged ('R') as different from the regular hierarchy or be treated as an A head. (References gathered at the end of the whole book will normally start with a chapter head, just as a bibliography would.)

The prevalent style in the references is clearly to invert authors' surnames and initials (though not the editors' names in entries for chapters in books). Some publishers and journals, however, prefer the style as typed in Sommer and Felipe (1967). Although inversion of the co-authors' names has no particular advantage, it looks more consistent.

As we saw in Unit 17, an ampersand (&) is often (but not necessarily) used for publishers' names. Certainly Routledge and Kegan Paul should be made consistent (one way or the other) in Dosey and Maizels and Leibman. To avoid possible ambiguity (as in my last sentence, for instance), some publishers and authors also like to use '&' between co-authors in parenthetic text references (so they would put '&' on ll. 8 and 11).

Technique

If the references come at the end of each chapter (or article), the suggested **ticking** procedure is sufficient to keep track. If, for example, you become engrossed in the subject matter, you may miss some references; these ticks (like the marking of note indicators you practised in Unit 18) enable you to double-check the text afterwards, scanning for any references you may have missed the first time. There is no need to delete the ticks before sending the typescript for setting.

If the references are gathered together at the end of the book, you need a more elaborate procedure. Tick the text reference in the same way, double-checking as usual at the end of each chapter. In the reference list, instead of just ticking the entry, note (in the margin) at least which *chapters* it appears in. This enables you to check back relatively easily if you discover a discrepancy late in the proceedings. (Some editors note *all* the folios on which each entry occurs. This is certainly worth doing when different contributors' references have been amalgamated into one list: if a contributor corrects a date or wants to add or remove an entry in response to a query, you need to know where to look for other references to that entry and related ones.)

You also need the ticks in order to raise as queries any entries in the reference list that you have *not found in the text* (unless, as we've seen, there are so many that it is clearly doubling as a bibliography). It may be that during the course of revision a section has been cut out and some of the references are redundant. (You do, of course, need to have double-checked to be *sure* a reference is not mentioned: far worse than unnecessary typesetting is the risk that a reader may come across an untraceable reference in the printed text.)

Raise a query (as here for Johns, 1970), rather than simply deleting, because the author may prefer to add a text reference instead of omitting the entry.

Answer to Exercise 19.1

(A) Personal space   (120)

Sommer (1969) has popularized the term 'personal space'. This
refers to 'an area with invisible boundaries surrounding a
person's body into which intruders may not come.' Sommer suggests
that one of the best ways of studying this personal space 'bubble'   5
is to observe people's behaviour when the bubble is violated.

    Thus, investigators have sat too close to people as they
were studying in a library (Sommer and Felipe, 1967); sat very
close to psychiatric patients on benches (Sommer, 1965); had
people walk over to hatracks and to people, to compare how close   10
they went (Horowitz et al., 1965; Dosey and Maisels, 1969);
had people manipulate models of various persons in various
situations (Little, 1965); had people reconstruct relationships
using felt model figures (Kuethe, 1962, 1964), to mention only
a few examples.   15

    Variables that have been shown to affect the size of the
bubble are situational — the physical context in which the
interaction occurs — for example, Little (1969) found that
open-air settings promote closer distances than contained
settings; personalistic — Felipe (1966) found that extroverts   20
appeared to tolerate physical closeness better than introverts;
acquaintanceship — Kuethe (1962) found that friends stand closer
to one another than strangers; and gender — Liebman (1970) found
that when intrusion of another's bubble is unavoidable, females
will intrude on another female's rather than on a male's.   25

(R) References   [Indent turnover lines 1 em]   (121)

? Dosey, M. and Maizels, M. (1969) Personal space and

(or 1970?) self-protection. In N. Cartwright and C. Jones (eds), _Environment
? and Behaviour_. London: Routledge & Kegan Paul. pp. 62-75 (and throughout)

✓ Felipe, N.J. (1966) Invasion of personal space. _Social Problems_, 14 (2): 206-14

✓ Horowitz, M.J., Duff, D.F. and Stratton, L.O. (1965) Body buffer zone. _Archives of General Psychiatry_, 11 (6): 651-6

✗ Johns, G.K. (1970) Closeness and gender. _Sociology_, 65 (2): 20-45

? Kuethe, J.L. (1962a) Further research on social object displays.
? _Journal of Abnormal and Social Psychology_, 64 (3):

✓? Kuethe, J.L. (1964) Influence of social schemata. In Hall and Friedrich (eds), _Thought Patterns_. New York: Norton. pp. 118-40

? Kuethe, J.L. (1962b) Social schemas and the reconstruction of social object displays from memory. _Journal of Abnormal and Social Psychology_, 64 (1): 71-4

✓ Little, K. B. (1965) Personal space. _Journal of Experimental Social Psychology_, 1 (3): 237-47

? Leibman, (1970) The effects of sex and role norms on personal
(or 1969?) space. In N. Cartwright and N. Jones (eds), _Environment and
? Behaviour_. London: Routledge & Kegan Paul. pp. 144-73

? Sommer, R. (1966) Man's Proximate Environment. _Journal of Social Issues_, 22 (4): 59-70

✓ Sommer, R. (1969) _Personal Space_. Englewood Cliffs, NJ: Prentice Hall

✓ Sommer, R. and N.J. Felipe, (1967) Research on personal space. _Journal of Social Issues_, 23 (1): 1-22

Queries for Exercise 19.1

PAGE	LINE	QUERY	RESPONSE
120	8	Confirm Felipe (one p) as refs	
120	9	Sommer 1965 as text or 1966 as refs?	
120	11	Dosey & Maisels or Dosey & Maizels as refs? - plse also rechk date (Leibman in same bk but given as 1970)	
120	12up &4up	Kuethe 1962 - which is a, which is b?	
120	8up	Little 1969 - not in refs	
120	3up	Liebman as text or Leibman as refs? - also plse rechk date (Dosey & Maizels in same bk but 1969)	
<u>Refs</u>			
121		Kuethe 1962a - pp?	
		Kuethe 1964 - eds' initials?	
		Leibman - initial? - also shd Jones initial be C (as in Dosey & Maizels)?	
		Johns 1970 not in text - OK to omit?	

Several missing references may come from the author at query stage. You then have to show the typesetter simply and clearly where to insert them. The example opposite indicates how this may be done. The original folio of references is fo. 109; in response to your queries, the author has sent you fo. 109A. (They are shown on one page here only to save space: in real life they would be two separate folios.)

The order of the lettering (A, B, etc.) should be consecutive on the *insert* sheet (fo. 109A), so that the typesetter, reading down fo. 109 and coming to insert D, for example, knows exactly where to look for it on fo. 109A. Don't forget to put the new references into style.

The example illustrates too how awkward it can be editing single-spaced reference lists (even with space between entries). Encourage authors to type references, notes and extracts double-spaced.

Styling the reference list

The detailed styling of the reference list is best done as a separate operation. The style conventions for author–date references differ in minor ways from short-title references, as Personal Space demonstrates. Within the system, however, there can be just as many different styles in relation to order and punctuation as we found in the short-title system.

For example, the date may not be in parentheses; it may instead appear as the Leibman reference was typed (sometimes with a stop rather than a colon). Book titles and journals are usually italicized in the familiar way. For journal articles and chapters in books, roman but without quotes is a common but not mandatory style. (Articles and chapters would always be treated the same in this respect.) Again familiarly, 'in' distinguishes chapters in books from journal articles.

Jaspars, J.M.F. and Fraser, C. (1983), 'Attitudes and social representations', In Social Representations, ed. R.M. Farr and S. Moscovici, Paris: Presses Universitaires de France.

D → Lévi-Strauss, C. (1967), 'The myth of "Asdiwal"', In The Structural Study of Myth and Totemism, ASA Monographs. London: Tavistock.

E → McKinlay, A. and Potter, J. (1987), 'Social representations: a conceptual critique', Journal for the Theory of Social Behaviour, 17: 471-488.

Moscovici, S. (1983), 'The phenomenon of social representations', In Social Representations, ed. R. Farr and S. Moscovici (eds), Cambridge: Cambridge University Press.

A → Musello, C. (1979), 'Family photography', In Images of Information, ed. J. Wagner (ed.), Beverly Hills, CA: Sage.

Perelman, C. and Olbrechts-Tyteca, L. (1971), The New Rhetoric. Notre Dame, IN: University of Notre Dame.

B → Potter, J. and Litton, I. (1985), 'Some problems underlying the theory of social representations', British Journal of Social Psychology, 24: 81-90.

Rose, R. and Kavanagh, D. (1976), 'The monarchy in contemporary culture', Comparative Politics, 8: 548-576.

Schwartz, B., Zerubavel, Y. and Barnett, B.M. (1986), 'The recovery of Masada: a study in collective memory', Sociological Quarterly, 27: 147-164.

F → Shils, E. and Young, M. (1953), 'The meaning of the Coronation', Sociological Review, 1: 68-81.

C → Vidal-Naquet, P. (1987), Les Assassins de la Mémoire. Paris: La Découverte.

Williamson, J. (1987), Consuming Passions. London: Boyars.

A Nairn, T. (1988), The Enchanted Glass: Britain and its Monarchy. London: Radius.

B Potter, J. and Wetherell, M. (1987), Discourse and Social Psychology. London: Sage.

C Wetherell, M. and Potter, J. (1988), 'Discourse analysis and the identification of interpretative repertoires', In C. Antaki (ed.), Analysing Everyday Explanation. London: Sage.

D Larrain, J. (1979), The Concept of Ideology. London: Hutchinson.

E Larrain, J. (1983), Marxism and Ideology. London: Macmillan.

McLellan, D. (1986), Ideology. Milton Keynes: Open University Press.

F Thompson, K. (1986), Beliefs and Ideology. Chichester: Ellis Horwood.

Technique for inserting late references

Full stops are often used *within* the entry as here. The colon between place and publisher is also common (and indeed is sometimes used in arts-style bibliographies too). Whereas with commas the order of place and publisher may vary, if a colon is used place *must* come first.

The journal volume, with number in parentheses, may be closed up, rather than spaced as it is in Personal Space, provided you are consistent. The colon (normally followed by space) before the page numbers is quite usual but this could equally well be a comma and 'pp.'

The rule (usually 2 ems) for a repeated name shown in the Sommer entry is quite a common style but you should be consistent – for Kuethe's publications, the name was repeated.

The *order* in which references are listed is normally (as in the Sommer entries) all works by the single author first (in date order); then all works by the author and others, arranged alphabetically by co-author. So Sommer and Felipe (1966) would come before Sommer and James (1960). (Sometimes, however, references called 'et al.' in the text are given in date order, ignoring the co-authors' names.) Where two references have to be designated 'a' and 'b' (as for Kuethe, 1962), they are usually put in alphabetical order by title (regardless of the kind of work).

Position and form of the reference in the text

- As we saw in Unit 11, if the author's name is already part of the sentence, you never need to repeat it in the parenthetic reference.

    According to Gerhardt (1962a: 162) myths reveal the essence of a culture.

    Myths reveal the essence of a culture (Gerhardt, 1962a: 162).

- The comma between surname and date is optional but you must be consistent. The page number following a colon is a common form: be consistent about whether there is a space after the colon or not. (Either style is possible but not both in the same book.) An alternative to the colon is a comma and 'p.', as we saw in Exercise 11.2 (Gender at Work). If volume is needed as well for a book (a multi-volume work), you usually put '1962b: I, 162'. (This style is fine when roman numerals are used for the volumes but ambiguous if book volumes are in arabic numbers.)

- If the same author's work is discussed over several

sentences there is no need to repeat the name each time; *nor* do you use 'ibid.' All you need is the date, with a new page number each time. (Sometimes the page alone is enough.)

- Where several works are referred to, the semicolon between them, as demonstrated in Personal Space, is standard. (In a case like 'Kuethe, 1962, 1964' a semicolon could equally well be used between the dates, again provided you are consistent.)

- What order is being followed in '(Horowitz et al., 1965; Dosey and Maisels, 1969)' (l. 11)? Again it is usual to demand consistency within the book: either follow **chronological** order as here (helpful as showing the development of thought through time) or **alphabetical** order (helpful to the reader wishing to find the references quickly in the list). Occasionally an author will depart from mechanical ordering:

    (on pottery, see Midas, 1990; on fine art, Chang, 1989)

Naturally, you mustn't annihilate such an intentional distinction.

- As we've seen, where there are several co-authors, the text reference is usually abbreviated to 'et al.' Like 'ibid.', this is often (though by no means always) set in roman, so that it does not stand out distractingly. (Remember that, unlike 'op. cit.', there is only one stop in 'et al.' – putting in two is a surprisingly common mistake.) Be consistent as to whether 'et al.' is used for *three or more* authors, or for *four or more*.

- Often a reference gives the source of a quotation. If this is an embedded quotation, you might have:

    As Gerhardt and Franks say: 'Myths reveal the essence of a culture' (1960: 162).

    or

    As Gerhardt and Franks (1960: 162) say: 'Myths reveal the essence of a culture.'

The first version tucks the reference away in the least obtrusive place (much as a note indicator is best at the end of a sentence). The second version conforms with the *general* rule of this system that the date should come as close as possible to the name (so that the reference may easily be looked up in the list). Provided the author consistently follows one or other of these systems, it is best not to interfere.

- Date and page number, however, should be *kept together* as in both these examples. (If you look back at Exercise 2.4, Caring, you will see that the editor did not do this – at proof stage it is often too late to make the change.) When you do move references, double-check that the *sense* of the sentence remains the same.

■ Finally, as we saw in Unit 11, publishers or authors may have preferred styles on the position and punctuation of references in relation to extracts.

They may favour always putting the reference at the end (the least obtrusive place) or, wherever possible, in the introductory sentence, following the author's name. (If the author is not mentioned there, you have no alternative but to put the reference at the end of the extract.)

Be consistent too about whether the parenthetic reference comes before or after the final stop of the extract. (Either style is possible.)

Now do Exercise 19.2

Follow the same routine: first check the reference list rapidly; then edit the text, cross-checking each reference as you come to it; tick if it matches and query any problems. Check too (as you did when matching up notes) that the reference seems likely in terms of subject matter and that the page given does fall within the page range. Look out particularly for the punctuation and position of the references in the text. Finally, style the reference list in accordance with the style sheet, looking out for any further queries such as missing details.

*This time formulate your queries on the assumption that the author will **not** be sent even a photocopy of the edited typescript. So, in addition to a column for your new folio number (continuous through the book), you will need a column for the author's original folio number (so that he or she can check against a duplicate). Remember that the author's copy will not have any of your editing on it.*

Review of Exercise 19.2

Check your work against the marked reference list and typed queries on the next two pages. Text changes are discussed below.

Since the dates are different, it is not essential but *is* helpful to distinguish the two Dawsons. Add 'T.' or 'T.J.' on ll. 3, 41, 102; Alan already appears in the text on l. 91. In that sentence the surname is repeated unnecessarily: *either* just delete the surname in parentheses *or* move the date and page to follow the full name on l. 92 (not forgetting in that case that the full stop must *precede* the closing quote on l. 93).

The stray '(p. 110)' after the embedded quote on ll. 20–3 has to join the date. Again you can *either* shift the page number so that l. 20 reads '(1983: 110)' (again remembering to add a full stop preceding the closing quote on l. 22) *or* put date and page together on l. 23.

There is no need to include such adjustments in your query list (even when the author will not see your editing) unless you think you *might* have misunderstood the sense. (Occasionally, for instance, a general reference might be intended for the first half of a sentence; the specific page reference might only relate to the second half.)

On ll. 42 and 52 we again have the date and page wrongly separated, before and after an extract. Following the preference expressed on the style

sheet, take both to the end of the extract, deleting the final stop. (The reference on l. 39 has to remain at the end of the extract, whichever system you follow.) Similarly, move the reference on l. 58 to the end of the extract (after l. 72), adding 'Taylor' because the name is not mentioned in the introductory sentence. Where the name *does* feature in the introductory sentence, there is no need to include it at the end, so on l. 80 you can delete Vandenbeld, as well as correcting the punctuation by adding a full stop at the end of l. 79 and deleting the one on l. 80.

Checking the punctuation of the text references, you should have added or substituted: colon l. 9; comma l. 28; commas and semicolon l. 41; comma and colon l. 83; comma and space after colon l. 90; comma ll. 96 and 102.

On l. 28 the order of references must remain as typed because 'see also' deliberately separates Hallam into a different category. On ll. 40–1 and 96, however, the order should change to the alphabetical style specified.

You will have noticed other minor editing points such as deleting the comma on l. 70 (unnecessary since a new sentence follows). In several other places additional commas are helpful; again, I wouldn't usually query such changes. On l. 53 you may have thought the sentence should have a verb. However, an occasional verbless sentence may be left if it is more effective than the alternatives – I'd keep it

Answer to Exercise 19.2

(R) References   [Indent turnover lines 1 em]   (169)

✓ Carey, S. Warren (1967) Proofs of the existence of Gondwana.
American Journal of Science 265: 509-40   N ← (and throughout)

✓(A) Dawson, Alan T. (1986) Development in young kangaroos. Australian
Geographic 1: 8-12

✓(T) Dawson, Terence J. (1977) Monotremes, marsupials and eutherians.
?   In/Hunsaker, D. (ed.), The Biology of Marsupials. New York: Academic Press, pp.
        Don

✓ Hallam, A. (1983) Great geological controversies. Oxford: Oxford
University Press

✓ Hume, Ian D. (1977a) |Digestive physiology and nutrition of
marsupials, in Hunsaker, Don (ed.), The biology of
marsupials. New York: Academic Press. pp. 263-89

✓ Hume, Ian D. (1977b) Joey's Second Birth. Australian Wildlife
20: 32-40

✓ Morgan, W.J. (1968a) Evidence for continental drift. Nature
211: 446-56

✓ Morgan, W.J. (1968b) Plate tectonics. Journal of Geophysical
Research 73: 1959-86

✓ Taylor, Jan (1987) Evolution in the outback: time in the North
West of Australia. Kenthurst: Kangaroo Press

✓ Tyndale-Biscoe, Hugh (1983a) Reproduction in kangaroos. In Ronald
?   Strahan (ed.), Complete book of Australian mammals. Sydney:

✓ Tyndale-Biscoe, Hugh (1983b) The reproductive system of
kangaroos. Journal of animal biology, 22: 148-65

✗ White, Mary E. (1986) The greening of Gondwana. Sydney: Reed

✓ Vandenbeld, John (1988) Nature of Australia: A Portrait of the
Island Continent. London: BBC Books

Queries for Exercise 19.2

OUR PAGE	YOUR PAGE	LINE	QUERY	RESPONSE
165	30	4	OK to add quotes round 'mammal'?	
165	30	9	Tyndale-Biscoe 1983 becomes 1983a	
168	33	9up	T-B 1983a becomes 1983b as style	
166	31	2	Carey 1968 not in refs Also Morgan 1968 – a or b? or both? And Hallam 1982 – shd this be 1983 as refs and p. 30 l. 7up?	
166	31	8 & 10	Confirm 'marsupials' and 'into' (not 'intro') in extract	
167	32	5up	Confirm Vandenbeld as elsewhere	
168	33	5	Confirm Hume 1977a ('Digestive...') (as p. no. & subject suggest)	
168	33	6	Suggest change 'the kangaroo' to 'kangaroos' (as 'wallabies')	
168	33	12	Confirm Hume 1977b ('Joey's...)	
168	33	9up	Which Hume 1977 – a or b?	

Refs

169	34		Dawson, T. 1977 – pp?	
			Tyndale-Biscoe 1983a (prev. 1983) in Strahan (ed.) – publisher?	
			White 1986 not in text – OK to omit?	

here. If you did change it, you should include this in the query list. I hope you corrected to 'forward' on l. 17 and 'drought' on l. 73.

Imposing a reference style

By now you are, I hope, becoming familiar with bibliographical details. Although styles vary, they do so within limits. Some information is essential, some optional; order and punctuation differ but patterns are predictable. Often you are not given a style sheet of features to be imposed but will be expected to act as you did in Personal Space: to notice all the details of an author's system and follow it.

Reference style sheets are extremely helpful as guidelines for authors, especially in a journal or multi-author book. However, it is sensible to be adaptable. As for other points of house style – and more than most – there are risks in imposing a reference system different from the author's own. If a typescript arrives that reasonably consistently follows one of the accepted styles, changing it could be time-consuming and messy.

Even when you are not imposing a different style but are expected to follow the author's system, do make yourself a reference style sheet, along the lines of those used in the exercises for this course, as a reminder of the system you are following.

UNIT 20

Making Cuts

To most people 'editing' *means* cutting a text (judiciously, of course). We think of the newspaper editor's blue pencil, slashing to the essentials. In this unit you have a chance to do likewise. Cuts may be required at any of the proof stages, in order to fit text and illustrations satisfactorily into the available space. At typescript stage you may have to cut either (similarly) because the author's original is overlength or because it is repetitious or verbose.

At paste-up or proof

Where text is set in columns, you often have to shorten or lengthen passages slightly when you check the designer's **rough paste-up**, or when you do your own layout, if this is part of your job. (With a desk-top publishing system you may be doing this on screen rather than on hard copy.) The aim is to achieve a pleasing page layout, with columns of even depth and illustrations as close as possible to the text discussion of them. Some books are planned from the beginning in double-page spreads but precise **copy-fitting** will often still be needed once the typeset text is available.

Similarly, if you go direct to page proof, the typesetter may note 'line short' or 'line long' on certain pages, for example where a subhead begins the next page. Variation from the standard page depth may occasionally be inevitable but, if you reasonably can, you will lengthen or shorten the text to fit. If you do have to leave pages long or short, it is best to make the facing pages of a spread the same (both long or both short).

The other alternative to adjusting the text is to adjust the spacing (before and after headings, extracts, etc.) and many publishers going direct to page proofs will instruct the typesetter that such spaces are **variable** (probably within limits). Most pages will then automatically come out the standard depth, although occasional short pages may still occur before a heading.

Time is usually at a premium when you check the paste-up, so you cannot re-read a whole page to see what material is most dispensable (if you are cutting) or what could be expanded (if you are adding). You have to take some short-cuts.

When you have to **save** (omit) a line or two:

- Look for a short line at the end of a paragraph.

- Read that para only and cut a word or phrase that will make it possible to 'take back' the last line of the para on to the line before. If it is a long para, the cut should be made towards the end; if it is short, the cut may be made anywhere in the para.

- Sometimes running on two paras can achieve your aim, but check carefully what the effect will be: this doesn't always save a line. Equally important, you have to do more reading round the cut to make certain you have not interfered with the logic of division into paras.

- Occasionally a gappy line can just be squeezed up.

When you have to **make** (add) a line or two:

- Look for a full line at the end of a paragraph.

- Again, read that para and add a word or phrase.

- Sometimes creating two paras out of one can make a line, but again you need to be sure that you are not disrupting the logical structure.

- Occasionally a tight line can be spread without any word changes.

Now do Exercise 20.1   [G]

Each sheet is going to be a full page of a book. (The illustration is incomplete because it continues on the facing page.) At the bottom the designer has asked you to make or save a line in certain columns, to bring them to the same depth as the others on the page. The alteration can be made anywhere in the column. But remember you do not have time to read the whole page or even the whole column.

Review of Exercise 20.1

On the first page (Dinosaurs), the obvious place to shorten col. 3 is in the first para. You could change (and improve) the last sentence, for example, to 'They had only 3 fingers on each hand.' (The number was 'reduced' only by comparison with creatures discussed earlier on the page.) Or change 'reduced to 3' to 'only 3'.

On the second page (Turtles), col. 1, the most likely candidate is para 3; for example, you could expand the last line to 'subclass of their own. This would be called Testudinata.' Alternatively, changing 'save' to 'except' on l. 3 of the para and adding 'is' on l. 8 would probably have the same effect.

In col. 2, spreading to make a new line can be done in para 3 *without* word changes, by taking over 'a', 'mar-', 'out-' and 'protection'.

In col. 3, shorten the first para about the cryptodira. You could cut 'and survive to this day' (ll. 2–3), perhaps adding 'indeed' before 'most modern' and cutting 'of them' from 'Many of them' on ll. 4–5. ('Venezuela' will not fit on the same line as 'South America' – never be over-optimistic about squeezing.)

On the third page (Seals), col. 1, the first para is the best candidate for making a line. Replace the commas round 'the cats, dogs and bears' on ll. 2–3 with those wonderfully long spaced em dashes.

In col. 3, you can save the last line of para 2 by changing 'the animal' to 'it'. (You'll notice you were not asked to adjust the middle column here because the rule serves as a final line.)

There was not much room to write round this exercise, as you will have found. In practice you would probably not be making these adjustments in the paste-up itself but in a **galley proof** to be returned to the typesetter with the paste-up. On the paste-up itself, to show you had dealt with the problem, you would note '+1' or '–1' against the relevant para and tick the instruction 'make line' or 'save line'.

Now do Exercise 20.2

---

*The typesetters have set the whole article but it will not fit into the available space. The latter half is therefore just labelled **overmatter** (left over). First count exactly how many lines you have to save, then edit the article so that it takes up precisely the right space (neither shorter nor longer than the present col. 1). None of your cuts should affect the usefulness or comprehensibility of the article. These are savage cuts by any standards: bold strokes of the pen are the only way.*

Review of Exercise 20.2

There are numerous different ways in which the right result can be attained but some are much more fiddly than others. Deleting a few words here and a phrase there is time-consuming, both for you and for the typesetter. There is (at least) one good bold solution that does the trick neatly.

First, you will have worked out that you have to save 15 lines (the number in the overmatter). The first para is purely introductory – of interest perhaps but not essential – and cutting it out saves 12 lines at a stroke. The omission necessitates a change at the beginning of the next para. For example, it could start 'A new scheme'. This will save you another line at the end of that para because '1980' will be taken back.

Looking for further cuts, your eye should quickly light on the examples in the overmatter, ll. 5–7. Anything in parentheses, or an illustration of a point already made, is fair game. If you cut the whole sentence you would be a line short (which would be equally undesirable) but you could change it to, say, 'An example would be an art gallery.'

Cutting the typescript

In the typescript, you have greater freedom to **tighten up** sentences, rather than (or as well as) making swingeing cuts. Satisfyingly, the effect of this form of editing can often be to improve the impact and clarify the message. Make sure, however, that you never distort the argument or take the colour and individuality out of the language.

Look for redundant adjectives, tautology, long-winded phrases, repetition of information. In the case of repetition, don't assume that the *second* mention is the one to delete. Think instead about the logical organization of material, paragraphing and so on.

Be careful to mark all your changes very clearly (as you learned in Unit 8), not forgetting to delete what you are replacing, and rechecking as you go that each edited sentence makes sense. When you are cutting extensively, consider whether certain paras should be run on or even put in a different order.

Now do Exercise 20.3

---

*Tighten it up as much as you think appropriate, without losing any of the information. **When** you have finished, read your version through out loud. (Better still, ask someone else to read it to you.)*

Further reading

Helpful practice and advice on this aspect of editing are to be found in:

H. Wendell Smith, *Readable Writing: Revising for Style* (Wadsworth, Belmont, California, 1985; distributed in the UK by Routledge, Chapman & Hall)

Leslie Sellers, *The Simple Subs Book* (Pergamon, Oxford, 2nd edition, 1985)

Ernest Gowers, *The Complete Plain Words*, revised by Sidney Greenbaum and Janet Whitcut (Her Majesty's Stationery Office, London, 3rd edition, 1986; Penguin, Harmondsworth, paperback edition, 1987)

UNIT 21

Tables

Tables, simple or complex, may occur at any level of non-fiction. Setting numbers out in tabular form often makes them easier to understand, but much depends on clear, logical layout – and that often depends on you. You have to check that the meaning of the table comes across clearly, that units of measurement are unambiguously stated and so on. You must also cross-check each table against the relevant text and against similar tables.

As with the heading structure (Unit 5) and extracts (Unit 11), the editor's involvement in **detailed marking up** of tables will vary. You may be asked to do the minimum and leave all decisions to the designer; or you may be given a detailed typo-graphical specification and be expected to mark every element on every table.

In this unit we take a middle course, ensuring that the tables conform to a style sheet, which will later be amplified by a general specification for all the tables. (In Unit 25 we look at both specific mark-up of tables and general specifications.) In your own work, make certain you know what you are expected to mark and what you should leave to the designer, if there is one. Find out too whether the designer will mark all the tables specifically or give general instructions. (If the latter, it will be particularly important to mention any unusual features in your notes on design, discussed in Unit 24.)

Now Look at the Style Sheet accompanying Exercise 21.1

Compare the style sheet with the printed version reproduced opposite. Typed labels in the margins of the printed version identify the different parts of a typical table.

The style sheet accompanying the exercise shows just one of several ways in which a table may be laid out. Although styles of layout may differ, the various elements of the table remain much the same. In this particular style sheet, we are asked to standardize the following points.

- The **main head** of the table is to be ranged left (not centred). The **table number** and **table title** are to appear on the same line, separated by an em space. (An alternative is to put them on separate lines.) The table number will be in roman type and the table title italic, with min caps.

- **Rules** (lines) are wanted above and below the **column head**s (which also take min caps but are roman). Below each column head (still between the rules) the **units** of measurement appear, in parentheses.

Authors often put in vertical rules (not usually favoured in print) or more horizontals than are necessary. For this reason, the typesetter should *ignore* all rules in the typescript unless you specifically mark them with a small circle, as shown. It is safest (though not essential) to write 'rule' as well. There is no need to delete unwanted rules.

- The **stub** (the side headings) gives the other dimension of the table. The column heads and stub together explain the meaning of the numbers.

- The style shows a half-line space separating the main part of the table from the 'bottom line', often a total, as here, sometimes an average. (Note that by no means all tables will have a bottom line in this sense.) Again, the typesetter should not put in any extra spaces (even when they

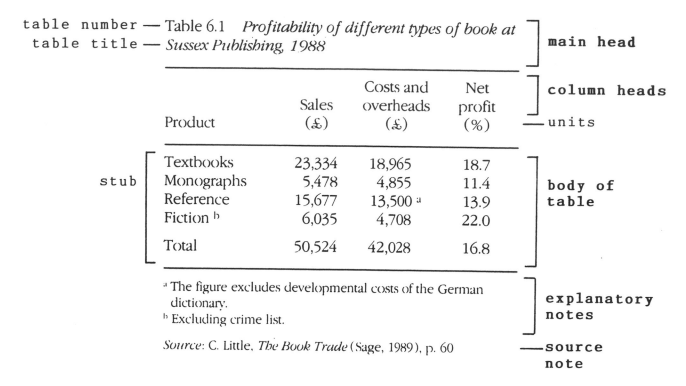

table number — Table 6.1 *Profitability of different types of book at*
table title — *Sussex Publishing, 1988* — main head

column heads / units

Product	Sales (£)	Costs and overheads (£)	Net profit (%)
Textbooks	23,334	18,965	18.7
Monographs	5,478	4,855	11.4
Reference	15,677	13,500 [a]	13.9
Fiction [b]	6,035	4,708	22.0
Total	50,524	42,028	16.8

stub — body of table

[a] The figure excludes developmental costs of the German dictionary.
[b] Excluding crime list.

— explanatory notes

Source: C. Little, *The Book Trade* (Sage, 1989), p. 60 — source note

Parts of a table

appear in the typescript) unless they are specifically marked.

- A third rule separates the body of the table from the notes. The note indicators are to be superscript roman a, b, etc. (rather than 1, 2, etc. or asterisks and daggers). This style is commonly, though not necessarily, followed in tables in order to avoid ambiguity – note indicators attached to numbers can look like indices ($3^2 = 9$) – and to distinguish table notes from notes in the text.
- Each explanatory or substantive note is to end with a stop, regardless of whether it is a full sentence (like a) or just a phrase (like b). Turnover lines are to have **hanging indention** (that is, the first word of the turnover line comes under the first word of the note).
- A half-line space also separates the explanatory notes from the **source note** (sometimes confusingly called a caption, a term best reserved for figures). The style shows the word 'Source' in italic, the rest in roman, except where the overall reference style for the book demands italic. (Notice in the typeset version that the convention is to print the colon roman (upright) after a run-on italic heading such as 'Source'.) Unlike the other notes, the source note is not to end in a stop. Remember that, where a table results from the author's own research, no source is required.

Now do Exercise 21.1

Check the table carefully as well as marking it to accord with the table style.

Review of Exercise 21.1

Check your work against the sample answer on the next page.

It is common (though by no means obligatory) to abbreviate the units that appear under column heads. Whether you do so may depend on the width of the column (here the numbers have only two digits) or the standard style throughout a book. As we saw in Unit 15, 'm' for million is closed up; 'bn' for billion usually follows suit. If you kept the word in full, you would keep a space between the dollar sign and 'billion' (without an 's'). You might also query whether the billions are American or European (see the *Writers' Dictionary*) but as they are attached to dollars this is hardly necessary. Indeed the European billion (a million million) is rapidly becoming obsolete and most English-language authors who

Sample answer to Exercise 21.1

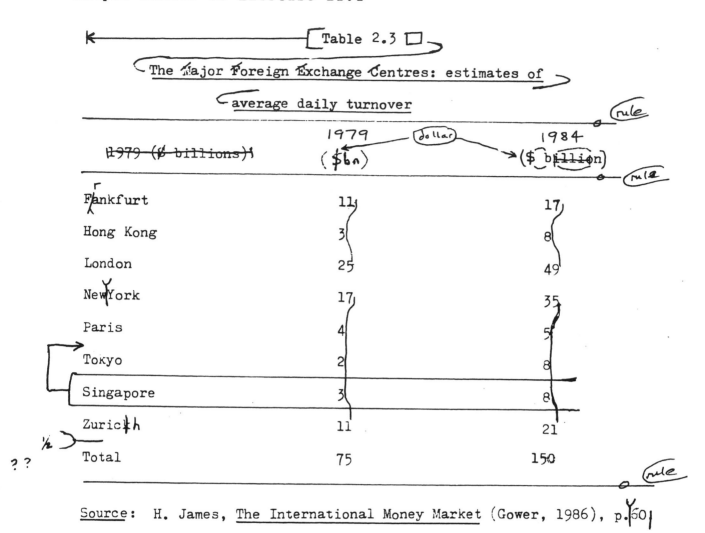

Table 2.3

The Major Foreign Exchange Centres: estimates of average daily turnover

	1979 ($bn)	1984 ($ billion)
Frankfurt	11	17
Hong Kong	3	8
London	25	49
New York	17	35
Paris	4	5
Tokyo	2	8
Singapore	3	8
Zurich	11	21
Total	75	150

Source: H. James, The International Money Market (Gower, 1986), p.60

use the term without explanation now mean the American billion (a thousand million).

A dollar sign, especially a handwritten one, can easily be mistaken for a deleted S. As we have seen, any character that might be ambiguous should be identified (either above/beside the symbol or in the margin).

Where the units are the same in each column, as they are here, they could equally well be put at the end of the *main head* (in parentheses). Whether or not you take this step may depend on the style in the surrounding tables.

You will see that correcting fluid has been used (despite my earlier strictures on obscuring the author's original) in order to make the column heads absolutely clear. In marking up tables, clarity for the typesetter is of paramount importance.

When you are editing a table it is helpful to know whether column heads are to be centred over the column or ranged left. The style sheet here shows a centred style, so you can safely write the corrections in this way.

You may have added a heading 'Foreign exchange centre' above Frankfurt (to match 'Product' in the style sheet). This is fine (though 'Centre' alone would be inadequate) but is not essential: if the main head makes the subject quite clear, there is often no need for a column head for the stub. Where there *is* such a heading, it is always ranged left, even when the other column heads are centred. (You might also have put hyphens in 'foreign-exchange centres', both in the main head and here.)

Mark the transposition of the whole row relating to Singapore as shown (rather than with the shorter bracketing marks recommended elsewhere), just in case the numbers get left behind. (Alternatively, the more elaborate proofreading style of transposition may be followed, see Unit 2.)

The reason for transposing Singapore is that the stub is clearly meant to be in alphabetical order.

This is not always so – the items might follow some other logic, say, regional order. In any table you need to work out what order was intended and check that it has been applied consistently.

There are alternative methods of indicating that the numbers in the columns must be **aligned right**. The line shown is the simplest and therefore the clearest but you could use the 'move matter right' proofreading symbol (see Unit 2). Ones must appear below ones and tens below tens in any such column of numbers. If there are decimals, numbers are aligned on the decimal point. In the style sheet you may have noticed '22.0': this form is used not just to give it the same number of digits as the rest of the column but because, as we saw in Unit 14, it shows that the number has been corrected to one decimal place. (If many of the tables in a typescript have been typed out of alignment, give a general instruction to align all columns on the decimal point.)

Instead of querying the totals, you may simply have corrected them but this would be wrong. In one or both cases the error may lie in one of the other numbers in the column, not necessarily in the total. So you must note a query for the author: 'Should 75 be 76 – or is another no. in the column wrong?' In some tables (though not, I think, in this simple one) such discrepancies may be the result of **rounding**. If that is the answer to your query, a general note should usually be added to say so.

I hope you *did* check the totals. This is always worth doing (with a calculator) whenever you reasonably can. (If the bottom line derives from a statistical formula, you may not be able to do so.) When you are checking a column of percentages, you will often find that they come to 99% or 101%. This is the inevitable result of rounding and you don't need to query it.

The purpose of tables

A table allows easy comparison: setting the data out in tabular form makes their relationships much clearer than packing them into continuous text. Once the details are separated out into a table, the accompanying text can just emphasize the most important or surprising information revealed. (Sometimes a graph may be clearer still: always think about the best ways of presenting information, particularly in textbooks.)

Now do Exercise 21.2   **G**

Tackle this in two stages. First read the passage and decide what information should go into the column heads and what into the stub. Column heads have to be kept short; in the stub you have more space. Decide too what the main head will be. In each case, make your wording as brief as possible, precise and unambiguous. **When you have drafted this framework, turn to the next page** *to check your own scheme against the suggestions given there; make any necessary amendments to your scheme. Then, as the second stage, insert the numbers in the correct places. All the statistics given in the passage should be apparent from your table.*

Review of Exercise 21.2

Precision of wording is quite difficult to achieve, both in the age groups and in the period for re-offending. For children we mean 'up to and including 10' but that is clumsy; '10 or under' would do if you prefer it. A mathematical symbol would be unambiguous (≤ 10) but probably inappropriate in this context.

The numbers in the table would be quite different if, instead of 'in 2–5 years', you said 'within 5 years' (including all the 'within 2 years' offenders as well). The recommended form gives more meaningful comparisons.

The suggested layout uses indents to indicate subheads under the major headings in the stub. The turnover line of each subhead is then indented even further. If this style is to be followed by the typesetter, the indents should be specifically marked (by you or the designer), probably with an em space for the subhead and a 2 em indent for the turnover. Alternatively, the two major headings could be distinguished from the subheads by using bold or italic (in which case, indents would be unnecessary except for the turnovers). As well, or instead, extra space may be added between the two sections.

The total number of adolescents (in the first section) and children (in the second section) put on probation must go in somewhere. You may have put in extra lines for these but much the neatest way is to put the total *on the same line as the major heading*. A total can just as legitimately come first, followed by

Suggested layout for Exercise 21.2

Table 1 <u>Re-offending among young people put on probation</u>
<u>in Chester, 1965–79</u>

Put on probation	1965–9	1970–4	1975–9
Adolescents (11–16)			
Re-offended within 2 years			
Re-offended in 2–5 years			
Children (up to 10)			
Re-offended within 2 years			
Re-offended in 2–5 years			

a breakdown of the figures (although you would not then apply the style sheet's extra half-line space between the body of the table and the total). So under '1965–9' you will have 100, 30, 20 for adolescents; 40, 16, 10 for children.

If the material had remained as a passage of text it is unlikely that the missing information (total number of children put on probation in 1970–4) would have been spotted. The muddled order in the passage, of course, complicates it unnecessarily, but creating a table makes the data much more accessible.

In the final column, 160 from the text has to be broken down into 83 and 77; the final number is 25 (subtracting 30 and 42 from 97).

The text relating to this table could now be shortened to the existing first sentence and one other, such as 'Table 1 shows a dramatic rise in re-offending, even among children, in the period 1975–9.' Remember that, as well as mentioning the table number in the text, you will also **key in** the tables, writing 'Table 1 near here' in the margin, as you learned to do for figures in Units 14–15.

Can you think of a way of making the table even more useful? One way would be to show percentages as well as numbers. Under an umbrella column head '1965–9' you could have two subheads, 'no.' (for number) and '%'. Sometimes where there are two (or more) levels of column head, an additional short rule (sometimes called a **spanner rule**) between the two levels can help to link the lower ones under the umbrella head.

Table notes

The final table exercise affords specific practice in dealing with table notes (both explanatory notes and the source) and also units of measurement.

Now do Exercise 21.3

Follow the same table style sheet as for Exercise 21.1. Aim for simplicity and the consistent treatment of similar data.

Review of Exercise 21.3

Check your solution to the various problems against the *typeset* edited version shown on the next page.

Avoid note indicators that interrupt the flow of a table title. One indicator is acceptable at the *end* of the title: the implication is that the note refers to the whole table. Alternatively, such a general note can appear below the bottom rule without any note indicator. (Since anything below this rule is understood to be a note, there is no need for the word 'Note', although some house styles insist on it.) Wherever possible notes are better attached to a specific part of the table, as the edited version demonstrates.

The note sequence ('a', 'b', etc.) should read across the rows. So if there were notes attached to '15.5' and 'Franco', they would be lettered 'c' and 'd' respectively.

In most cases you can safely convert an author's asterisk system to 'a', 'b', and so on as here. The exception is **levels of probability**. These usually appear thus:

$$* \, p \, < \, .05 \quad ** \, p \, < \, .01 \quad *** \, p \, < \, .001$$

The varying number of asterisks will then appear beside different figures in the body of the table. This is a standard convention and must be preserved. Notice too that probability is one area in which many authors prefer to have no 0 before the decimal point.

The source may be taken down to the bottom either by transposition or by deletion and rewriting. (Do be careful not to introduce errors if you rewrite.) In the typescript version, the publisher's name was missing and you will have noted this as a query.

I hope you noticed the inconsistent use of capitals in the column heads and corrected to min caps. You may also have followed the *Writers' Dictionary* to hyphenate 'sea level', unlike the typeset version. 'Average' height is more accurate, especially since fields are not necessarily contiguous.

Always check that units are specified. Query them if you cannot reliably deduce them (as you can here, for example, for 'Size of farm'). Note, however, that no units are required for a column headed 'ratio' or 'proportion'.

The abbreviation 'kg per ha' could be used instead of 'kg/ha', although the solidus for 'per' is quite common. Use SI units wherever possible, abbreviating them in the standard way. Remember that such abbreviations should never take an 's' in the plural.

Did you work out what order was being followed? It is not alphabetical here but by size of farm, so there is no need for any transpositions. This time the clearest way to mark the alignment of 15.5 is with the standard proofreading symbol for 'move matter right'. 'Data', as we saw in Unit 7, normally takes a plural verb.

The **horizontal alignment** of column heads should be standard throughout a book. This table style sheet shows column heads aligned at the bottom and that is how both the tables on pp. 113 and 118 have been typeset. This style is widely favoured because it brings the heading close to the column and so makes reference to it easy. Alternatively, column heads may be aligned at the top, which may seem more logical. Although a general specification will set the style, deviations in the typescript are worth marking specifically.

Consistency

Authors should provide each table on a separate sheet, preferably grouping all the tables at the end of the relevant chapter. As you read the chapter, you will be comparing each table with the text to make sure that everything is clearly explained and that there are no discrepancies.

Once that is done, you will need to look at the tables again *as a group* to check for consistency. For example, are similar details given in the main heads or does one specify the place and dates of a study (as in Exercise 21.2) and another only the place? Does the wording of column heads in similar tables vary for no good reason? For example, in giving subjects' age groups, one table may have '30–9', '40–9', etc. and the next '30–40', '40–50', etc. The former is to be preferred – there is an ambiguity in the latter over which category a 40-year-old would fall into. (But see Unit 27 for conventions on bands of rainfall and the like.) In making such details consistent, you need to be sure that you are not standardizing studies conducted on different bases. For example, you cannot assume that 'the UK' and 'Great Britain' mean the same thing; the latter may exclude Northern Ireland.

Typeset edited version of Exercise 21.3

Table 8.2   *Average yields of the farms in Ripallo district, 1980*

Household [a]	Size of farm [b] (ha)	Average height above sea level (m)	Soil type	Main crop	Average yield (kg/ha)
Soldi	20	300	chalk	hay	15
Tamara	18	150	loam	maize	56
Patio	15.5	180	clay	maize	52
Araba	13	245	chalk	hay	20
Franco	12	200	loam	maize	38

[a] Three households were excluded from the survey results because data on them were incomplete.

[b] Farm is defined as the property of one household; fields are not necessarily contiguous.

Source: Marcello Bruno, *Italian Smallholdings* (Oxford University Press, 1986), p. 25

UNIT 22

Poetry and Drama

Like all creative writing, poetry and drama demand an editor attuned to the author's intentions. As with tables, however, you also need to be thinking about the technicalities of the work's appearance on the typeset page, and coordinating your efforts with the designer's. Even if you are not involved in publishing poetry, plays or discussions of literature, you may from time to time come across poetry (for example in an epigraph) or extracts set in drama style (for example an interview).

Poetry

Classical forms of poetry usually follow a regular pattern of scansion and rhyme. Sometimes (though by no means necessarily) the indention of the lines will indicate which ones rhyme: so the first and third might rhyme with each other and start full out; and the second and fourth, again rhyming with each other, be indented.

In a book of poems it is usual to centre each poem on its longest line. If you are giving the instruction to centre, be sure to specify 'centre block on longest line'; otherwise the typesetter may centre *each* line (a more straightforward command to most machines). The simpler alternative for the typesetter is to set a standard indent (perhaps 2 or 3 ems) from the left margin. Which style is chosen will usually be a design decision and will often be made after you have done your editorial work.

Now do Exercise 22.1   **G**

Look for the patterns and adjust anything that does not seem to follow them. The problems are very few, so this should not take long.

Review of Exercise 22.1

All the lines begin with a capital except l. 9. You may safely correct this: in classical poetry, each line starts with a capital. (Some modern poetry has abandoned this convention and instead follows normal prose rules.)

The typesetter should be given a general instruction to set poetry **line for line**. Therefore if the typed line of a poem continues on to a second line only because it is very long, you must mark a run-on. (Because of the regular pattern in this poem, we know l. 9 isn't a turnover line.) Mark the run-ons throughout, even though you know some of the lines will inevitably have turnovers in print as well.

Although there often *is* a punctuation mark at the end of a line of poetry, unlike the capital at the beginning it is there only when the sense requires. So ll. 7 and 8, for example, correctly have no punctuation. On l. 13 you should delete the comma and on l. 18 change the full stop to a question mark. The colon and semicolon on ll. 9 and 11 are unusual although they are in fact in the original. (In a new poem you'd query them at least.) The capitals on ll. 13 and 21 are used for emphasis, on l. 8 perhaps more as a title. There is a spelling mistake on l. 11.

I hope you were checking that similarly indented lines did rhyme throughout. The mistakes here were on ll. 13 and 19, which should both be marked full out. On l. 19 you may also have thought 's' was required after 'contain' (though, of course, it can't be added because of the rhyme). In fact 'to' is understood here. Nor need we query the fact that the sentence has no main clause: even in prose, as we saw in Exercise 19.2 (Marsupials of Australia), this is allowable for special effect.

Do you need to mark spacing and indents? This may depend on whether a designer will go through the typescript in detail after you. If not (and perhaps even if so), mark a space between verses and use the square box (quad) to show each indented line.

In concrete poetry (where the lines make a shape, perhaps creating a diamond or forming a tail) you might just give a general instruction to follow the original as closely as possible. If the unusual features are few, it is best to mark them specifically.

Now do Exercise 22.2   **G**

Again there are only a few mistakes and fewer conventions.

Review of Exercise 22.2

If there is any likelihood that the heading will be set with cap sig wds, as well as coding it 'A' you should mark which letters are to remain caps (N, R, D). The different number of lines in verses 1 and 2 is unusual but in such free form not worth querying.

On l. 10 mark an em space between the words to show the typesetter that this oddity is to be reproduced. (It shows someone reading aloud that each word requires emphasis.)

The reason for the indent on l. 22 is not obvious (except perhaps to give weight to a short last line) and you might suggest ranging it left like all the others. If the indent is to stay, it should be marked.

Clearly the conventional capital at the beginning of each line has been rejected, probably in favour of normal prose use of capitals (to begin sentences). Change to 'beauty' (l. 15) and 'but' (l. 22) (perhaps asking for confirmation in your query list).

The end-of-line punctuation seems conventional, so add a comma to l. 7 and perhaps l. 21 (but not l. 14). Mark spaced ellipses as usual. Finally, the correct spelling on l. 18 is 'pavane'.

Drama

The drama exercise that follows is accompanied by a style sheet showing both a typeset version and the marked typescript it comes from. In real life you are most often expected to follow the style of an existing book or **specimen pages** (advance setting to approve the design of the particular project). Just as we saw for tables in Unit 21, it is very helpful to know, as you edit the text of a play, what the layout is going to be.

Precisely what you mark and what the designer marks may vary. For example, here spaces between speech and **stage directions** have been marked by the editor; the designer will then give a general instruction on whether to leave a line or half a line throughout.

The names of the characters are often picked out in a special way typographically, not only in the **speech prefix** at the beginning of each speech but every time they are mentioned in stage directions. This is to enable each actor to find all references to his or her actions quickly, even when they occur during someone else's speech.

Now do Exercise 22.3

Refer back to the style sheet as you do the exercise, looking especially carefully at the use of capitals and punctuation. Use a ruler to underline whole sentences for italic; mark for small caps by hand. There is likely to be a short list of queries.

*You will probably recognize the characters' names. The passage is not, however, from Shakespeare's **Hamlet** but from a modern play (which may also be familiar) that takes two of its minor characters and promotes them to centre stage.*

Review of Exercise 22.3

Check your work against the sample answer (for the first folio only) on p. 122.

It is usual to specify a standard indent (1 em or 2 ems) for turnover lines as a general instruction. The alternative of varying the indent according to the length of the speech prefix (as typed on l. 14) is less common in print. This correction may either be marked as in the sample answer or be shown as a run-on from l. 13 to l. 14, as for poetry.

If the typescript consistently had characters' names (both in the speech prefixes and elsewhere) in capitals, you could give a general instruction that they were to be set in small caps, rather than marking each one. (Typesetting in full caps is, of course, also possible but looks heavy. 'Caps and small caps' is, sadly, out of fashion.)

Stage directions are often set in italic as here, in addition to being separated from the text by either parentheses or square brackets. **Scene-setting** at the beginning of an act or scene is similarly italic but *not* usually in brackets. The brackets themselves are set roman (upright): on l. 19 this is best shown by (for once) using correcting fluid. Similarly, if speech prefixes were set in italic (rather than small caps as here), the colon would still be roman (as we saw for 'Source' in Unit 21).

Entrances and action between speeches are usually set on a new line, often indented (either the same amount as turnovers or further), sometimes (as here) with extra space above and below. Notice that spaces are marked even when they occur in the typescript: as we saw in Unit 21, the typesetter should not leave extra space unless instructed. It is particularly important to show that l. 19 is not just a continuation of Rosencrantz's speech. (Both characters are involved, so it is best treated as action between speeches.)

Actions of other actors during a speech (for example on l. 27) are, by contrast, usually run on. Picking out the character's name in small caps (or sometimes in u/lc roman) is particularly helpful here.

Two different forms of **exit** are shown in the style sheet: a brief one such as Penelope's is ranged right, *without* a closing bracket; a longer sentence is treated the same as an entrance. This distinction is quite common. Note that 'exit' (not 'exits') is the singular form; 'exeunt' the plural, following the original Latin.

Keep a sharp eye on entrances and exits to make sure that none of the characters has lines when not on stage. This is the problem on l. 25. Almost certainly the change is correct (Hamlet was already at Elsinore, so the line would not make sense coming from him) but it is worth asking for confirmation. Similarly, you would also check that each character appears in the **dramatis personae**, or cast list, at the beginning of the play.

The query on l. 3 is again a request for confirmation. 'Deciphering' is more usually applied to written material but in a play as beautifully wrought as this you should secure the author's agreement to any wording change, even in a stage direction.

The other essential query will be the repetition of the same speech prefix on l. 34. Do not just delete it and run on: there could equally well be a missing line of speech by Rosencrantz.

The punctuation of stage directions, as I hope you deduced from the style sheet, varies as follows. A complete sentence (for example, ll. 5, 17–18, 27–8, 55) begins with a capital and ends with a stop. An incomplete sentence (a phrase or word) requires no punctuation (see l. 13); it begins lower case *unless* it follows a full stop. So all instructions on ll. 32–40 should start lower case except 'Picking' (l. 36). (The stop after 'up]' here must also be deleted.) The punctuation round such interpolations should read normally, so add commas before 'for' on l. 33 and before 'then' on l. 41.

The other point to note when you are looking at a style sheet for guidance is whether a stage direction at the beginning of a speech *follows* or *precedes* the colon. Either style is acceptable but you must be consistent (see ll. 12, 29).

The abbreviation of some, but not all, of the speech prefixes may have worried you. It is valid when, as here, two main characters dominate the play and the others appear only occasionally. In some plays all will be spelt out in full; in others most may be abbreviated. The short form used must always be the same (so change ll. 50, 52). The style of spelling the names out in full only at the top of a folio (ll. 29, 31) cannot be retained: the printed pages will fall quite differently. (Nor is this common even in print.)

Although there is little difference between an ellipsis (l. 12) and a dash (l. 42) at the end of a sentence, it could be that one is a tailing off and the other a dramatic pause: I'd leave the variation. A final dash is usually treated like any other dash (a spaced en in this style).

On l. 47 a comma is needed after 'going' and an 'a' should be added at the end of the line. You could query whether 'further' on l. 54 might not be better as 'future'. Italic has to be added for stage directions on ll. 29, 39, 55. Indention should be marked for ll. 30 and 53–4.

You will, I hope, have checked the left/right, east/west convolutions in ll. 32–42. Even though they will be spoken too fast for the audience to spot errors, and it's all meant as nonsense, remember that the actor will have to rehearse the actions carefully, so it is important that the script is right. (The simplest way to check is to sketch a compass on paper, stand up and perform as instructed.) In fact, all is well.

Further reading

For editing poetry, plays and literary work generally, including annotated editions of texts, see Butcher, *Copy-editing*.

Answer to Exercise 22.3

(A)   ACT TWO

HAMLET, Rosencrantz and Guildenstern are talking. Their

? conversation, on the move, is ~~indecipherable~~ *indistinguishable* at first.

HAMLET: Gentlemen, you are welcome at Elsinore. Your hands,
   come then. [He takes their hands.] You are welcome. [About
   to leave] But my uncle-father and aunt-mother are deceived.

GUIL: In what, my dear lord?

HAMLET: I am but mad north-north-west; when the wind is southerly
   I know a hawk from a handsaw.

   [POLONIUS enters as Guil turns away.]

Polonius: My Lord! I have news to tell you.

HAMLET: [mimicking] My lord, I have news to tell you...

POLONIUS: [As he follows HAMLET out] The actors are come hither,
   my lord.

HAMLET: Buzz, buzz.

   [Exeunt HAMLET and POLONIUS.]

Ros: He's at the mercy of the elements. [He licks his finger
   and holds it up, facing the audience.] Is that southerly?

   [They stare at the audience.]

GUIL: It doesn't look southerly. What made you think so?

ROS: I didn't say I think so. It could be northerly for all
   I know.

GUIL: I wouldn't have thought so.

ROS: Well, if you're going to be dogmatic.

? ~~HAMLET~~ GUIL: Wait a minute — we came from roughly south according
   to a rough map.

ROS: I see. Well, which way did we come in? [GUIL looks round
   vaguely.] Roughly.

UNIT 23

Lists

In educational and technical books lists occur frequently; in all areas of publishing they crop up occasionally. Like headings (as we saw in Unit 5), the function of lists is to organize the material into a logical, orderly and clear presentation of the information.

Now do Exercise 23.1

G

First read it through; then think about the logical grouping of the information and the order in which it is presented; finally rearrange and edit it as you think best. At this stage, although you should mark the script as clearly as you possibly can, don't worry if it becomes a trifle messy.

Review of Exercise 23.1

As the introduction to the exercise may have warned you, it is easier to decide what to do with this passage than to demonstrate clearly to the typesetter how you want it to look. This kind of material is far easier to deal with if you have it on disk and can rearrange as you edit.

Having access to a word-processor, I have been able to do just that. On the next page, you will find two alternative 'tidy' versions of the same material. These are only two of the innumerable ways in which the passage *could* be improved (it could hardly be worse) and you may have made even more changes.

Essentially, both 'tidy' versions group ll. 2–6 as general appearance and ll. 7–13 with ll. 17–18 as the content of the letter. Version A makes ll. 14–16 a separate section; Version B just adds it as a final caveat. Within each grouping the order has been changed to a 'first things first' approach, which is usually best in 'how to' books. So, you select the notepaper before laying out the letter; you put the reference number after the address and before starting to make your points (not necessarily a 'request' if we are dealing with business letters in general).

The first version uses B heads, which simplifies the layout so that only one level of list is needed. Since they are parallel lists (on the same level), they must be treated the same, *either* both with numbers *or* both with '(a)', '(b)', etc. The numbers could have stops if that is your preferred style; it is less usual to have parentheses round numbers. If you are using letters, a parenthesis before as well as after is generally preferable.

Although the first, or only, level of list *can* use letters it is very common to differentiate (as Version B does) and use '1', '2', etc., for major points and '(a)', '(b)', etc., for subdivisions within them (and sometimes for minor points elsewhere). A hierarchy is created, much like the heading hierarchy.

In Version A you have no options as far as punctuation and use of capitals are concerned. The items in the list must all be full sentences, beginning with a capital and ending with a full stop.

In Version B the '(a)', '(b)', etc., subsections all form part of the overall sentence beginning at '1' (or '2'). They therefore begin lower case and end with a semicolon (except the last, which concludes the whole sentence with a full stop). If each item in the list was just a word or two (rather than long phrases), a comma would be quite sufficient.

Like punctuation introducing an extract (Unit 11), the punctuation introducing the list does not have to be standardized but may depend on the form of the sentence. So in Version B the introductory sentence breaks off without punctuation in point 1, but there is a colon in point 2.

Sample answers to Exercise 23.1 (retyped)

(A) HOW TO WRITE A BUSINESS LETTER   **Version A**

(B) General appearance

1 Use headed notepaper, if possible, because it gives a more
  professional impression.
2 Lay the letter out carefully. Choose appropriate margins and
  allow plenty of space.
3 Type accurately. Recheck your work at the end.

(B) The letter itself

1 Address a specific individual. If necessary, ring to find
  out the name of the person responsible.
2 Include any relevant reference numbers.
3 Make your points clearly and briefly.
4 End with 'Yours sincerely' (to a specific person) or 'Yours
  faithfully' (if you have not managed to find out the name).
  (Never use 'Yours truly'.)
5 Remember to spell out your name as well as signing, however
  clear your signature is.

(B) Finishing touches

Having done all this, don't spoil everything by sellotaping
up the envelope scruffily. They all seem to have lost their
stickiness these days, but do use glue.

(A) HOW TO WRITE A BUSINESS LETTER   **Version B**

1 Pay attention to the general appearance of the letter by
  (a) using headed notepaper, if possible, to give a more
      professional impression;
  (b) laying the letter out carefully (choosing appropriate
      margins and allowing plenty of space);
  (c) typing accurately, rechecking your work at the end.

2 In the letter itself:
  (a) address a specific individual (if necessary, ringing
      to find out the name of the person responsible);
  (b) include any relevant reference numbers;
  (c) make your points clearly and briefly;
  (d) end with 'Yours sincerely', to a specific person, or
      'Yours faithfully', if you have not managed to find out
      the name (never 'Yours truly');
  (e) remember to spell out your name as well as signing
      (however clear your signature is).

Having done all this, don't spoil everything by sellotaping
up the envelope scruffily. They all seem to have lost their
stickiness these days, but do use glue.

What is important is that the grammatical form of each item within any specific list should not vary. So in Version B, point 1, each item begins 'using', 'laying', etc., so that it reads smoothly on from the introductory 'by'. In point 2, each item in the list begins with a straightforward command. On l. 11 'you should' has been omitted because, although it does still read on, the change of grammatical form creates unnecessary confusion.

Although the style is not demonstrated here, it is also perfectly acceptable to have an introductory sentence ending in a colon, which is then followed by numbered (or lettered) points containing complete sentences (with a capital and full stop).

On l. 14 I hope you noticed the dangling participle, which you learned about in Unit 7. The suggested change is by no means the only way of solving the problem and you may hesitate to *introduce* the colloquial 'don't' (though you might accept an author's use of it). In the context 'do not' would sound heavy, but you'd need to check whether shortened forms occur elsewhere in the book. An alternative change would be: 'Even when you have done all this, it is still possible …'.

Many editors would use a capital for 'Sellotaping' as well as correcting its spelling (or would ban the verb and convert to 'use Sellotape'). My own view is that, if you accept such a word as part of the language (rather than a trade name) by making it into a verb, you can also lower-case it. The same would go for 'hoovering' and so on.

As we saw in Unit 5, instead of either numbers or letters, you can use bullets for lists. Equally, in many contexts you can leave lists unpunctuated (as I've done in this book where list items consist of phrases).

If the material is not on disk and we cannot afford to have it all retyped, how can we make clear to a busy typesetter what layout is wanted? On the next page you will find a sample marked-up typescript for Version B only. As you see, I have shown a **list style** at the bottom. A little sketch like this (relating either to a whole typescript or to a particularly messy page) can save a thousand technicalities of marking. You *do* need to mark the indents in the typescript as well (as this sample shows) but the sketch giving a visual clue to the desired layout is invaluable.

As we saw in Unit 21 (Tables), this layout is called **hanging indention** (as opposed to **para indention**, where only the first line is indented, like an ordinary para). The vertical lines in the sketch, and the vertical (or where necessary curving) lines marked in the text itself, show which words should align.

Neither of the sample answers discussed adds to the information given in the passage but you may quite rightly have filled it out by mentioning the recipient's address, the date, more about the content of the letter, etc. You would also want to illustrate the passage with a sample letter.

Now do Exercise 23.2

This is not an instructional piece – the purpose is not to teach the reader how to make carpets – but it should convey information in a clear and readable way. So, although some set-out lists will be helpful, other points may be better run on as part of the text (where they can still begin '(a)', '(b)', etc., if you wish). Think about logical paragraphing and varied language as well as about the lists.

You will see that a folio of figures is included: don't forget to check them and key them into the text, as you learned in Units 14–15.

Review of Exercise 23.2

The two lists on the first folio are parallel and should follow the same system (either numbers or letters, preferably numbers). The list on ll. 26–8 is probably best run on in the text as an ordinary sentence, without any numbers. At ll. 40–1, I would keep the points run on, but here the '(a)' and '(b)' do serve a useful purpose, if the sentence remains unchanged (see below). There seems no particular reason for setting out ll. 45–7 as a list: the points are better run on.

On ll. 9–13 there is another list, run on in the text, and again best kept that way. You do, however, need to make it consistent, *either* as one sentence divided by semicolons *or* with each item forming a separate sentence. Also, as we've seen elsewhere, you should consistently include or exclude a comma after the word that indicates that this is a list (including 'finally').

Then there is that contentious word 'firstly'. Some (including myself) argue that this is a reprehensible word-form and 'first' is preferable. Some (but here I wouldn't agree) go on to argue that, if you change

Marked copy for an answer to Exercise 23.1 (version B)

(A) HOW TO WRITE A BUSINESS LETTER

1 Pay attention to the general appearance of the letter by

☐ (b) Lay the letter out carefully, (Choose appropriate margins, and allow plenty of space);

☐ (c) type accurately, rechecking your work at the end.

☐ (a) If possible, use headed notepaper, which generally gives a more professional impression;

2 In the letter itself:

☐ (a) address a specific individual (if necessary, ringing to find out the name of the person responsible);

☐ (c) Make your points request clearly and briefly;

☐ (f) you should include any relevant reference numbers;

☐ (d) sign off 'Yours sincerely', (to a specific person), or 'Yours faithfully', if you have not managed to find out the name (if not) (never 'Yours truly');

Having done all this, it is still possible to don't spoil everything by sellotaping up the envelope scruffily. (They all seem to have lost their stickiness these days, but do use glue.)

☐ (e) remember to spell out your name as well as signing (however clear your signature is).

List style:

1
☐ (a)
   (b)
2

to 'first', you also have to change to 'second', etc. My own preference is for 'first' followed by 'secondly', though I wouldn't nowadays impose it on an author unless he or she had been inconsistent. (You'll recall that Unit 7 gives a further reading list of the various authorities on such points.)

The first list (ll. 4–8) is a mixture of complete and incomplete sentences. You could convert all the items into complete sentences like 1 (beginning with a capital and ending with a stop) or all into phrases like 2 and 3 (beginning lower case and ending with semicolons until the final stop). Even if you use sentences, the colon on l. 3 can remain (though some editors would prefer a full stop).

There's that ubiquitous word 'use' again: I hope you will have disposed of at least *some* of its occurrences in the exercise, and of other instances of repetition, as well as some of the passives. For example, l. 14 could be 'The illustrations show the tools needed.'

'Kinds of' came up twice (ll. 3 and 25), once with the singular following it, the other time with the plural (see Unit 7). If you kept both instances, the usage should be made consistent one way or the other. On l. 25, however, a better option might be 'Two different knots'.

On l. 30 'the latter' is probably all right but on l. 33 'the former' would be better changed to 'the Turkish' (and the 'knot' at the end of the sentence can be omitted). These rather heavy expressions ('the former', 'the latter') are best avoided except where they save ugly repetition. If you keep them, make sure they are unambiguous.

A new para is probably appropriate at l. 9. An introductory sentence would help to bring together the para starting at l. 34, for example, 'The designs follow traditional conventions.' The new para at l. 42 is odd: its first sentence is more closely connected with the preceding para (we are already discussing prayer rugs) and its second sentence moves on to other kinds of rug. The best solution may be to run the whole of ll. 34–47 on (so that the last sentence is just hooked on to a para all about design). Alternatively, a new para could start at the end of l. 38.

Standardize the use of italic: is it for Turkish words, or is it for the main word(s) in each item of a list, or both? The system of using italic for the first mention of a foreign word and roman thereafter is possible, but it is generally better to be consistent throughout. (Similarly, avoid capitals for first use only, ll. 26–32.) I'd just have italic for Turkish words here (so cancelling the underlining of 'knot knife' on l. 15 and adding underlining for Turkish words on ll. 9 and 22). An English plural on a foreign word (*kirkits* on ll. 20, 22) is usually italicized too. Make sure that an author is consistent about whether plural forms follow the original language or are anglicized.

Note the **diacritics** required in Turkish (the comma shape – not a cedilla – under 'c' and 's', for example, converts them into 'ch' and 'sh'). There is a difference too between an 'i' with a dot and one without. (So even a capital 'I' will often have a dot.) If, for consistency, you converted 'woof' on l. 12 to atkı, remind the typesetter 'no dot', and do the same on l. 6.

As we saw in Unit 15, in addition to identifying them in the typescript, you should make a list of **special sorts**. French and German accents do not usually need listing, nor do the commonest maths symbols (+, =, etc.), but anything beyond those is worth mentioning.

In the margin (in a circle or box) you will have keyed in the figures by writing 'Fig. 1 near here', etc. The placing in the eventual book does not have to be precise (as it might, say, in a woodwork manual or geometry textbook) but should be as near to that text passage as is practicable. If, for example, the relevant text comes near the bottom of a page, the figure will have to appear on the following page. (If positioning had to be precise, you would need to make cuts or additions in proof, as we saw in Unit 20, to achieve the correct layout.)

On the figures themselves, it would be helpful to **label** each section of Fig. 5 ('Single-stepped niche', etc.), to make the text on ll. 40–1 clearer. The two plain designs would also be better placed above the two stepped ones. Knots are notoriously difficult to portray in two dimensions but the dotted and solid lines of Fig. 4 could perhaps be explained (in a **key** or **caption**), or two separate stages might be shown for each knot. (Figures and their labels and keys are discussed in more detail in Unit 27; captions in Unit 28.)

UNIT 24

Design and Layout

In this unit we look at general design considerations: first the editor's briefing of the designer, then the wider design decisions such as format, layout, typeface and type size. Unit 25 goes on to more specific typographical mark-up. Whatever your degree of involvement in, or isolation from, design aspects, you should find a basic understanding of them helpful.

Briefing the designer

Either at a preliminary meeting or on paper (or both), a designer has to be briefed on general points: the market, likely readers, suggested format, expected extent, general feel (spacious or close-packed), tightness of budget and so on. Ideally designer and editor will work together closely from the beginning.

The editor's specific **notes on design** accompanying the typescript will then cover its main (and particularly any unusual) features, giving a typical folio, or (if the feature is rare) all folios, on which it occurs. These show the designer how far you have already marked up the typescript and what remains to be done or to be mentioned in the general specification. Features usually covered in notes on design are:

- **headings**: what codes have been used; whether all, or any, headings are very long or very short (often giving an example of longest and shortest); whether text should/may run on after lower levels of heading (Unit 5)

- **display in text**: extracts, poetry, drama-style extracts, lists, examples, maths formulae, etc.

- **other passages needing special treatment**: boxes, reading passages, questions, etc. (explaining any use of highlighters)

- **tables**: where they are to be found, any particularly awkward in shape, any likely to have to go **landscape** (that is, be **turned** to run up the page)

- **illustrations**: including much the same details as for tables, although often there will be a separate brief for these, specifying requirements or suggestions on the size and treatment of each (as we'll see in Unit 26)

- **endmatter**: notes, references, appendices, answers, etc., either at the ends of chapters or at the end of the book

- **special sorts**: mathematics, phonetics, foreign accents, etc.

Sometimes these notes on design are prepared at an early stage and accompany a duplicate unedited typescript (with only the main features marked); sometimes they will accompany the fully edited typescript.

In publishing firms without specialist design departments, design is sometimes handled by the production department; alternatively, it may become an editorial responsibility. If you are a production editor, for example, you may well wear both hats.

Even if you are responsible for both aspects, try to keep them apart in your mind and tackle them as separate operations. The editorial function is concerned with analysing the logical structure and determining which features should be treated alike. The design function is to decide how best to demonstrate those hierarchies, similarities and differences on the printed page.

Typesetting specification

The designer draws up a typesetting (or typographical) specification, usually known as the **type spec**. This will include instructions on how to handle all the detailed features you have listed (as we shall see in Unit 25) but it also has to deal with the broader questions we look at below.

In more complicated books, the spec will be accompanied by a **layout**, or sample pages from a similar book, or specimen pages typeset in advance for this particular project (as we saw in Unit 22).

Terminology and units of measurement

The illustrations on the next spread show four different typefaces, two of them with **serifs** (little 'ears' on the letters), two **sans serif** (without serifs).

■ **Picas** (shown in the rule at the bottom of each illustration) are the standard unit of measurement for the length of a line of type from left margin to right margin, the **measure**. (There are 6 picas to an inch; a pica is approximately 4.2 mm.)

■ Type size is given in **points**. (There are 12 points in a pica.) However, as you can see from the illustrations, the same point size can look very different in different typefaces. This is because the point size is determined by the overall measurement (in fact, the height of the piece of metal block to which each letter was traditionally attached). But typefaces vary greatly in the proportion of the **x-height** to the **ascenders** and **descenders**. (You met these terms in Unit 2.) Sans serif typefaces, for example, can often appear larger than their point-size equivalents with serifs.

■ Most of the examples shown (headed 10 pt to 14 pt) are set **solid**, that is, without any extra space between lines. (A descender from one line almost touches an ascender on the next.)

■ Such solid setting is rare: more often a small amount of extra space, or **leading**, is introduced. The first example in each typeface demonstrates 10 on 12 pt (also written as 10/12 pt). This means that the type size is 10 pt but the distance from one **baseline** to the next baseline (called the **linefeed**) is 12 pts. The extra space (2 pts) is the leading. (Confusion can arise because the term 'leading' is increasingly used to mean 'linefeed', especially on some computer systems.)

■ The illustrations also demonstrate that, even in the same point size, different typefaces will give a different number of characters per line. (Compare the line endings for Times and Palatino.) So the other measurement a designer may need for a given typeface and size is **characters per pica** (abbreviated to **C/P**).

■ All the examples show **justified** setting (that is, the right margin forms a straight vertical, just like the left). As you will recall from Unit 2, the alternative is **unjustified** (also known as ragged right) setting.

Tools

A **pica rule** enables a designer to decide, or an editor / proofreader to check, the measure (line length).

In addition, the designer has to know *how many lines* will fit on a page or in a column. This can be calculated with a **depth scale** (illustrated on p. 132) and ruler. Remember that the depth scale does not show the point size but the linefeed (baseline to baseline). For example, in the 12 pt column you can measure with a ruler to find out that 44 lines would take up 186 mm. This will be so whether the type size chosen is 10/12 pt, $10\frac{1}{2}$/12 pt or 11/12 pt. (Specification in $\frac{1}{2}$ pts, for both type size and linefeed, is quite usual.)

For editors and proofreaders, depth scales are helpful for checking the type size (or, to be more precise, the linefeed) and / or the number of lines on a page of proofs.

An aid to checking the point size of the type itself is given on a **typescale** (or **H scale**) shown on p. 133, which also usefully combines a pica rule and short depth scale. (Confusingly, a depth scale may also simply be called a typescale.)

As we have seen, typefaces may look different, and take up different space, even when they are the same point size. Different typesetting systems have minor variations even within the same typeface, so it is best to use the typesetter's own samples for design where possible. There are also books of typefaces available on particular machines such as the Linotron. Separate sheets showing a typeface in different sizes are particularly useful for tracing title pages, chapter headings, etc., for which **display typefaces** (generally more elaborate than ordinary text typefaces) are often used.

Layout

What does a designer have to think about when setting the general specifications for a book or journal page?

■ The first decision concerns the **format**, for example Demy Octavo or Crown Quarto. As we saw in Unit 3, the choice will depend partly on the market and production cost, but also on the kind of material in the book: maps, tables, illustrations, etc.

The format is specified precisely by giving the **trimmed page size** in millimetres. Remember that the page size is always expressed with the *vertical* measurement first. It is important to follow this convention because some books are wider than

PALATINO

PALATINO

The Linotron 100 is a digital, laser phototypesetter which consists of a laser recording unit, a Motorola 68000 microprocessor and two mini floppy disc drives. It is a slave typesetter and is further equipped with 512k of RAM memory for the storage of programs, fonts and text that has been transmitted for typesetting. The Linotron 100 supports RS232C serial, asyn-

10 POINT
The Linotron 100 is a digital, laser phototypesetter which consists of a laser recording unit, a Motorola 680 00 microprocessor and two mini floppy disc drives. It is a slave typesetter and is further equipped with 512k

11 POINT
The Linotron 100 is a digital, laser phototypesett er which consists of a laser recording unit, a Mot orola 68000 microprocessor and two mini floppy disc drives. It is a slave typesetter and is further

12 POINT
The Linotron 100 is a digital, laser phototype setter which consists of a laser recording uni t, a Motorola 68000 microprocessor and two mini floppy disc drives. It is a slave typesette

14 POINT
The Linotron 100 is a digital, laser phototypes etter which consists of a laser recording unit, a Motorola 68000 microprocessor and two min i floppy disc drives. It is a slave typesetter and

PICAS   5   10   15   20

TIMES

TIMES

The Linotron 100 is a digital, laser phototypesetter which consists of a laser recording unit, a Motorola 68000 microprocessor and two mini floppy disc drives. It is a slave typesetter and is further equipped with 512k of RAM memory for the storage of programs, fonts and text that has been transmitted for typesetting. The Linotron 100 supports RS232C serial, asynchronous input. The

10 POINT
The Linotron 100 is a digital, laser phototypesetter whi ch consists of a laser recording unit, a Motorola 68000 microprocessor and two mini floppy disc drives. It is a sl ave typesetter and is further equipped with 512k of RA

11 POINT
The Linotron 100 is a digital, laser phototypesette r which consists of a laser recording unit, a Motoro la 68000 microprocessor and two mini floppy disc drives. It is a slave typesetter and is further equipp

12 POINT
The Linotron 100 is a digital, laser phototypes etter which consists of a laser recording unit, a Motorola 68000 microprocessor and two mini floppy disc drives. It is a slave typesetter and i

14 POINT
The Linotron 100 is a digital, laser phototypese tter which consists of a laser recording unit, a M otorola 68000 microprocessor and two mini flop py disc drives. It is a slave typesetter and is furt

PICAS   5   10   15   20

Two serif typefaces
The first passage shows 10 on 12 pt across 24 picas. The other examples show how much would fit across 20 picas (or 24 in the largest one). (These have no leading, so they would be called, for example, 10 pt solid.)

OPTIMA

OPTIMA MEDIUM

The Linotron 100 is a digital, laser phototypesetter which consists of a laser recording unit, a Motorola 68000 microprocessor and two mini floppy disc drives. It is a slave typesetter and is further equipped with 512k of RAM memory for the storage of programs, fonts and text that has been

10 POINT

The Linotron 100 is a digital, laser phototypesetter which consists of a laser recording unit, a Motorola 68 000 microprocessor and two mini floppy disc drives. It is a slave typesetter and is further equipped with 5

11 POINT

The Linotron 100 is a digital, laser phototypesett er which consists of a laser recording unit, a Mo torola 68000 microprocessor and two mini flopp y disc drives. It is a slave typesetter and is furthe

12 POINT

The Linotron 100 is a digital, laser phototyp esetter which consists of a laser recording u nit, a Motorola 68000 microprocessor and t wo mini floppy disc drives. It is a slave types

14 POINT

The Linotron 100 is a digital, laser phototypes etter which consists of a laser recording unit, a Motorola 68000 microprocessor and two mi ni floppy disc drives. It is a slave typesetter a

PICAS 5 10 15 20

UNIVERS

UNIVERS 55

The Linotron 100 is a digital, laser phototypesetter which consists of a laser recording unit, a Motorola 68000 micro-processor and two mini floppy disc drives. It is a slave typesetter and is further equipped with 512k of RAM memory for the storage of programs, fonts and text that has been

10 POINT

The Linotron 100 is a digital, laser phototypesetter which consists of a laser recording unit, a Motorola 68000 microprocessor and two mini floppy disc dri ves. It is a slave typesetter and is further equipped

11 POINT

The Linotron 100 is a digital, laser phototypese tter which consists of a laser recording unit, a Motorola 68000 microprocessor and two mini floppy disc drives. It is a slave typesetter and is

12 POINT

The Linotron 100 is a digital, laser phototy pesetter which consists of a laser recordin g unit, a Motorola 68000 microprocessor a nd two mini floppy disc drives. It is a slave

14 POINT

The Linotron 100 is a digital, laser phototyp esetter which consists of a laser recording u nit, a Motorola 68000 microprocessor and t wo mini floppy disc drives. It is a slave types

PICAS 5 10 15 20

Two sans serif typefaces
The first passage shows 10 on 12 pt across 24 picas. The other examples show how much would fit across 20 picas (or 24 in the largest one). (These have no leading, so they would be called, for example, 10 pt **solid.**)

6	7	7½	8	8½	9	9½	10
6 PTS	7 PTS	7½ PTS	8 PTS	8½ PTS	9 PTS	9½ PTS	10 PTS

10½	11	11½	12	12½	13	13½	14
10½ PTS	11 PTS	11½ PTS	12 PTS	12½ PTS	13 PTS	13½ PTS	14 PTS

Geliot Whitman
HERSCHELL ROAD
LONDON SE23 1EQ
081-699 9262

Geliot Whitman
HERSCHELL ROAD
LONDON SE23 1EQ
081-699 9262

A depth scale (front view and back view)

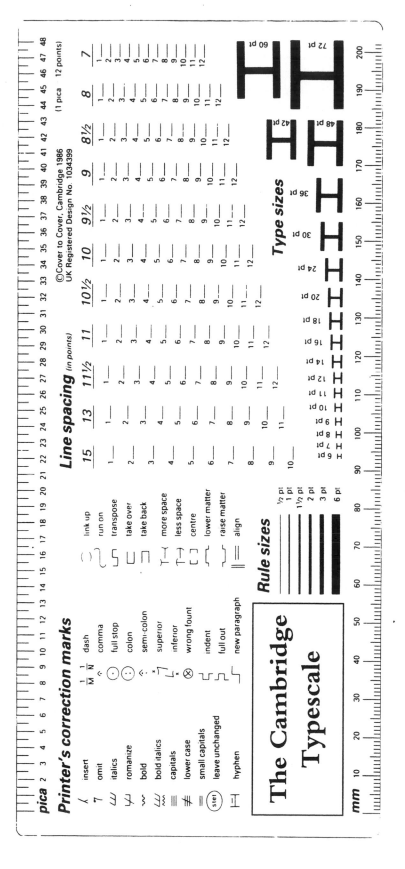

A typescale (combining pica rule, guide to type sizes and a small depth scale)

they are high: you cannot just assume the longer measurement is always the vertical one.

- The next decision will be the number of **columns** on the page. This depends on the complexity of the material, the age group it is aimed at, etc. In the illustration opposite (alternative layouts for a Crown Quarto book) the shaded areas represent typical illustrations. As you can see, varying shapes of illustration can easily be fitted into such multi-column books. In a smaller format, as in most fiction or academic books, you would only have one column.

  Books for very young children usually stick to one column too for clarity (whatever the book size) and might have type of 15/18 pt. At late primary and early secondary level, a large format with two columns and type of around 12/14 pt might be used. Glossy trade books often have two or three columns in a large format suitable for lavish illustrations. A common layout for these is the one-third/two-thirds style (the bottom layout shown).

- Once the number of columns is settled, the measure and number of lines are specified. Together, these details define the **text area**. Finally, the **margins** (measured either in picas or in millimetres) will position the text area on the page of the printed book. Margins cannot normally be checked on proofs; at that stage you are concerned only with the text area. The designer specifies **head** (top) and **back** (inside) margins only. The printer will set these up as standard when photographing the CRC (camera-ready copy) and will then trim off the **bottom** and **foredge** (outer) margins to the trimmed page size.

- The choice of text typeface will be governed largely by aesthetic appeal, clarity and suitability for the intended market. It must, however, also contain all the special sorts you require, especially in complicated maths setting, for example, for which Times is often recommended. In books for the very young you may need a special 'educational face', in which 'a', '4', '9', etc., look as they do in handwriting rather than in standard print.

  For most book work serif typefaces are more common than sans serif: they are thought easier on the eye for continuous reading, though tradition probably has as much to do with the choice.

- Around seven words per line of unjustified type is said to make the easiest reading. However, many of the books (as opposed to magazines and newspapers) you read as an adult will have around eleven words per line. The more formal justified type is generally favoured too, especially in multi-column work.

- Books for adults (novels, biographies, academic works, etc.) often have 1, $1\frac{1}{2}$ or 2 points of leading. In books for younger children, or in work such as chemistry where superscripts and subscripts abound in the text, there may be 3 or 4 points. A densely packed reference book or dictionary, by contrast, might be set in 9 pt solid.

Now do Exercise 24.1 G

Ideally you should have a pica rule and a depth scale (or a typescale, which combines the two) to help you. However, extra information is given to enable you to perform the calculations without them, if necessary. The illustrations in this text unit are full-size, so you may be able to use them to help you as well.

Design considerations at proof stage

The proofreader's main concern is to check that words, numbers and symbols have been accurately set, that word-breaks are acceptable, widows are avoided, etc. (as we saw in Unit 2). However, layout is equally important in conveying the book's message and the proofreader is often the only person going through the book in sufficient detail to notice minor problems such as incorrect type sizes, inconsistent indention, or tables rendered incomprehensible by an inappropriate layout.

As we have seen, a typescale and depth scale help the proofreader to check type sizes, measure and number of lines per page. It is very useful too to have a copy of the type spec, not necessarily for checking every detail – after some experience, inconsistencies leap to the eye – but for reference, so that you know what was intended.

Text area: full page

Text area: two columns

Text area: three columns

Text area: one-third/two-thirds

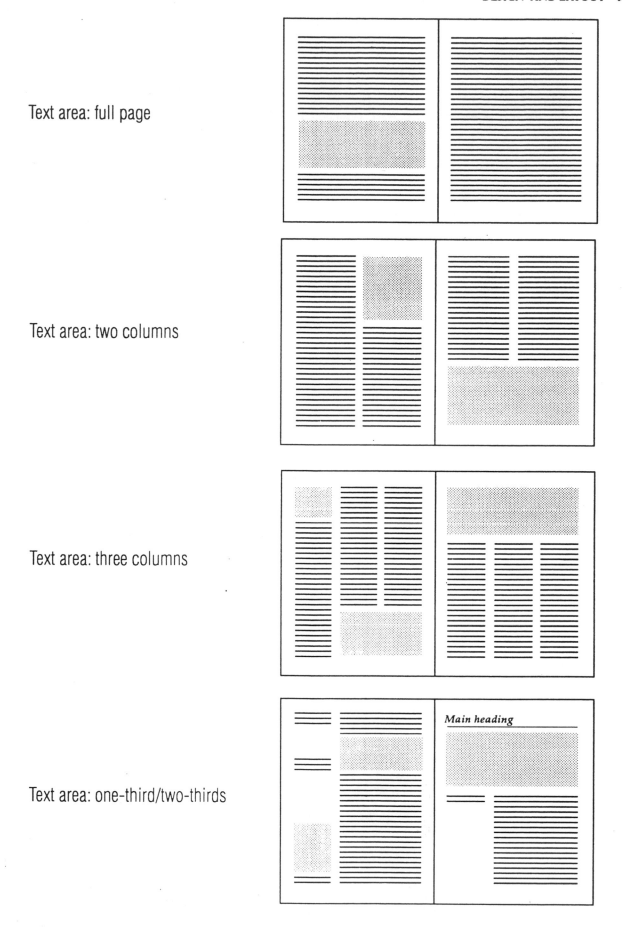

Four typical design layouts

Paste-up

Doing a rough paste-up for the typesetter to follow (as we saw in Unit 20) is usually the designer's task, but sometimes it falls to the editor. If you are responsible for it, use **pre-printed grids** whenever possible. These are similar to the layouts shown above (without the indications of how illustrations might go). They are ruled in pale blue (because it does not reproduce when photographed) to show the lines and columns as they would appear when full of text type. If pre-printed grids are not available, draw up a master grid carefully (a single page or preferably a double-page spread) and clip each tracing-paper sheet to it in turn as you work on it. Be methodical, keeping track of everything that has to go in. The composition of each spread should be as varied as possible, to keep the reader's interest, and tables and illustrations have to be positioned close to the relevant text.

More often the editor's role is to check a paste-up done by a designer. You will then be checking the same points: that page layout is varied and interesting and that tables and illustrations are suitably positioned and sized (Unit 26 below). You will also be making and saving lines as requested (Unit 20 above), perhaps finalizing the numbering sequence and captions (Units 26 and 28), even adding sections or suggesting other illustrations to fill major gaps.

If you are working with a DTP system in house, all this work of trying out different layouts and editing text to fit round illustrations may be done much more quickly on screen.

Jacket/cover design and illustration

Briefing the jacket/cover designer and illustrator cannot be discussed in any detail here. I would only stress the need for adequate briefing on market, general feel and any ideas you already have, as well as budgetary constraints such as the number of colours. The designer will usually also need to see a 'blurb' or description of the book, perhaps the introduction, or even the whole typescript.

Further reading

This section serves Units 24–5 as both are concerned with typographical design.

Because of its newspaper orientation, helpful guidance on type size and weight, etc., is given in:

Leslie Sellers, *The Simple Subs Book* (Pergamon, Oxford, 2nd edition, 1985)

An exhilarating and eye-opening vision of what design can do for communication emerges from:

Jan V. White, *Editing by Design: A Guide to Effective Word-and-Picture Communication for Editors and Designers* (Bowker, New York, 2nd edition, 1982)

Though based on magazine work, its message is equally relevant to educational and trade books.

UNIT 25

Specific Mark-up

This unit addresses marking up a typescript in accordance with a designer's typographical specification. We look first at ordinary text, then at tables. Even if such detailed marking up is not your responsibility, the basic practice offered here should help you to interpret a type spec, a useful skill for any editor or proofreader.

Generic and specific mark-up

As we saw in Unit 4, an editor may either code the typescript generically or mark it up specifically to conform with a particular type spec. Even when a typescript has been specifically marked throughout, the type spec should accompany it to the typesetter.

For many projects, generic coding of the typescript, together with a detailed type spec (preferably accompanied by a layout or specimen pages), is all that typesetters need. They can set up a standard style for A heads and B heads, for example, and the typesetting machine will apply that style throughout; similarly, before starting to typeset a group of tables, they can set up certain details of the layout as standard.

Nevertheless, specific marking up is sometimes required and may be done by a production editor (for example on a journal) or by the designer. A proofreader needs to understand both the marked-up typescript and the type spec to ensure that instructions have been carried out.

Now Look at the Examples on the Next Two Pages of a Marked-up Typescript and a Type Spec

You will recognize the typescript as Exercise 4.2 (Sartre on Freedom), marked specifically rather than generically. (Your own marked copy will show you the differences.) Read each individual instruction in the type spec and then look across to the typescript to see how it has been marked.

The type spec may be a printed (or typed) form, which is then completed by hand, as in the example. In that case, you can see the other options available to the designer. Alternatively, if the form is stored on a word-processor, only the selected style will appear on the final version.

■ The type spec (as we saw in Unit 24) first establishes the overall **text type** (typeface, size and measure). This is normally only marked at the beginning of each chapter (or the beginning of the book if the design is uncomplicated). Once the text type is established, variations in size are shown (in this case, 13/15 pt for A heads and 10/12 pt for extracts), without repeating 'Palatino' each time. Nor does the typesetter need a specific instruction to revert to the text type size

(for example after an extract), provided you show clearly, by your marginal line, where the extract ends. Setting a standard text type size also means that a standard *space* of 1 text line has been established.

■ For any section of text the spec will indicate justified or unjustified setting. Again, you only need to indicate a variation from the overall instruction (in this case, for extracts).

■ The spec shows whether each level of heading is to be centred or ranged left (or even set in the margin, as it might be, for example, in the one-third/two-thirds layout shown in Unit 24). If it has been correctly positioned in the typescript (as the A and B heads have been here), there is no need for any marking.

Chapter 5

JEAN-PAUL SARTRE ON FREEDOM

The Paradox of free will

To what extent are we free? What are we really free to choose? If we are to any degree free to make choices, does it make sense to chose one thing rather than another? In this chapter we must attempt to find out Sartre's answer to these questions. For in that answer lies the chief message, if we may so call it, of his existentialist philosophy.

Sartre appears to be committed to two incompatible views. On the one hand, we truly apprehend our own impotence: we are born in a certain place at a certain time with certain characteristics which are not of our choosing. On the other hand, we are free to be what we choose to be. There is indeed no other sense, for the existentialist, in which we 'are' at all.

So Sartre seems to be faced with an acute version of the familiar paradox: human beings are both free and not free. How does he solve it?

Sartre's Solution

Motives and actions

Without motives there would be no actions. By a motive Sartre means a consciousness of something to be done. For example, if I am very cold and get up to put more wood on the fire it is not the cold which leads to my action but my apprehension of the cold as something to be overcome.

Sartre takes examples from history to illustrate the way in which motives arise out of situations, e.g.:

It is by a pure wrenching away from himself and the world that the worker can posit his suffering as unbearable suffering and consequently can make of it the motive for revolutionary action. This implies for consciousness the permanent possibility of effecting a rupture with its

TYPESETTING SPECIFICATION

Composition   Typeface: *Palatino*
Text type size: *11* on *13* pt
Measure: *24 ½* picas justified/~~unjustified~~
Paragraph indent: *1* ems of set, except after headings
Figures: lining/~~non-lining~~
Special sorts: *none*

Chapter heads   Chapter begins ~~new recto~~/new page/~~runs on~~
Heading centred/~~ranged left~~
Number and title on sep lines/~~run on~~
Drop from trim to baseline of ch number: *5* picas

Ch number typeface and size: *Optima bold 16/18 pt*
number arabic/~~roman~~/~~spelt out~~

Ch title typeface and size: *Optima bold 16/18 pt caps*
space below: *24* pts

Subheads   A head typeface and size: *Palatino 13/15 pt u/lc (cap sig wds)*
~~centred~~/ranged left/~~in margin~~
space above: *1 ½* text lines   space below: *½* text lines

B head typeface and size: *Palatino 11/13 pt bold ital u/lc (min caps)*
~~centred~~/ranged left/~~in margin~~
space above: *1* text lines   space below: *½* text lines

Extracts   Typeface and size: *Palatino 10/12 pt* ~~justified~~/unjustified
indented left: *2* pica ems   indented right: *1* pica ems
space above: *1* text lines   space below: *1* text lines

The large square brackets around the chapter head in the example indicate that it should be centred (see the proof-correction symbols in Unit 2). The instruction 'centred' is therefore, strictly speaking, redundant but unfortunately the symbol is not universally understood – I suggest you use the word as well (or even instead) until a less ambiguous centring symbol is established.

■ Specific marking for bold, italic and capitals in subheads is usually best done, as here, following the standard conventions (wavy line for bold, etc.). However, chapter heads are sometimes set in display faces, which may come in several different weights – not just roman and bold, but also medium, medium bold, extra bold, etc. – so it is often better to treat these terms as part of the specification of the typeface (as has been done for Optima bold in the chapter head here).

■ You'll recall from Units 4–5 that u/lc means any kind of upper- and lower-case setting, whether cap sig wds or min caps. The decision on which style to follow is sometimes left to the editor, sometimes included in the type spec.

■ Where two headings occur together, the specification of space above one and below the other may conflict. For example, here there should be $\frac{1}{2}$ line below an A head and 1 line above a B head, but we certainly don't want both (making $1\frac{1}{2}$ lines) and have to decide (consistently through the book) whether to have $\frac{1}{2}$ line or 1 line. (The type spec will often give an additional instruction to the typesetter on how to resolve this conflict.) The space below the chapter head normally remains constant whether the chapter begins with text or with an A head.

■ Notice that in addition to the indents on the left and right of the extract, the different measure is shown ($24\frac{1}{2} - 3 = 21\frac{1}{2}$ picas). This helps to avoid the potential confusion between a **pica em** and an **em of set**. A pica em is a fixed length the same as a pica (that is, 12 points). But if you specify an indent of '1 em of set' (for example for paras), you mean that the indent should be in proportion to the particular type size, whether it is 10 pt for text or 8 pt for notes. The square box (quad) symbol does not distinguish the two, although normally an em of set should be assumed.

This Sartre passage is likely to be in a book going direct to page proof. Pagination will be automatic and spacing variable within specified parameters so that, even though one heading is 13/15 pt while the rest of the text is in 11/13 pt (making 2 points extra), all the pages ought to come out the standard depth.

In work set in columns (often going through a paste-up stage) it is essential to fit the precise page depth in terms of text lines. The heading specification therefore often follows a different form, stating the **text lines occupied** by the whole heading, the size of type and the space below. (Whatever remains is the space above the heading.)

Technique

It is unwise to attempt a specific mark-up at the same time as editing the text: treat them as separate operations and tackle the editing first. As you edit, code the headings, extracts, etc., generically in the way you have already learned. (You can do this in pencil if you want to remove the coding later – but it may quite helpfully remain.) This allows you to decide on the heading hierarchy as you read, to add or omit headings, run on or set out extracts and lists, etc. More important, it is difficult enough to follow the argument and sort out inconsistencies and reference problems all at the same time; trying to mark up specifically as well would impair your efficiency.

When you do come to the mark-up stage, keep your marking as clear and as simple as possible. A different colour of pen is helpful: use green (if no designer is involved) or red (if it has not been used for the regular editing). In the example, the longer instructions at the beginning are circled but the minor spacing and type-size instructions elsewhere are not. In the original the different colour used would show clearly enough that they were not setting copy.

Now do Exercise 25.1

First edit the passage, coding generically as you go. Remember to cross-check references and text; also check rapidly that the tables (which you will find in Exercise 25.2) accord with the text, but without looking at them in detail at this stage. You'll need a query sheet as usual. Then mark the passage specifically to follow the type spec supplied.

Review of Exercise 25.1

Check your work against the sample answer (for the first folio only) on p. 142.

Rewriting the chapter number, centred above the chapter title, is the clearest method, but you can simply mark a new line. Always show unambiguously whether you are marking the distance to a baseline (as here for the **chapter drop**) or between the bottom of one line and the top of the next (for other spaces, such as the one below the chapter head).

Because some paras have been typed blocked (l. 33) and some indented (l. 67), it is best to mark them all. You don't have to show that the text should start full out after a heading, unless it has been typed indented (as on l. 53). Nor, strictly speaking, do you need to close up between paras (or below the B head on l. 6) since the typesetter should only leave spaces when specifically instructed to do so. However, if you are marking all the para indents, you may as well close up at the same time.

It *is* essential to show whether l. 19 starts a new para or not. (Query it with the author if you are unsure yourself: I decided a new topic – the export of pollution – was being introduced.)

Circling the typed instructions that key in the tables (ll. 25 and 39) ensures that they will not be set by mistake, and makes them stand out better. Never put space marks round such instructions: the space to be allowed between text and table is always given as a general instruction or indicated on layouts.

You *do* need to show that a line space is to be left before the B head on l. 26; this may be done either at the top of fo. 201 or bottom of fo. 200. (The same applies at the top of fo. 203 or at the bottom of fo. 202.)

Some decisions had to be made on heading hierarchy. The typing may at first have suggested that three levels were required ('A' at l. 5, 'B' at ll. 6, 26 and 40 and 'C' at ll. 44 and 52). As you read the passage, I hope you will have realized that the argument fell into two major parts, 'Crisis in the Forests' and 'Pollution of the Atmosphere' (hinted at in the introductory sentence on l. 4). Making ll. 5 and 40 into parallel A heads and the rest B heads is much the neatest solution. The 'References' head, as we've seen, may also be treated as an A head. Min caps had to be marked on l. 52.

The singular/plural problem on l. 9 could equally well be resolved the other way, by making 'level' singular. (The problem cropped up again on l. 57.) Beware of such recurring slips by the author, especially a word wrongly spelt throughout, as 'Scandinavia' was here.

Names of chemicals are normally lower case and roman (l. 10) (unlike the botanical names we came across in Unit 10), although their abbreviations as chemical formulae are mostly in capitals. Only proprietary drugs (such as Valium) begin with a capital.

As we have seen, you should always mark subscripts and superscripts (even when they are typed that way) to show that, as well as being set low or raised, the number/letter should be small (ll. 10 and 54). Note, however, that if a capital letter is set subscript, it should never be marked as a small cap.

I hope you noticed that 'oxygen' on l. 41 should be 'nitrogen'. Even if oxygen did not immediately strike you as an unlikely substance to be polluting the atmosphere, you should have checked back to l. 10 and either silently corrected the word or noted a query for the author.

Other minor editing points were: on ll. 21 and 38 standardize either to 'table' or 'Table'; on l. 26 delete the stop; make 'rainforests' consistent (probably without the hyphen) on ll. 26 and 29 and in the main head of Table 2; on l. 30 write 'fifty' in words (as ll. 3 and 36); on l. 31 add 's' to 'hundred'; apply -ise spellings on ll. 50 and 72; also on l. 50 the dash is better converted into a full stop and new sentence; l. 56 should be 'glass'; on l. 61 space 'the century'; on ll. 62–3 'in' has inadvertently been repeated; on ll. 67–8 add commas round the parenthetic 'which' clause; finally, the colon on l. 71 should be a semicolon (or comma).

In the extract on ll. 58–66 you had to resist editing, for example 'Poles' (which would usually be lower case). More seriously perhaps a **temperature interval** is given (on l. 62) as though it were a temperature reading: in scientific work the convention is to distinguish 'warmer by 2 or 3 deg C' from 'the patient's temperature was 38 °C'. As we saw in Unit 15, even where the degree symbol *is* appropriate, views on the correct spacing differ. Since you probably cannot rely on the author to have followed the original precisely on such a point, you could standardize to an overall style.

You should have listed as a query the missing page reference for this extract (l. 66). Even though the reference list was so short, I hope you remembered to check quickly through it first (as you learned in Unit 19). You would notice at that stage that '(eds)' should be added on l. 81 and '(1988)' after 'James' on l. 84 (even though it already appears later in the reference). The method of listing the edited volume as a separate entry can save space where chapters from the same works occur frequently in a list. When editing in detail you will have underlined the subtitle on l. 82 and indented l. 83.

Just as for para indents, an em (or 2 ems) of set is usually specified for indents in reference lists and (especially important) indexes. In these sections (often set in 8, 7 or even 6 pt type) a pica em indent looks very deep and wastes space. As we saw in Units 17–19, the instruction on turnovers is best written at the top of each reference section, for example, 'Indent turnover lines 1 em of set.'

Picas, points and lines

You may have noticed in the type spec that some spaces or distances were expressed as picas, some as points, some as text lines. Why the variation?

- Picas are widely used for measure. It is also common to specify the chapter drop in terms of picas (or millimetres), as you do for the head and back margin of ordinary text pages of the book (as we saw in Unit 24). (Alternatively, the position of the chapter head may be specified by saying, for example, 'set on the 3rd text line'. This has the advantage of keeping the rest of the page in alignment.)

- In specifying or marking up title pages, chapter heads and similar places where display faces are used and/or type size is changing frequently, the safest method is to use points.

- For the space above and below subheads, extracts, lists, etc., it is quite common to use line spaces as the unit of measurement. Between *different* sizes of type, as we have seen, this should be interpreted by the typesetter as a space the size of the text line. However, *within* a small-type passage (for example an appendix, notes or index), a line space should be interpreted as a line of that type size. (If there is likely to be any confusion, mark in points.)

- Points are always used for very small spaces. For example, if additional space had been wanted between the entries in the references in Exercise 25.1, it would have been specified as 2 or 3 pts. (Line measures are appropriate down to $\frac{1}{2}$ lines but not for smaller spaces.)

6 picas from trim

6 ↓

Optima bold 14/16 centred

new page

ø

THE ENVIRONMENT

36 pts)

Text Times 10/12 x 24 picas just.

Human exploitation of the world's resources, especially over the past fifty years, threatens the future of the planet. Our activities endanger its flora and fauna, and its very atmosphere.

1½)

line)

Ⓐ ## CRISIS IN THE FORESTS   5

Ⓑ ### Acid rain

( )

In Germany and Scandinavia the pine forests are dying and the fish population of many lakes has been virtually wiped out. The increasingly high acid levels in rain have been traced to sulphur dioxide (SO_2) and nitrogen oxide (NO) emissions from   10 burning fossil fuels in industry and from motor-car exhausts.

line)

9/10½ x22

(ext)

While the causes of acid rain are more or less understood, its effects are still hotly contested. Certainly acid deposition is responsible for the death of fish in thousands of lakes and streams across substantial areas of northern   15 Europe and North America. However, its effect on forests and crop lands is a grey area that has spawned scientific controversy. (Hinrichsen, 1988: 66-7)

line)

The controversy is exacerbated by the fact that the industries responsible are not necessarily in the country said to be   20 affected (see Table 1). Scandinavians, for example, bitterly resent denials by some scientists that emissions from British factories can be the cause of the environmental damage in Scandinavia.

[Table 1 near here]   25

■ To avoid confusion, always write '2 pts', etc. (except for type sizes, such as 10/12, where the form makes 'pts' unnecessary). For lines, $\frac{1}{2}$ and $1\frac{1}{2}$ are unmistakable but for 2 or more it is safest to include the word 'lines' (or abbreviation 'l'). To save writing 'line' each time you want a 1 line space ('1 l' is too ambiguous), you can give a general instruction that *all* space marks should be interpreted as 1 line unless otherwise indicated.

Alternatives to 'line', '$\frac{1}{2}$', '$1\frac{1}{2}$', etc., as used here, are '1#', '$\frac{1}{2}$#', etc. (the old proof-correction mark for space) or '1 wh', '$\frac{1}{2}$ wh', etc. (meaning 'white').

Now do Exercise 25.2

Check the sense and consistency of the tables (as you did in Unit 21) and cross-check their sources with the reference list in Exercise 25.1, as well as marking them up in accordance with the specification.

Review of Exercise 25.2

Check your work against the sample answer on the next page.

To stretch these tables to the full text measure would leave a huge gap between the names of the countries and the column of numbers, so clearly they count as **narrow tables.** Sometimes you may be expected to decide and specify the appropriate measure for each individual table. Often it proves more satisfactory to leave the decision on the precise measure of a narrow table to the typesetter's judgement. (Similarly, if it is obviously going to be difficult to fit in a complicated table, you can instruct that the type size may be 'reduced as necessary to fit'.)

Note (from the entries for Ecuador and Mexico in Table 2) that the number should always be on the turnover line, not on the first line, of the heading in the stub. Indenting the turnover line makes the table easier to read. (Again your marking should be interpreted as 1 em of set.)

Details such as whether a space is to be left before the 'bottom line', whether turnover lines in the stub or in notes should be indented and whether the source should end in a stop are not included in a type spec. They may instead be demonstrated in an accompanying sample table, or they may be shown in a table style sheet of the kind used in Unit 21. With or without such style guidance, you as editor must make sure that these details are *consistent* throughout the edited typescript.

As elsewhere, if the typed style is correct there is no need for any marking, provided the typesetter has a type spec (and preferably a sample table as well). For example, the column heads in Table 1 are already typed with each line centred over the column.

The type spec offers three different options for column heads from which this style, 'centre each line', was chosen. The typed version of Table 2 demonstrates the second option, 'range left', which gives a bizarre effect here but may be suitable when most column heads are short and most numbers have four or five digits. The third option is to range left but centre the whole block over the column, so that it looks less incongruous.

The other decision about column heads, as we saw in Unit 21, concerns **horizontal alignment**. Again, the typed style demonstrates the difference: Table 1 was correctly typed to align at the bottom; Table 2 is typed to align at the top, so you have to mark the change.

In marking the column heads to be set in italic, take care not to include the note indicator. If italic *is* wanted for the 'a', etc. (a possible option, although roman is more common) put a separate short underline under it, both in the column head and in the note. Whether roman or italic, the two must match up. (A note *number* would always be roman.)

It is quite common (though not essential) to distinguish the thickness of the different rules as here. If you look back at the typescale illustrated in Unit 24, you will see what 1 pt and $\frac{1}{2}$ pt rules look like. Alternatively, the specification may just say 'medium' (abbreviated to 'med' in mark-up) and 'fine'. (Often the type spec will also cover the space – usually 2 or 3 extra points – to be left above and below each rule.)

Remember that wherever five-digit numbers appear in columns with four-digit ones, as in Table 1, you must retain a space (regardless of the style followed in the text) so that all the numbers line up. (You came across this instruction in the house style used for Exercise 14.3, Canadian Architecture.) I hope that, if you had access to a calculator, you did check

Sample answer to Exercise 25.2

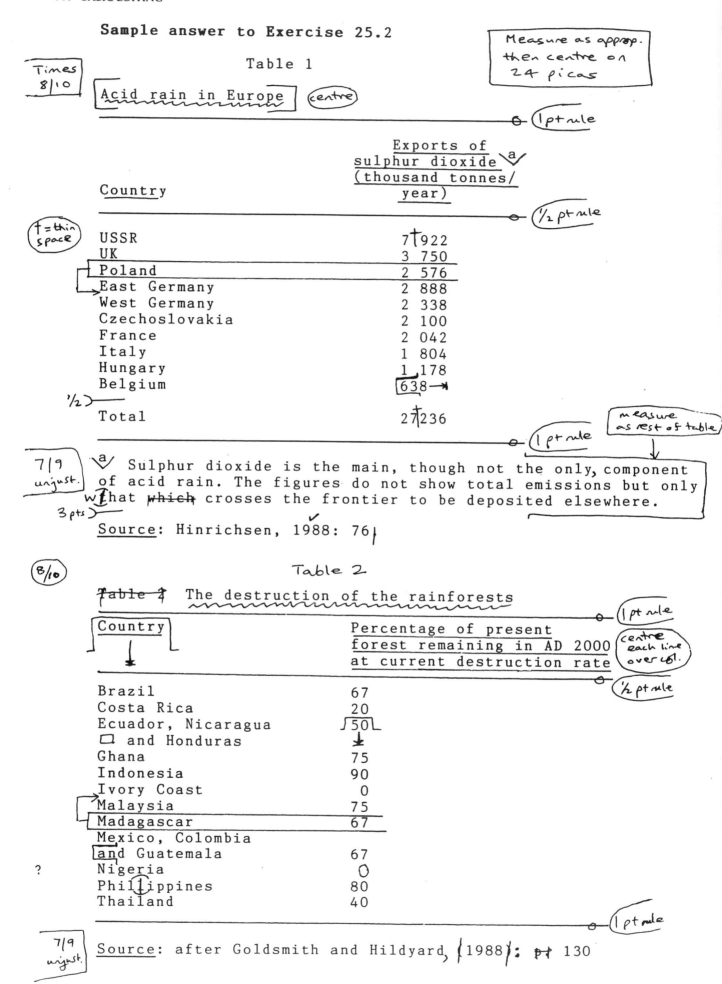

Times 8/10

Measure as approp. then centre on 24 picas

Table 1

Acid rain in Europe   centre

○ 1pt rule

Country	Exports of sulphur dioxide [a] (thousand tonnes/ year)
	○ ½ pt rule
USSR	7 922
UK	3 750
Poland	2 576
East Germany	2 888
West Germany	2 338
Czechoslovakia	2 100
France	2 042
Italy	1 804
Hungary	1 178
Belgium	638
Total	27 236

t = thin space

½)

○ 1pt rule   measure as rest of table

7/9 unjust.

[a] Sulphur dioxide is the main, though not the only, component of acid rain. The figures do not show total emissions but only what ~~which~~ crosses the frontier to be deposited elsewhere.

3 pts)

Source: Hinrichsen, 1988: 76

8/10

Table 2

~~Table 1~~ The destruction of the rainforests

○ 1pt rule

Country	Percentage of present forest remaining in AD 2000 at current destruction rate
	centre each line over col. ○ ½ pt rule
Brazil	67
Costa Rica	20
Ecuador, Nicaragua and Honduras	50
Ghana	75
Indonesia	90
Ivory Coast	0
Malaysia	75
Madagascar	67
Mexico, Colombia and Guatemala	67
Nigeria	0
Phillippines	80
Thailand	40

?

○ 1pt rule

7/9 unjust.

Source: after Goldsmith and Hildyard, (1988): ~~pt~~ 130

the total in Table 1 (though there was no problem).

In the note to Table 1 you could equally well change to 'those that cross' (though 'what crosses' seems neater). You may well have decided to recast part of the unwieldy column head in Table 2 as a note. (AD *before* the date is correct.)

It would be equally good to convert both Ivory Coast and Nigeria in Table 2 to an en rule (or em rule), to show a blank, rather than to '0' as in the sample answer. Be careful, in general, though, about such changes in the name of consistency. It is certainly correct here to standardize the two entries since the numbers are equally approximate projections; and similarly in many typescripts you may find one table with blanks and the next with zeros for no good reason. But some authors will be making a deliberate distinction (for example, showing '0' for a tiny number that has been rounded). As the question mark shows, you should ask for confirmation of any such change in your query list.

Always preserve the similar distinction between zero (or blank) and 'n.a.' (or 'N/A'), both of which, confusingly, may mean either 'not applicable' or 'not available'. (The abbreviation must therefore be explained in a table note, at least the first time it occurs in the book or article.)

Finally, giving a source as 'after' or 'based on' another work indicates that the present author has adapted it in some way, either simplifying it or perhaps converting a figure into a table. See Unit 30 for the permissions implications.

UNIT 26

Illustrations

As we saw in Unit 3, illustrations may include technical figures (diagrams, graphs, maps and so forth), creative artwork (original drawings, perhaps of people or animals) and photographs. Unit 27 examines more closely the editor's involvement in technical figures; this unit focuses on creative artwork and photos.

Creative artwork

The extent of briefing required for creative artwork varies greatly. For a children's story, for example, an artist may simply be given the typescript and a budget and/or ideal numbers and sizes of illustrations. He or she also needs practical details such as the format and text area, and whether all the illustrations can be in full colour, or some sections must be in black and white because only certain **signatures** (see Unit 3) are to be printed in colour.

In educational books, however, the author and/or the editor have to specify much more precisely what is to be illustrated. Together you build up an **art brief** (see the example below). This is usually done (in draft at least) during the editing stage, although in some cases the artist may not start work until the typeset text is pasted up, when the exact spaces available are known.

The golden rule for briefing artists (and similarly picture researchers and photographers) is to tell them, not only what illustration you want, but *what it is to show*. If (in the example) you wanted the first illustration to show in detail what a hoe looks like, you would have to mention this in the brief. Similarly, if the purpose of an illustration is to show

PRIMARY SCIENCE

Art brief

1   Children working in a school garden, one setting up
    bamboo canes for runner beans to grow up (see sketch
    attached), one hoeing weeds, one spraying an apple   *full
    tree (photo ref of suitable type of spray can   page*
    attached), one tending a compost heap. Others perhaps
    in background. Neat rows of vegetables, season is   *colour*
    spring. Some boys, some girls, age about 10, varied
    ethnic origins.

2   Garden pests – slug eating a hosta, greenfly on rose,   *½ p*
    caterpillar on cabbage, finch pecking at raspberries
    (artist to find refs) – make into single picture if   *colour*
    poss.

3   Gardeners' friends – worm aerating soil, ladybird   *½ p*
    eating greenfly, bee pollinating rhododendron (artist   *colour*
    to find refs) – again as single picture

4   Boy and girl at work bench in lab, analysing sample   *¼ p*
    of soil in test-tube (sketch attached shows equipment)   *b/w*

the sequence of letters on a typewriter keyboard, don't just ask for a photograph of a typewriter.

Artists will sometimes be able to research their own **references**, particularly if they specialize, for example in botanical drawing or medieval history. Normally, however, it is the editor (with recourse to the author as necessary) who provides the artist with references – photos and photocopies showing the details and the colours of essential elements in the drawing, a Viking helmet, perhaps, or the colours and insignia on a Zambia Airways aeroplane.

If you are showing an experiment in progress, you will need a sketch (a **rough**) of the apparatus at a crucial stage. Remember that you can annotate an author's rough (or your own, if it doesn't turn out quite as you meant) with circled instructions to the artist (for example 'these lines should be parallel'). Providing good references is a key skill for an editor in educational publishing: the more visual guidance you can provide in advance, the fewer corrections should be required to the artwork roughs.

Check the **artwork roughs** that come from the artist very carefully. Show them to the author and any technical advisers as well, since major changes can only be made at this stage. If you aren't satisfied with some of the details, provide further references. At final artwork check the appropriateness of the colours, at proof the reproduction quality.

Now do Exercise 26.1   G

Feel free to take a medical, botanical or comical approach, whichever you think would make the most marketable book.

Briefing for photographs

Similarly, the author and/or editor will usually draw up a **picture list** (or **photo brief**). An **art editor** may be involved in briefing (as well as in selection). The photos may then either be collected by a **picture researcher** from photo libraries, art galleries, etc., or come from a photographer commissioned to take specific subjects and scenes. If you are doing the picture research yourself, it is still worth making a picture list to keep track of progress. (When the photos come solely from the author, as they might for a medical treatise or an autobiography, there will be no briefing stage.)

Drawing up a picture list is much the same as preparing an art brief, although in this case it is often wise not to be *too* specific. Whereas in the art brief the illustration is (to an extent) being made to order, in a picture list you are usually asking for a selection of photos – of Everest, perhaps, or of a tiger – from which you (and/or the art editor) can choose the best. Don't therefore specify which face of Everest or the tiger's pose unless these are essential features. Do, as in briefing an artist, say what the photo is illustrating, for example the tallest mountain, the fiercest animal. Then if what you ask for cannot be found (or proves too expensive for the budget), the picture researcher may be able to offer an alternative that makes the same point.

If something specific is wanted, for example a particular painting or sculpture, provide (or ask the author for) full source details – ideally the location of the original, alternatively a book in which it is illustrated (where the location will be given).

Permission is usually thought essential for the reproduction of all photos and few of them will come free. Payments include both **reproduction fees** (permission to use the picture in your project) and the **purchase of prints** or **hire of transparencies** (popularly known as 'trannies'). The contract commissioning creative artwork and photos will similarly cover permission to reproduce the work, as well as the preparation of the work itself. Artists' and photographers' names must always be stated. (We return to acknowledgements in Unit 28 and to permission-seeking generally in Unit 30.)

Selecting photographs

When several photos have been collected for each item on your picture list, you (and the others involved) will judge not only which one best illustrates the subject but also which one will reproduce best. If several are suitable, the final choice may be left to the designer at rough paste-up. It is particularly helpful for the designer to have a choice between a **portrait** photo (deeper than it is wide) and a **landscape** photo (wider than it is deep) as they will fit very different spaces.

For colour reproduction, transparencies usually give the best results; for black-and-white photos, either prints or negatives may be used. When you are selecting photos, or judging the acceptability of an author's photos, look for sharp definition of black and white if general effect is what you want, but a good range of grey tones if the reader is to pick out detail. Good focus is always essential.

The photos will be converted into **halftones** by the printer (or a repro house), using a **screen** of the appropriate density of dots for the paper on which they are to be reproduced. Screens normally range from 100 to 150 dots per inch but may be finer still; the better the paper, the more dots are used. Halftones are often integrated with the text, so that they come as close as possible to the relevant discussion, either by printing them on ordinary text paper or, much more expensively, by printing the whole book on **coated** or **art paper**. Alternatively, all the photos may be gathered into special **plate sections** on coated paper. These are wrapped round or inserted into a signature of text paper. They will appear in the finished book as groups of 4, 8 or 16 pages (each page often containing several photos), separated from the relevant text. (See the original page numbering and marginal notes in Exercise 12.3, Arab Geography.)

Photographs from published books and magazines will already have been screened when made into halftones for that publication. Provided they are reasonably clear, they can be reproduced again **dot for dot**: the quality will not improve but should not get worse. Obtaining the original is, however, usually preferable.

Handle all photos with the greatest care. Keep them between card; do not attach paper-clips to them or write on the back. To identify them, either put each photo into an envelope (or see-through folder) labelled with its number and brief caption, or write these details on an adhesive label, which you can then stick on the back of the photo.

Cropping and sizing

Cropping (or **masking**) a photo means shading any parts that are not to be reproduced, *either* on a photocopy *or* on an **overlay** (a transparent sheet covering the photo). The overlay protects the surface of the print as well as being useful for indicating areas to be cropped and (as we shall see) reproduction size. It goes over the top of the photo to be lightly fixed to its back. (Never mark or cut the photo itself; if you are using an overlay, note carefully the technique discussed below.)

If a photo is a work of art in itself, you should not crop it in any way without the photographer's permission. For more technical purposes, or for amateur photos, however, it is often helpful to crop background or extraneous detail in order to emphasize the precise point being illustrated. Be careful

not to crop *too* close to the focus of interest. More mundanely, you may need to crop a photo in order to fit it on to the page at the best possible size.

The appropriate reproduction size will depend partly on the importance of the subject to the text and partly on the constraints of the format and layout. If, for example, the layout is one-third/two-thirds (see Unit 24), you will have three size categories, often designated 'A' (full-page width), 'B' (two-thirds, that is, the text width) and 'C' (one-third, in the margin). Which category a photo falls into is partly an editorial decision (relevance of subject matter) and partly a design decision (quality and shape of photo). In other layouts, the choice may lie between one column width and two. Sometimes photos can be **bled** (allowed to extend outside the text area to the full trimmed page size), although this is more expensive.

Photos are normally printed upright, rather than turned on the page, unless that is the only way to show some important detail. Remember – in general, not just in relation to photos – that a turned figure or table must take up most of the page since there can be no ordinary text on the same page. The bottom of a turned figure or table should always be on the right of the page.

It is usually more satisfactory to reduce than to enlarge: an enlargement can just go fuzzy; reduction often sharpens the image (although excessive reduction will, of course, lose detail). A reduction (or enlargement) may be expressed as a percentage; for example, 'reduce to 70 per cent' means that the width (and depth) of the printed illustration should be 70 per cent of the width (and depth) of the original. (It is important to specify '*to*', since reduction '*by*' 70 per cent would give a very different result.) A common alternative is to specify 'reduce to 25 mm width' (or depth – whichever is the critical dimension to fit your layout). The abbreviation **s.s.** means 'same size' (that is, without reduction or enlargement).

Technique

Sizing will often be done by a designer, sometimes by an editor. In any case it is useful to know the basic procedure. (There are quicker ways, which we look at later.) First examine your illustration. Is it portrait or landscape? Then look at your page size or design layout. Decide (by eye) whether the photo is likely to fit best upright or turned on the page, across two columns or within one column. From this you should be able to see which is the **critical dimension** (vertical or horizontal).

The example opposite demonstrates how you can then size the photo precisely. The desired

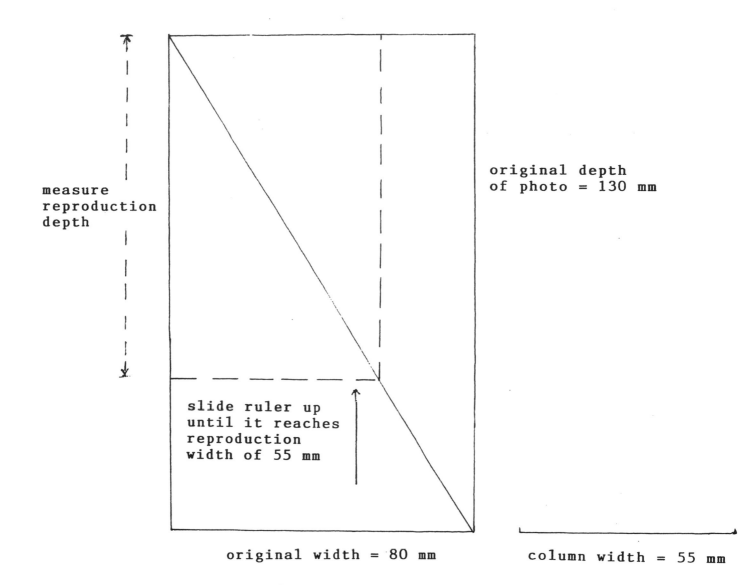

measure
reproduction
depth

original depth
of photo = 130 mm

slide ruler up
until it reaches
reproduction
width of 55 mm

original width = 80 mm

column width = 55 mm

Sizing a photo

On a photocopy or overlay, draw in the **diagonal** as shown, then
slide your ruler up, keeping it parallel with the bottom line.
(Using a set square rather than a ruler helps.) If you draw
in the **horizontal** at the required spot, you can label it 'reduce
to 55 mm width' to show the printer the **reproduction size.**
Measuring the **reproduction depth** shows you how much of the
printed column the photo will occupy. (The illustration assumes
that the width is the critical dimension; for another photo
it might be the depth.)
    If you are sizing or cropping on an overlay, remember to
remove the photo before you draw lines or write on the overlay.

Sizing a photo

reproduction size may be shown, like cropping, either on a photocopy of the print (the safest way) or on an overlay. Alternatively, you can annotate a picture list with instructions such as 'reduce to 70%' or 'reduce to 40 mm depth'.

To work out the reduction as a percentage of the original, calculate

$$\frac{\text{reproduction width (or depth)}}{\text{original width (or depth)}} \times 100$$

(Or on a calculator: reproduction width (or depth) ÷ original width (or depth) %.)

Remember that you must never write on a photo; still less should you press on it to rule lines. If you are using an overlay (rather than a photocopy), take the greatest care. First position the transparent paper over the photo and, extremely lightly, mark the corners. Remove the overlay before you draw in lines to join the corners, insert the diagonal, etc.

Similarly, to shade an area to show that it should be cropped, position the overlay over the photo and lightly mark the edge of the area to be omitted. Remove the overlay before you convert this into a firm vertical (or horizontal) line and add diagonal shading to the area not to be reproduced. Once the cropping is marked, you can size the photo in the usual way by drawing a diagonal between the corners of the uncropped area.

Now do Exercise 26.2

Imagine that the photo is an actual print and take great care not to harm it. You will need two overlays (sheets of paper thin enough to see through).

Review of Exercise 26.2

Although the photo is landscape, it would, as we have seen, be unusual to turn it on the page (the only way you could reproduce it in the largest possible version). More likely our choice lies between one column (generally more suitable for a portrait photo) and two columns (usually better for a landscape photo such as this). The critical dimension is the width (242 mm in the original) and, if it is to go across two columns, the printer has to reduce this to the width of the text area, 160 mm.

Your ruler will have shown you that, without cropping, this will give a reproduction depth of 112 mm (so the photo would take up more than half the text area of the page). This is a reduction to 66 per cent (a sizeable reduction but not unusual).

Some cropping might, however, make the main subject (the van and its attendants) more prominent. The half-visible notice on the left may be better omitted (probably by shading up to the next upright); if you did this, you would probably crop a little at the right as well in order to maintain balance. However, cropping the sides makes the photo more awkwardly square. To redress this, part of the blank foreground can certainly be cropped and you will need to omit some at the top as well. This could leave an original width of around 200 mm and depth of around 140 mm. Across two columns, these dimensions would translate into the same reproduction depth of 112 mm but with a much less drastic reduction, to 80 per cent of the original.

You might, on the other hand, decide that a photo taking up over half the page (not allowing for a caption) leaves too little room for text. A reduction factor somewhere between our two extremes, with less cropping at the sides, may be the answer.

Often you will want to experiment with different options in this way and clearly you need a quicker method than drawing on photocopies or overlays. Many photocopiers now have useful reduction and enlargement facilities for speedy trials. DTP systems, as we saw in Unit 3, can scan photographs and show them in varying sizes. If these high-tech methods are not available, a **proportional scale** (shown opposite) is very helpful. The illustration shows the scale set to the dimensions of the sizing example on the previous page; the window indicates that this requires a reduction to 70 per cent. A turn of the wheel (say, lining up the original width *when cropped* against the same column width) quickly shows the reproduction depth and reduction following that option.

Often a batch of photos or figures have to have the *same* percentage reduction so that the camera does not have to be adjusted for each one. Again the proportional scale can help you to crop and size to a given reduction.

Numbering photographs

Creative artwork is rarely numbered in the final book, although numbers are helpful for identification in the art brief. For photos there are various options.

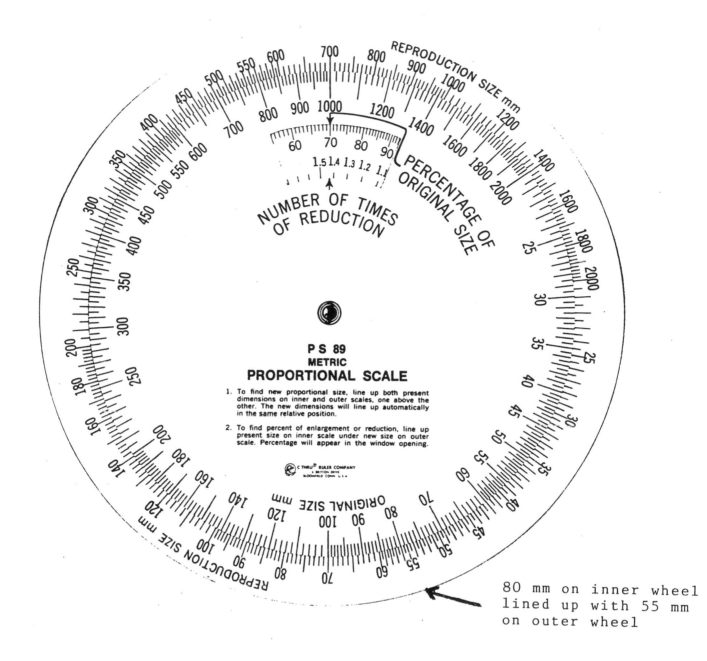

80 mm on inner wheel
lined up with 55 mm
on outer wheel

The inner wheel (original size) moves independently of the outer wheel (reproduction size). The added arrow shows that the scale has been set to the same dimensions as our earlier example for sizing a photo: original width 80 mm, lined up precisely with the desired reproduction width, 55 mm. Knowing that the original depth was 130 mm, you can immediately read off the **reproduction depth**, 92 mm (check on the example, which is drawn s.s.) and also (in the window) you are told that this is a **reduction** to 70 per cent of the original size.

Using a proportional scale

- They too may appear unnumbered in the book, when there is no need for specific references to them in the text. Again identification numbers are helpful in the picture list. When such numbers are for identification only, you *don't* have to renumber if you change the order of the photos in the book. Indeed it is better to keep the identification numbers the same, regardless of order, to avoid confusion.

- If they are to be numbered in the finished book, photos may have their own sequence, separate from other figures. They may be referred to as plates (even when they are not in a plate section), photos or illustrations. The numbering system may continue through the book or begin again in each chapter.

  If there are to be two separate sequences for photos and figures (not to mention one for tables), it is often useful to distinguish their form. So in a geography book, for example, you might use simple numbers (Pl. 1, Pl. 2, etc.) for photos, and numbers incorporating the chapter (Fig. 2.1, Fig. 2.2, etc.) for diagrams and maps. (The abbreviation 'Pl.' or 'pl.' may be used even though the photos do not appear in a separate plate section. Alternatively, they may be called 'photo 1', etc.)

  Photos are usually given their own sequence in this way when the picture collection is organized by the publisher (rather than the author). The order of the photos and therefore their final numbers in the book are not known until paste-up stage. (You still need identification numbers in the earlier stages but have to keep identification and final numbers separate, both in your mind and in your records.)

  The designer, as we have seen, will make choices between photos of different shapes illustrating the same subject, and may have notes from the editor on which ones are essential and which may be left out if necessary, or places where the order is significant and others where the photos only have to be fitted within a particular section. When you check the paste-up, you will finalize the numbers and captions, and insert or renumber any text references to the photos in the relevant galley proof.

- In a book where all the photos are an essential part of the text exposition, for example in a medical book, they and the other figures are usually numbered in a single sequence (generally by chapter). Such photos, as we have seen, often come from the author with the typescript.

Further reading

If you undertake picture research yourself, as many editors do, you may find this comprehensive tome helpful:

Hilary and Mary Evans, *Picture Researcher's Handbook: An International Guide to Picture Sources and How to Use Them* (Van Nostrand Reinhold, Wokingham, 4th edition, 1989)

UNIT 27
Figures

In this unit we turn to diagrams, charts, graphs, maps, technical drawings in general, all of which may be called figures. As we have seen, photos and creative artwork (Unit 26) may also be called figures but tables (Unit 21) are usually distinguished. In many areas of publishing the successful integration of figures and text is one of the most important and satisfying aspects of editorial work.

Roughs

Technical figure roughs should come from an author with the typescript. Although not often sufficiently finished for direct reproduction, the roughs (of graphs for example) should be accurately drawn and unambiguous.

As when dealing with tables, your tasks are to

- scrutinize the roughs and clarify where necessary
- standardize the layout and wording in parallel figures
- cross-check to ensure that they match up with the text and with each other
- key them into the text

After editing, the figures are often separated from the text and tables, to be prepared by a technical artist or artwork studio rather than by the typesetter. If the book is being prepared on a DTP, or if the figures are simple (for example, just words with vertical or horizontal arrows and/or boxes round them), the whole project may stay together.

Distinguishing figures from tables

Anything containing columns of numbers is clearly a table; any visual representation of the relations between objects or concepts is clearly a diagram. There is, however, a substantial grey area in between.

For example, the vocabulary in a reading passage, divided into grammatical categories (nouns, verbs, adjectives, etc.) could *either* be treated as a table,

with rules round column heads and so on (as discussed in Unit 21) *or* be laid out as a diagram, in boxes perhaps, with arrows showing which categories are most closely allied.

I prefer to make the decision on whether to treat such information as a 'table' or as a 'figure' solely on the grounds of its appearance in the final book, rather than on the process it happens to have gone through (tables to the typesetter, figures to the artwork studio).

The overriding consideration should be that similar information must appear in similar form throughout the book. So, to continue our example, don't lay out the vocabulary sections as tables in the first half of the book, because they are simple, and as figures in the second half, because they have become more complex.

As we have seen, simple figures can often be set by a typesetter (or DTP system). Equally, artwork is occasionally required in text (or tables): unusual special sorts, diacritics and arrows may have to be provided as artwork (or added to the CRC). Even vertical rules (as we saw in Unit 21) can be a problem for some typesetters; certainly diagonal rules or arrows often have to be artwork.

Maps

Like photos, maps are sometimes included with other figures in a single numbering sequence, sometimes separately numbered. Again the separate sequence may take a different form, perhaps running throughout the book as Map 1, Map 2, while other figures incorporate the chapter number, Fig. 2.1, Fig. 2.2.

Labels

Figure **labels** (also known collectively as **annotation**, or **anno** for short) are any words on the diagram, graph or map except the caption. The caption (which we'll look at in more detail in Unit 28) tells the reader what the figure shows (like the main head of a table) and may also contain a source and possibly other explanatory notes. Whereas the labels are usually dealt with by the artist or artwork studio, the captions often go with the text to the typesetter.

A **key** (or **legend**) may be included either with the labels (if it is to appear as an integral part of the figure) or with the captions (if it involves extensive typesetting).

Sometimes you will be expected to type up **label copy**; usually it is enough simply to mark any amendments to the labels on the roughs themselves. Maps in particular may require separate label copy, especially if the roughs are labelled by hand, or if only a selection of the names shown on the rough (perhaps a photocopy from another work) is to appear in the finished artwork. Type the label copy

in categories (separating river names, country names, etc.) so that the designer (or you) can specify distinct typographical styles. This is especially important for maintaining consistency across a range of maps taken from different sources.

In addition to making the style of labels consistent (the use of capital and lower-case letters, roman and italic, etc.), standardize the position of similar labels in different figures, for example on graph axes. Although the artist may decide to change your system to improve the effect, he or she needs to know what information in each figure is parallel. As with tables, it is occasionally clearest to delete (or even use correcting fluid) and rewrite, making certain that you do not introduce errors. (Ensure first that you have a clear duplicate set of the author's original roughs in case you need to check back.)

Now do Exercise 27.1

Assume that all these figures are to appear in the same book, unlikely as that may seem, and make them consistent in style. (They are squashed on to two pages here simply in order to save space; encourage authors to supply roughs on separate sheets, except where the figures are very small.) Don't forget to check the meaning and logic of each figure: there are some serious flaws. Mark the labels in place: no separate label copy is necessary. You will need a query sheet.

Review of Exercise 27.1

A and B – graphs

Most graphs have a vertical axis and a horizontal axis. Unless the graph is purely algebraic (in which case the vertical axis is y and the horizontal is x), the **axis label** often consists of an identification and the units. As with column heads in tables, these units are usually given in parentheses, normally abbreviated. (Where the indicators along an axis just show years, rather than numbers, no axis label is necessary.)

The position of axis labels should be consistent. They may be either (most commonly) centred on the axis (reading up the page, in the case of the vertical axis) or at the end of the axis (at the top of the vertical; to the right of the horizontal). The two elements (identification and units) are usually best kept together, although occasionally the identification is centred and the units (without parentheses in that case) are positioned at the ends of the axes.

Clearly the axis labels in A and B required attention. You could change the vertical axis label in A into 'Charge (£)' (deleting the original and rewriting

it to run up the page). The abbreviation is actually clearer in this case, to avoid the ambiguity of 'pounds'. In B the vertical axis is better as 'Weight (g)' (identification as well as units) and again could run up the page.

Similarly, the two elements of the horizontal axis label in B are best brought together: 'Age (days)'. Abbreviation of units on the two horizontal axes is more problematic: the standard SI abbreviation for 'hours' is 'h' (rather than the more familiar 'hrs') and 'days' are rarely shortened. Since they form a matching pair, I'd leave these spelt out.

Labels should consistently start lower case *or* start with a capital. Exceptions can be (and often are) made for axis labels and/or explanations in keys, which often start with a capital even when all other labels start lower case.

In A you should query (or in real life check against the relevant text) which line represents Alf and which Bill: the position of the labels is ambiguous. The text discussion (or related question) must match the figure. (The graph is about three men, electricians perhaps, who charge at different rates. For example, Charlie charges a minimum of £10 for the first hour and then £10 an hour; one of the others charges a £30 minimum but that will cover up to three hours' work. There might be an accompanying question asking which one you would employ to do a job that you estimated would take a certain length of time.)

A key is sometimes helpful on a graph, and frequently helpful on a map (though the word 'key' or 'legend' is now normally omitted). But avoid unnecessary keys: graph B is much easier to read if the labels are not in a key but next to the relevant lines on the graph itself, as in A.

In A two of the lines are solid and the one crossing them is differentiated with dashes. In B three different kinds of line (solid, long dashes, short dashes) have been used, in order to distinguish between them in the key. If you eliminated the key, as suggested, they could all be solid. Usually simplicity is best: make distinctions only where necessary (because lines cross each other, or to match lines up with a key).

Whether the labels always run horizontally (the most common style) or follow the angle of the line is likely to be the subject of a general design instruction, or very often it will be left to the artist's judgement.

There were several problems with the **scales** on the axes. Be consistent about whether 0 is included or excluded. (Either style is acceptable, though inclusion is preferable.) In mathematical works you may also need to identify whether it should be zero or cap O, for origin. Ensure that scales (for example on the vertical axis in A here) continue as far as necessary to read the graph easily. (On this point, of course, they do not have to be made uniform with each other.)

In B you have to *query* whether (on the horizontal axis) '30, 40' should read '25, 30', or whether that section of the graph needs to be redrawn. Scales must never change in the middle like this (from 5, 10, etc., to identically spaced indicators showing 20, 30, etc.). It may be that the animals were weighed less often as they grew older but the slopes of the lines are misleading if the scale doesn't reflect the time intervals accurately.

These graph roughs are on plain paper but authors sometimes use graph paper in order to plot the points accurately. In that case be sure to instruct the artist whether or not the **grid** should be reproduced and, if so, in what detail (centimetre squares for example). Ensure that a standard grid is used throughout the book, or at least for groups of similar graphs. Such a grid often *is* required in school maths books; a tint or second colour helps to show that it is just a background. In most other books, the standard practice is simply to show the axes, divided by short indicator lines as here.

C and D – diagrams

The flaw in C can be corrected by redrawing the top of the balance at a steeper angle: the strings holding the two pans must be of equal length. (The string doesn't lengthen as the pan goes down.) There is no need to query this. We cannot tell without the text but the drawing is presumably intended to show that volume is different from weight: coal will weigh more than its equivalent volume of peanuts. If so, you'd probably need to instruct the artist to draw the content of the pans more carefully to look the same in volume, as well as looking more realistic.

D's fatal flaw (literally: errors of this kind could have serious consequences) is the transposition of the labels for the earth (the striped wire) and the live wire. As we saw in Unit 14, the publisher can be held responsible for negligence.

More prosaically, the order and style of the labels (kind of wire and colour) should be standardized. For example, the kind of wire could be in small caps (usually preferable to full caps on a diagram) and the colour lower case (if you make this distinction, no parentheses are needed); or both could be in roman (retaining the parentheses round the colour).

E – map

The key shows that the map is about rainfall (the only data measured in mm, or inches, per annum). For rainfall, temperature, contours, etc., the convention is that shading (tints) should be *graduated* from dark (heavy rainfall) through to light (sparse rainfall). Here, however, the bands alternate between light and dark. Such a shading style can be effective where no gradation is involved (for example to distinguish neighbouring countries or provinces) but is inappropriate for rainfall.

All you can or should do to indicate the problem is to add an instruction to the artist to graduate the tints, using the darkest for the heaviest rainfall. (Any attempt to alter the rough by hand would just cause confusion or obscure the precise boundaries.)

In addition, the key doesn't extend to the lowest rainfall category (0–200 mm p.a.) but a small region in the far north of Kenya is shown untinted, which probably indicates this level. (The straighter edge shows you it is not a lake.) Because lakes (including several small unnamed ones) are also untinted, it may be advisable to suggest a pale tint even for this lowest level. (Alternatively, the lakes might have a special tint.)

Data have not been included for countries outside the East African region (Rwanda and Burundi on the left – the distinctive border lines tell you that these are countries). You might think it more consistent to omit the border lines between the two countries and land to their west, although they are quite helpful in showing that this is not just another large lake.

Whether or not the border line should be included in the key will depend on the context: it is a conventional one and you certainly wouldn't need to explain it on *each* map throughout a book. A north point is not usually included either. Do, however, insist on a *scale* for every map, preferably a visual one (rather than a ratio), so that it remains accurate when reduced or enlarged. (See Exercise 5.1, Reading Maps, for some examples of visual scales.)

On the rough, italic is used for lakes, italic capitals for the ocean. Italic is conventionally used for all kinds of water, especially rivers. (Small caps for the islands is less common but not wrong.) Since you weren't asked to type separate label copy, you just need to clarify any obscure labels (perhaps 'L. Turkana' at the top).

You may have noticed that the rainfall bands are given in the key as '200–400 mm, 400–800 mm', etc. In Unit 21 I castigated authors who use '20–30, 30–40' for age groups ('20–9', etc., avoids any ambiguity). Measurements such as rainfall and temperature, however, are conventionally banded in this way.

The rough seems to come from a printed book. In such cases in real life, remember to check that the source is acknowledged in the caption (even though the map is to be redrawn) and that permission has been obtained.

Cross-checking text and figures

Both figures and tables must be checked against the relevant section of text to make sure that the information given matches up. You also have to key them into the text. As we saw in Units 14–15 this usually means writing 'Fig. 2.1 near here' in the margin. If the author has included a typed note of the desired position (as in Exercise 25.1, Environment), you can just ring that instruction.

In a project going direct to page proof, the keying in instructs the typesetter where to place the figure (or table). In addition, you should ensure that there is a text reference to each, so that the reader can easily follow the argument. Standardize the style ('Figure' or 'fig.', etc.) and check that the numbering sequence does not skip or repeat.

It will not always be possible to position each figure (or table) precisely where it is most relevant. (The mention may occur low on a page, so that the figure will not fit in until the following page.) So you must replace such phrases as 'In the figure below' with 'In Figure 2.3', etc.

Now do Exercise 27.2

Code the headings generically. The lowest level may either be coded or (if no extra space is wanted) be marked specifically for bold or italic.

Review of Exercise 27.2

We don't know whether this is a new chapter or a section of a chapter, so it is safest to start the heading hierarchy with an A head (l. 1); you will then have B heads on ll. 6, 10 and 14. The lowest level ('Clasping roots', etc., which are all types of aerial root) may be coded 'C' or (preferably) just standardized to bold (or italic) with a normal para indent. If so, 'Prop roots' (l. 20) and 'Buttress roots' (l. 23) should be indented and marked bold; and 'roots' on l. 28 marked bold.

As well as changing text references to figures to conform with the style instruction, you had to consider their position. Normally such parenthetic references come before the final stop of the relevant sentence (just like the author–date references for

embedded quotations that we dealt with in Units 11 and 19). Like a note indicator, wherever possible a parenthetic reference to a figure or table should come at the end of the sentence, rather than in the middle. It can, alternatively, be an integral part of the text sentence: 'As Fig. 7.1 shows ...'. The reference to Fig. 7.2 must move from l. 12 to l. 13 and (new) Fig. 7.7 is better mentioned towards the end of l. 25, paralleling l. 28.

You will have noticed the misnumbering of the figures from l. 23 onwards. (There are eight in all, not seven.) Once this is put right in the text (with Fig. 7.6 on l. 24, at the end of the sentence), the diagrams can be identified. They are (top to bottom): (left column) 7.7, 7.1, 7.8, 7.3; (right column) 7.5, 7.4, 7.2, 7.6. (Correct any figure numbers you got wrong – both on the illustration sheet and in the text –

before you continue to the next unit because we look there at the captions that might go with this passage.)

The figure label style has to be standardized, preferably to start lower case. It is probably best to add 'root' where it is missing (on Figs 7.1 and 7.5) and add 'clasping' (on Fig. 7.3) and 'prop' (on Fig. 7.4). You *could* also add a label 'fibrous root' on Fig. 7.2 but it is not necessary. Correct the spelling of 'epiphyte' on Fig. 7.3.

The punctuation of the list (ll. 2–5) had to be standardized. I hope you also remembered to change 'page 132' on l. 5 to 'p. 000'. We cannot tell for sure whether this parenthetic reference is best taken into the sentence before it, lower-casing 'see' (this would be appropriate if that folio deals only with storage), or left as a separate sentence, transposing the closing parenthesis and full stop (appropriate if that folio deals with root functions generally). I would guess the former from its present position (if it related to the whole list, it should be on a new line) but in real life you would check fo. 132 to find out.

The use of italic and an initial capital for botanical names in Latin is demonstrated again here (ll. 7, 25 and 28, where the italic had to be added). Although the same name is used for them in English, the red and black mangroves are in fact different species. Finally, on l. 29 add 'e' to make 'breathe'.

Position of figures

If a figure or table appears in the middle of a paragraph in the typescript (rather than on a separate sheet), you need to mark the text to run on round it. Often, as we saw in the type spec in Exercise 25.2, the typesetter is asked to put tables and figures at the top or bottom of the printed page.

If a project goes through a galley proof stage, followed by paste-up, you have to key in the figures (and tables) on the galleys, so that the designer doing the paste-up knows where to position them. Often the same rules apply (all text references should be by number; tables and figures will be put at the top or bottom of a page). However, with a paste-up stage or working on a DTP, you have the option of **precise positioning**, which can be extremely helpful in instructional books, whether at school or adult level.

For example, in a book on practical origami, you may want to say, 'First fold the paper like this', 'Then join the two ends together', following each instruction with the relevant diagram. This style is more direct and easier to follow than 'First fold the paper as shown in Fig. 1', 'Fig. 2 shows the two ends joined together', etc.

However, precise positioning involves extra work: always consider the necessity carefully. At paste-up, lines will have to be saved and made (Unit 20), figures reduced or enlarged, text rewritten, so that each figure appears precisely at the point where it is mentioned in the text.

Figures (and tables) need not in that case be numbered in the finished book (unless it is useful for cross-referencing), although identification numbers are helpful for keying in.

Sizing

If the figure roughs are good enough to reproduce direct (perhaps just relabelled), they will be sized in the same way as photos (Unit 26). If they are to be redrawn, the artist may just be told the text area and asked to fit the figures as appropriate; alternatively, you may be expected to suggest actual sizes. It is certainly worth indicating which ones should go upright (portrait), which ones should be turned on the page (landscape), which should occupy one column, which should extend over two.

UNIT 28

Captions

In the last of these units focusing on illustrations, we look at the style and content of the captions, which identify and sometimes comment on photographs, maps or diagrams.

As we have seen, labels and keys (sometimes typed up as separate label copy, sometimes just marked in place) usually accompany the figure roughs, to be typeset and positioned on the artwork. Typed caption copy for both photos and figures, however, more frequently goes with the text to the typesetter. (A DTP system may eliminate the need for such differentiation.)

In the printed book the caption is usually positioned below (rather than above) the illustration. Alternatively, for example in a one-third/two-thirds design, it may appear in the margin beside it.

Style and consistency

In children's stories, as we saw in Unit 26, illustrations are usually unnumbered. Frequently they have no caption either, because to someone reading the story the illustration speaks for itself. Captions are often equally unnecessary in school textbooks. If you look back at Exercise 5.1 (Reading Maps), for example, you will see that the two maps and compass have no captions (although I did mention that 'The village of Isla' and 'Cross-section' were effectively captions). The figures are to be positioned precisely (so numbers are unnecessary) and the surrounding text and questions explain fully why they are included and what the reader is to look for in them.

When they *are* used, captions may consist of a number and description, or a description alone, or a number alone. So in a maths or philosophy book, 'Figure l' or 'Figure 2.1', with no further description, is sufficient to direct the reader's attention to each figure at the appropriate stage in a complex argument.

In most books and journals, however, a few words are included to identify the subject of the illustration. If some figures or tables in a book have such descriptive phrases and others are simply numbered, it is usual to ask the author to supply the brief descriptions that are missing in order to make the book consistent.

When you are editing caption copy, look for consistency in the information given and probably the order in which it is given. Sometimes strict uniformity will be too boring: you may want to vary the format in order to keep the reader's attention. Usually, however, a predictable order helps him or her to grasp the differences between similar illustrations quickly.

Predictably, you will be looking too for consistency in the punctuation system and general layout.

If you have a type spec or sample book to follow you will know the caption style. For example, the number ('Figure 2.1') might be italic and the rest of the caption roman, with turnover lines full out. (The details you need to know are the same as for a table main head, see Unit 25.) If the design has not yet been finalized (or if you are not expected to mark up such features), simply make the typed caption copy consistent.

Now do Exercise 28.1

This is the caption copy for the figures in Exercise 27.2 (Roots). Check each caption against your **corrected** *version of that exercise, looking both at the drawings and the text. Edit the captions as necessary.*

Review of Exercise 28.1

The first two captions should be in the same form (preferably both following the pattern of Fig. 7.1). As you know from the text, these are the two most common root systems; the remainder of the diagrams show examples of aerial roots.

For the rest of the captions, you had to decide whether the type of root or the name of the plant should consistently come first. My preference would be the type of root, as the main purpose of the illustration, but you may think that starting with the plant is more interesting.

Although it is perfectly acceptable to mix captions that are complete sentences (Fig. 7.5) with ones consisting of phrases (the remainder), a few exceptions to an otherwise uniform pattern will look odd: I would make them all phrases here.

Whether or not they form sentences, captions should end in a consistent way (always with or always without a full stop). In a book where most of the captions are short, they often end without a full stop. Longer captions (consisting of several sentences) *may* similarly end without a final full stop, but the modern trend, especially in books where long captions predominate, is to include the full stop throughout.

The style specified in Exercise 27.2 for text references to these figures was 'Fig. 7.1'. This does *not* necessarily mean that you have to abbreviate 'Figure' to 'Fig.' for the caption number itself. (Conversely, the text reference to a photo might take the form 'see Plate 3' but the caption could just read '3 The Blue Mountains'.)

A full stop (or less frequently a dash or colon) between number and caption is an acceptable style but I'd standardize here to the prevalent form, marking an em space and keeping the capital that follows.

You will have noticed that the captions for Figs 7.7 and 7.8 should be transposed. The Latin name for the red mangrove is probably best omitted; if you retained it, you should have added *Avicennia* to the parallel caption. 'Epiphytic' is misspelt again, and so is 'mangrove'.

Content of the caption

Remember that most readers will flick through a book looking at the illustrations and glancing at their captions *before* they get round to reading the text (or even before they buy the book). So it is important that the captions should be self-explanatory.

Now do Exercise 28.2 G

Make a query list of any points you would raise with the author to ensure that the captions are self-explanatory and complete. Edit the captions as necessary.

Review of Exercise 28.2

Most of these illustrations appear to be photos, many showing original painted portraits. In this context it would not be wrong to keep 'Map of' in Pl. 1, although in general such obvious information is usually better omitted. (You wouldn't, for example, want 'Portrait of' throughout; certainly if several of the figures were maps you should delete 'Map of'.)

Most of the captions mention the person's relationship, or the place's relevance, to Jane Austen, the subject of the book. This is essential if the numerous portraits of people and pictures of houses are to be meaningful, especially to someone who has not yet read the text. In the same vein, it would be helpful to know who Edward Austen was (Pl. 6); and to have the relationship of Lefroy (Pl. 14) explained. (The caption for Pl. 2 indicates that the families were related.)

You might think that an explanation of Steventon's significance is needed for Pl. 1 or 2 captions (not both). Personally I think its repeated occurrence is sufficiently clear indication that this was where Jane Austen lived (reinforced by Pl. 7); I would just add to Pl. 9 that this was the Austen family home.

For completeness you would probably ask for the author of *Fables choisies* (Pl. 8; note the lower case 'c') and for Engleheart's first name (Pl. 14). (Pl. 4 is almost certainly anonymous.)

The general style here is to separate the source (Pls 2, 4 and 14) from the main caption by a full stop. (We look at sources in more detail below.) You would have to check whether the illustration in Pl. 2 was one drawing of cottages or, as the source suggests, several drawings. Pl. 3 *could* be converted into the same format of subject and source but, since the illustration seems to be included more for its own sake than for the relevance of its subject matter, the different form is preferable.

Apart from this source information, each caption is a single phrase *or* sentence; the mixture of the two is quite acceptable here. The semicolon in the Pl. 15

caption would probably be better as a colon, following the pattern of Pl. 13. A full stop is evidently intended at the end of each caption: add one to Pls 1 and 14.

Words such as '(left)' often appear in italic but this would be a design decision. The titles of paintings (Pl. 3), as of books, are set in italic. ('Dancing' in Pl. 4 need not be made consistent: it indicates the subject of the painting, not its title.)

Sources of photographs and paintings

The source information included in Exercise 28.2 only offers a brief indication of origin, for the reader's interest: it does not give all the details of where the original may be found (an art gallery, a private collection, a library).

Sometimes this detailed information *will* be included in the caption; other **credits** such as the photographer's name may appear as well. Occasionally indeed **copyright-holders** (those giving permission for the use of material) insist that such information should be given in full on the same page as the illustration.

More frequently the captions are kept uncluttered. The details must, however, be included somewhere in the book, usually *either* as expanded entries in the **list of illustrations** *or* as part of the **acknowledgements**. Both of these would normally be in the prelims but, if long, they may go in the endmatter.

Sources of diagrams, maps, etc.

In school texts and general books for adults, the sources of figures are often similarly confined to the acknowledgements. In more academic books, however, they are usually included in the caption (either as well as or instead of in separate acknowledgements).

If the figure is taken from another work (a book or journal article perhaps), follow the short form of reference used elsewhere in the book (see Units 18–19). So in the author–date system the caption might read:

Fig. 2.12   Chevron-pattern frieze on a dressed stone wall (Garlake, 1973: 50, Fig. 9)

or in the short-title system:

Fig. 2.12   Chevron-pattern frieze on a dressed stone wall (Garlake, *Great Zimbabwe*, p. 50, Fig. 9)

In the short-title system, as you'll remember, such a reference would normally be found in a note, not in parentheses in the text. You (or the author) might suppose it would be neater simply to attach a note indicator after 'wall' and include the details in the notes. However, this cannot be done if (as is usual) notes are numbered through the chapter. This is because figures cannot usually be positioned precisely, so several notes might have to be renumbered at proof stage.

As we saw in Unit 25, a figure (or table) adapted from its source is given as 'after Ajayi, 1988: 206'.

If many of the sources are cumbersome you may decide to follow a style more like a table source:

Fig. 2.12   Chevron-pattern frieze on a dressed stone wall

Source: Garlake, *Great Zimbabwe*, p. 50, Fig. 9

The source information would probably then be set in smaller type. Explanatory details about the figure or a key (perhaps to abbreviations used on it) may be treated in a similar way.

Discursive captions

Explanatory details of this sort added to a caption would be set in smaller type because they are, in effect, (unnumbered) notes. Many books, however, have long captions that impart information as well as identifying the subject of the illustration. (The whole caption would then be in the same type size.) So a photo of a rabbit in a school textbook might have the caption:

Fig. 1   The angora rabbit has very fine hair, which is used for making woollen jumpers. These animals can be delicate and require careful monitoring for disease.

Such information may be additional to the text – specific details perhaps about a painting – or it may bring out and reinforce the main message.

Look at Exercises 12.3 (Arab Geography) and 20.2 (Change of Use) for examples of lengthy captions, which are very common in illustrated books. Taking seriously the fact that captions are normally read first (though often *written* last, after the final photo selection), discursive captions aim to whet the reader's appetite, stress the most important points brought out in the text (even, cynics might say, substitute for reading the text). The text and caption may overlap in content but should never duplicate each other.

Now do Exercise 28.3

UNIT 29
Editing the Index

This book makes no attempt to teach you how to compile an index: although it is sometimes tackled by the editor, indexing is a quite separate skill. Instead, in this unit we look at techniques for checking and marking up an index compiled either by a professional indexer or by the author.

Such an index may arrive as a typescript or as a hard-copy printout accompanying a computer disk. Many indexers have invested in software packages specifically developed to handle some of the more routine tasks of indexing. (Again not covered here are the rather different problems that may arise in indexes prepared mechanically by the typesetting machine.)

To edit an index well you need to know something of the art of indexing, and you must be sensitive to fine distinctions the indexer may be making. The practice offered here aims to set you on this road.

Alternative layouts

The index often contains both names and subjects. Alternatively, a name index (or author index) may be separate from the subject index. Although indexes are usually typeset in two or three columns, the *typescript* should be in a single column.

Most general or subject indexes will consist of numerous **main entries**, some of them subdivided into **subentries**. (More complex ones may have sub-subentries as well.) The layout of the main entries and subentries is either **set out** or **run on**.

Set-out style

peach trees, 29, 49, 53, 56,
    174
    fruit, 177, 179
rocks
    arrangement of, 20, 112,
      158–61
    as bridge, 143
    caves/caverns, 36, 113

Run-on style

peach trees, 29, 49, 53, 56,
    174; fruit, 177, 179
rocks: arrangement of, 20,
    112, 158–61; as bridge,
    143; caves/caverns, 36,
    113

In the set-out style, the different levels of entry are shown by indention: each subentry is indented and turnover lines (both of the main entry and of subentries) are indented further (sometimes to the same position as here, sometimes with a deeper indent for the subentry turnover).

In the run-on style, punctuation performs the same function. So each semicolon indicates the beginning of a new subentry ('fruit', etc.). In 'rocks' the list of subentries begins with a colon because there are no page numbers relating to rocks in general. No such colon is necessary in 'peach trees'.

In either style, the comma between an entry (or subentry) and the first page number relating to it is optional: an en or em space may be left instead. In some indexes each main entry begins with a capital but lower case (except for proper names) is now more common. Most publishers prefer unjustified setting so that the lines don't look too gappy.

Fitting the extent

The reason for choosing one or other layout often comes down to the space available. As the examples show, a set-out index is clearer for the reader; a run-on index occupies significantly less space.

Indexing normally takes place at page-proof stage. (A draft can be prepared earlier, for page numbers to be inserted when known, but tackling the whole operation at page proof is usually more satisfactory.) When the page proofs arrive, you will be able to calculate the closest **even working**, normally a multiple of 32 or 16 pages (see Unit 3).

For example, the text might take up pp. 1–236 inclusive and the prelims might be numbered up to xii. What is the closest even working? You already have 236 + 12 = 248, so the nearest even working (in 32s) is 256. This leaves 8 printed pages available for the index, which will probably be enough to allow it to be set out. If you found you had 4 pages, you would opt for a run-on index.

Tell the person preparing the index how many printed pages are available, and send a sample page of an index set in the likely type size, so that he or she can, as far as possible, tailor it to fit. Squeezing the index is by no means the only way of making a book fit into an even working: often you can also rearrange the prelims so that they take up less space (as we shall see in Unit 31).

Checking the index against the proofs

The indexer is often working from an uncorrected set of page proofs. Therefore part of your task will be to check that all proof corrections are reflected in the index. For example, the author or proofreader may have spotted a name incorrectly spelt in the proofs. Again, if lines have to move from one page to another, perhaps to bring an illustration closer to its text reference, you will have to look for index entries that may be affected.

As we shall see below, you will also be checking back from time to time on style points: Does 'government' take a capital; should it be 'judgment' or 'judgement'? If there is an inconsistency within the index, the reason is often a lurking inconsistency in the book, which you may also be able to set right now. Remember that, whatever your personal preferences, the index (which is only in typescript or on disk) must be made consistent in style with the book (which has already been typeset). Factual or spelling errors, of course, have to be corrected.

Whenever you do not understand an entry, or its relevance to the subject matter, you will check back to the page proof: it may be that clarification of the entry would be helpful or that a typing error in the index has misled you.

This cross-checking activity cannot be reproduced in the exercises, so you just have to imagine that you have the **collated marked set** of page proofs beside you. The various cross-checks are normally sufficient to *spot-check* the accuracy of the index. If the result gives you cause for concern, you may have to investigate further or return the index to its compiler for revision. The task of editing the index *doesn't* normally entail checking the accuracy of every page reference (a very time-consuming job).

Technique

You are looking for accuracy and consistency on all levels but must take care not to blur intentional and useful distinctions. Because it is not easy to grasp the shape of a normal-sized index, I advocate tackling the task in stages. In time you may find that a different way of dividing up the tasks suits you better, but for now I suggest that you use this one.

1 Read through, correcting spellings (and / or checking them against the marked proof), ensuring consistency of punctuation, elision of numbers, etc. At this stage just put a pencil question mark in the margin next to any entries you do not immediately understand (and a pencil cross against any entries obviously out of order).

2 Double-check the order and elision of page numbers within each entry or subentry.

3 Check the alphabetical order of main entries. (Indexes prepared with the aid of an indexing software package shouldn't require more than a spot-check for obvious oddities of alphabetical ordering.)

4 '**Read back**' and check the order of subentries, marking up as necessary. (This stage is explained after Exercise 29.1.)

5 By this time you should have a good idea of the overall content and balance of the index. Read through again more quickly to ensure that the index is logically organized, that **headwords** are sensible and do not overlap and that parallel entries are treated similarly, looking up in the page proofs any entries you still don't understand. Clarify or adjust where (but only where) necessary. If you change wording, remember to recheck the alphabetical order. (Sometimes you may have to prune as well to fit the extent: again do so with caution, taking care not to introduce inconsistent treatment or imbalance.)

6 Finally, check the **cross-references** for accuracy of wording and general usefulness. This has to be the last job in case you have reworded any entries in the course of 5.

Now do Exercise 29.1

The layout of the index is run on. Concentrate on stages 1–3 and 6 above, although you may also find a couple of improvements at stage 5. In real life you would have the whole index and the relevant marked page proofs to hand: note down on a separate sheet any points that you would cross-check.

Review of Exercise 29.1

Compare your work with the sample answer, and list of the further checks needed, on pp. 164–6.

As for bibliographies (Unit 17), a general instruction on indention of turnovers, with specific marking of any that have been wrongly typed (for example in 'Ming dynasty'), is usually sufficient in a run-on index. As we saw in Unit 25, in small type sizes (common in indexes) an em of set generally looks better (and wastes less space) than a pica em. The space between **letter blocks** will normally be a line but may have to vary to create even columns or to save space. (A *full* typographical mark-up of the index would, in addition, include specification of the type size, instructions to set in columns of a specific measure, etc.)

The conventions on alphabetical ordering of names, especially foreign ones, may be found in Anderson, *Book Indexing*. Chinese names, for example, are *not* inverted. Therefore, Ni Tzan is correct but Marco Polo (a Venetian) should appear under P.

Authors and editors are sometimes puzzled by an indexer's apparently haphazard indexing of names. The index does not have to include every proper name in the book (although, if you or the author want that, you can ask for it). The usual convention is only to index **significant mentions**. So a discussion of a scholar's work (either in the text or in a note) would be indexed, but a reference (either in parentheses or in a note) or a listing in the bibliography would not.

Missing initials (or a first name), as in the Plaks entry here, occur frequently, usually because no specific work by that person is listed in the bibliography. If it is someone famous, you or the indexer may be able to supply the initials or name; if not, you will have to ask the author. If no first name can be traced in time, 'Dr' or 'Mr', etc., is preferable to the surname alone.

The distinction between, for example, '58–9' and '125, 126' (under 'Ming dynasty') is deliberate: I hope you were not tempted to annihilate it by shortening to '125–6'. The meaning of '58–9' is a continuous discussion of the topic over those pages;

whereas '58, 59' would indicate two separate mentions.

On the other hand, '101ff.' (in '"natural" vs "artificial"') is no different in meaning from '101–3' or '101–20' (or wherever the discussion ends). Sometimes an author's index will follow this rather unsatisfactory style throughout. If you have to accept this, remember that 'ff.' means 'and following pages' and 'f.' means 'and following (single) page'. Occasionally the Latin word *passim* can be helpful (it means passing mentions throughout a long section of text) but is generally best avoided.

An unnecessary number (such as '113' in 'pavilions') is not unusual, often resulting from the amalgamation of two overlapping entries. Repetition of a number (such as '147' in 'paving') could just be a mistake but it is worth checking the page proofs (as the list of further checks suggests), in case a handwritten number has been wrongly typed (the probable explanation of the transposition of '95' and '98' in 'mountains'). Similarly, in 'pine trees' a typing error is more likely than the inadvertent transposition of '177, 176'.

The parentheses around the dates of the Ming dynasty helpfully distinguish them from page numbers. The same style is often followed for Acts of Parliament, etc.

Note the distinction of meaning between '*see*' (all relevant page references are found under another headword) and '*see also*' (for *additional* page references), a distinction we came across in Unit 14. Although in 'mountains' the cross-reference appears at the end of a long entry, '*see*' is correct: all the page references about that particular subentry appear elsewhere. Before '*see*', there is usually a comma (or no punctuation); '*see also*' more often follows a semicolon, like a subentry. (Italic is commonly, though not necessarily, used for both.)

The entries for 'peach' and 'plum' are exact **parallels**, and as such they must be treated the same, probably retaining 'trees' (as for 'pine'). You would, of course, have to look through the rest of the index for other similar instances.

The long string of undifferentiated page references in 'pine trees' is not very satisfactory: if you had time to look them up, you might be able to create

Sample answer to Exercise 29.1

THE CHINESE GARDEN

[as ch hd]

Index

[Turnovers indent 1 em of set throughout]

Marco Polo, 57, 58, 173 [throughout]

meaning, 193–200; _see also_ symbols/symbolism

miniaturisation, 37, 158–59

Ming dynasty (1403–1644 AD), 13, 16, 58–9, 108, 115, 125, 126, 176

Mountains, 35–40, 101, 103–4; erosion problems, 91, 92, 95, 97, 98, 175; inspiration from, 80, 99, 112–13, 155; miniature, _see_ rocks, piles of

mushrooms of immortality (lung-chieh), 37, 176

nature/natural, 9, 29–30, 94, 120–125, 161, 167, 168

'natural' vs 'artificial', 10, 42, 59, 90, 101ff, 138, 187, 193–195

Ni Tzan, 106–8, 114–15

nursery gardens, 24, 39, 160, 174

[reorder as shown]

(3) ostentation, 15, 40, 42–3, 88, 137; _see also_ extravagance

(2) orchids, 32, 153, 175, 187–88

(1) orchards, 34, 53

paths, 142, 144; _see also_ paving, designs of

pavilions, 10, 60–3, 112–14, 131, 135, 140, 164, 167–70, 190–191

Further checks needed

[The order follows the suggested technique. The number in the margin indicates the stage at which the query emerges.]

	Entry affected	Check to be made
[1]	miniaturisation	-ise or -ize spellings in prfs?
	'natural' vs 'artificial'	final p. no. of discussion beginning on p. 101
	petromania (no pp.)	look out for mention in prfs and/or chk w. indexer/author (if no success, x-ref. to rocks poss., or omit whole entry)
	Plaks (no init.)	look in bibliog./refs. If no success, ask author
[2]	paving (2 refs to 147)	any mention on 149?
	pine trees (177, 176)	chk mentioned on both 176 & 177 (if not, chk 172, 178)
[5]	rocks (subentries)	chk prfs in case subtle distinction between heaps and piles
[6]	meaning	chk x-ref. to symbols/symbolism
	ostentation	chk x-ref. to extravagance
	peonies (x-ref. to moutan)	look out for mention of moutan in prfs and/or chk w. indexer/ author (if no success, omit x-ref.)

some helpful subentries (not necessarily *exactly* the same as for blossom-bearing trees). If an index is full of such strings of page numbers, return it to the indexer or author for further work.

In 'rocks' the subentries 'heaps of' and 'piles of' are synonyms, that is, they have the same meaning (though you would check the page proofs to make sure that no subtle distinction was being drawn). It doesn't matter that 'heap' may be used on one page and 'pile' on another: if the *concept* is the same, one subentry will do. Indeed having two subentries is more confusing than helpful. You can amalgamate the page references *either* under 'heap' *or* under 'pile' but remember to adjust the cross-reference in 'mountains' as necessary to match.

'Reading back' the subentries

Read back from each subentry to the main entry to ensure that it makes sense. For example, under 'rocks' in Exercise 29.1, read back:

> arrangement of (rocks); (rocks) as bridge [there's rarely any need for 'a', 'the', etc., in indexes]; caves/caverns [a specific kind of rock]; petrified trees [ditto]; piles of (rocks) …

Because the headword is 'understood' in so many cases, it should never be *repeated* in the subentry. This is why, in the sample answer, 'rocks' has been removed from 'single' and 'symbolism of'.

Notice too that the reader is expected to understand immediately whether the headword should be read before or after the subentry. If when you have tried both ways you still cannot fathom the relation of subentry to main entry, check the relevant pages of the proofs.

Prepositions (such as 'in') or **conjunctions** (such as 'and') should in general be included only where their omission could lead to ambiguity. A preposition at the end of a subentry is usually more dispensable than one at the beginning. For example, in the 'rocks' entry, 'of' *could* in each instance safely be omitted (provided you applied this change in the same circumstances elsewhere in the index). Conversely, if a subentry is unclear or ambiguous, adding a preposition can often solve the problem. To take an example used below, 'perception, approaches' would be less quickly understood than 'perception, approaches to'.

Order of subentries

There are several different ways of ordering subentries. If the ordering is **alphabetical**, it may be *either* strictly alphabetical *or* alphabetical ignoring prepositions and conjunctions. Compare:

perception, 20, 25–7	perception, 20, 25–7
and past experience, 43–5	approaches to, 32–4
and sensation, 34, 36–7	criteria for, 46
approaches to, 32–4	of objects, 32–58
criteria for, 46	of others, 59–70
of objects, 32–58	and past experience, 43–5
of others, 59–70	selective, 43–7, 70–6
of self, 77–82	of self, 77–82
selective, 43–7, 70–6	and sensation, 34, 36–7

The strictly alphabetical version (left) may look neater but, if a reader is looking for a specific connection (for example, perception as it relates to sensation), being able to jump straight to the 's's in a long entry saves time.

Sometimes non-alphabetical systems are used for ordering the subentries. In a biography or history some groups of subentries might be arranged **chronologically**. Another system is to arrange by **first page number** thus:

> perception, 20, 25–7
>   approaches to, 32–4
>   of objects, 32–58
>   and sensation, 34, 36–7

Although simplest for the indexer to apply, the method is not generally recommended.

Usually when you are editing an index, you will work out which system the indexer is following and check that it has been applied consistently.

Marking up the index

As we saw at the beginning of the unit, a set-out index has a more complicated layout, requiring the specification of indents for subentries (normally 1 em of set), turnover lines of main entries and turnover lines of subentries. (In the example both of these were indented 2 ems of set.)

If the index has been typed in a consistent way (or is on disk), general instructions about indention (on the first folio) will be enough, with specific marking of any places where the typesetter may be confused about whether to run on or to start a new line.

If the index is inconsistent or messily typed, it should be marked throughout. Use a *different* colour to mark the indents so as to avoid confusion with any transpositions to correct the alphabetical ordering. (As in a run-on index, a fuller typographical mark-up, by editor or designer, would indicate the type size and measure, etc., as well as the indention.)

Now do Exercise 29.2

Edit and mark indents in this set-out index. This time, go through each stage of the suggested routine. Again list any points you would have to check against the proofs or other parts of the index copy.

Review of Exercise 29.2

Check your work against the sample answer on pp. 170–1. Your marked script should look less confusing than this because you will have used a distinctive colour to mark the indents. The question marks indicate the further checks needed (not listed this time but discussed below).

Under 'action', it is just possible (though unlikely) that what was intended was a large entry all about *collective* action (including its consequences and purpose) and just one page number relating to individual action: in that case you would add a comma after 'action' and run on the next line. (A glance at the relevant pages of the proof would tell you whether this interpretation was correct.)

The entry 'behaviour' followed by a solitary page reference seems odd. Clearly *much* of the book concerns behaviour (actions, choices, etc.) so you should look up p. 8 and *either* add an explanatory phrase *or* transfer the p. 8 reference to another suitable heading (eliminating this entry). The fact that p. 8 is early in the book suggests that this might be a category the indexer started with and then forgot or rejected.

The question mark beside 'choice, maximization of' is just a reminder to check for -ize or -ise spellings in the proofs (many people automatically type such words in their own way). The other queries involve oddities in page numbers.

The general instruction to use an en rule for a range of numbers does not, of course, cover en rules between words: 'cost–benefit analysis' must be specifically marked.

Remember that many classical names, such as Aristotle, require no first name or initials; even in more modern times the same would apply to Michelangelo or Madonna.

Headwords and order

There are options in the treatment of 'chosen' but a change of some sort is obligatory. A headword may be a noun or a compound of adjective (or noun acting as adjective) *and* noun ('nursery gardens' and 'peach trees' in Exercise 29.1; 'Christian Science' and 'cost–benefit analysis' here). A **purely adjectival headword**, however, is not good indexing practice. The reason for this is that each entry must be a logical unit: the only connection between 'chosen lifestyle' and 'chosen people' is linguistic. Similarly,

common: law, 20; sense, 60; toad, 85

or

nursery: gardens, 20; songs, 60

would be nonsensical.

One solution for 'chosen' is shown in the sample answer. A preferable alternative might be to index 'lifestyle, chosen' under 'l' and/or to add 'of lifestyle' as a subentry under 'choice'. You would have to check the relevant proof pages before deciding on the best solution. The familiar phrase 'chosen people', however, would *not* be right under 'p' as 'people, chosen'. In making such decisions, think which headwords are most likely to occur to the reader.

As you will see from the entries beginning 'charity' and 'Christian' there is no reason why consecutive entries should not start with the same word. Indeed proper names (such as the Charity Commission) *must* constitute separate entries. ('The' is not required except where the title of a poem is indexed; in that case the word will be included – either at the beginning or after a comma at the end – but ignored for alphabetical ordering.)

'Christianity' and 'Christian Science' demonstrate the difference between two methods of putting entries into alphabetical order: **letter by letter** and **word by word**. The sample answer, by leaving 'Christianity' before 'Christian Science', opts for letter-by-letter order ('ni' comes before 'n S'); the word-by-word system would switch them because the word 'Christian' on its own comes before the word 'Christianity'. Either system is acceptable provided it is consistently applied. The reckoning of alphabetical order in an index always stops at the first comma in an entry. For example, if 'charity, and justice' was 'charity, not justice' it would still come before 'Charity Commission' in *both* systems.

It is usual (though not essential) to be consistent about whether the abbreviation comes first in an entry, with the explanation in parentheses (as for CIA here) or the full version first with the abbreviation in parentheses (perhaps generally a preferable style). You can, however, legitimately vary the style according to which is more likely to be looked up (so here the abbreviation is more familiar than the full name). As in the text, unexplained abbreviations should be avoided.

Where the abbreviation comes first, it is usually ordered (as here) just like other words; alternatively, all abbreviations may be listed at the beginning of the relevant letter block.

Cross-checks

'Reading back' from subentries to main entries must not involve reading the headword twice, as in '[choice], and autonomy over [choice]'. The subentry may have a clarifying conjunction or preposition *either* at the beginning *or* at the end, but not both.

Although, as we have seen, the reader may be expected to switch without difficulty between understanding the headword before and after the subentry, the headword should consistently be treated *as a noun*. In one of these subentries, 'choice' had to be understood adjectivally ('choice maximization'); with the addition of 'of' it reverts to being a noun ('maximization of choice').

In checking the subentries you will have noticed several **reciprocal** or nearly reciprocal entries. The most precisely reciprocal pair was 'choice, and autonomy' and its converse, 'autonomy, choice as'. In such a pairing the page numbers listed should be the same.

Other similar instances were not precisely reciprocal: 'action, and consequences' has many of the same references as 'consequences' alone but there is no need to worry that it does not have them all (although it could be worth checking whether '121'

should be '121–2'). In real life cross-checking such entries within the index *systematically* is impracticable but you may happen upon them.

In your regular checking of cross-references remember to ensure, not only that the entry is there and that spelling and wording tally, but that it is *useful* to the reader. For example, the cross-reference in 'agreement' has been deleted because it offers no additional page numbers. Alternatively, you could eliminate the page numbers after 'agreement' and simply put *'see* consensus'. If the entry for 'agreement' had to take up three lines (as 'consensus' does) that would be the better option. However, a single-line entry that gives the reader information, rather than redirection, is often preferable.

'Agreement' and 'consensus' provide another example of synonyms, but in this case of main entries. Synonymous *sub*entries, as we have seen, are best amalgamated ('heaps of'/'piles of' in Exercise 29.1 and 'choice, as aim', 'choice, as goal' here). For synonymous main entries, the aim is rather to avoid a **split entry**, where some page numbers appear under one of the synonyms and some under the other. Instead, *either* include all the page numbers under one of the words and have a cross-reference under the other word (in case some readers think of that one first) *or* list all page numbers in both places (in which case no cross-reference is needed). This was the course chosen for 'agreement' and 'consensus' in the sample answer.

You may have thought 'choice, increase in' and 'choice, maximization of' were synonymous subentries too, but the meaning may not be quite the same – the first could be outside the individual's control, whereas the second implies will-power.

More complex layout

When you are reading the proofs of a set-out index, check carefully that the instructions on the indention of subentries and turnover lines have been followed throughout. In a more complex index there may be not just main entries and subentries but also **sub-subentries**. As with subentries, the distinctions are made clear either by punctuation or by indention. So both levels may be run on, with different punctuation; or both may be set out with different indention; or (perhaps most satisfactorily) you can adopt a mixed style with the subentry set out and the sub-subentry run on.

General principles of indexing

Despite the points made about 'behaviour' in Exercise 29.2, in general do resist the temptation to

Sample answer to Exercise 29.2

(ch hd)   INDEX

Accountability, 129, 131

action

? □collective, 2, 200   (en rule throughout)

and consequences, 1, 3, 4, 9–12, 69–70, 75–7, 90, □ 121, 195, 200

and purpose, 4

action │ individual, 199

agreement, 61–4, 66–7, 178 │ see also Consensus

altruism

③ □and self-interest, 10–12, 132, 202

② satisfaction from, 81, 84

① the limits of, 15–16

Aristotle, on justice, 31, 32

autonomy

□choice as, 98, 102, 112–15, 117

and rights, 124–5, 133–4, 137

? behaviour, 8

Buddhism, and morals, 57, 69–71

capitalism, and morals, 63, 65–6

censure, social, 21–2

certainty, 201

charity, and justice, 43–4

Charity Commission, the 64, 80

A │ Christianity, and morals, 60–68

Christian Science, 70–2

to fo. 2

Main entry turnovers indent 2 ems of set throughout

Subentry turnovers indent 2 ems of set throughout

amalgamate. Good indexing practice avoids amalgamation into lengthy entries under a few headwords; it favours division into small but meaningful categories. Cross-reference between them is kept to a minimum. After all, at some level everything is connected with everything else or it would not be in the same book: only the closest connections are worth noting.

A good index breaks the subject matter up into logical components, under the headwords most likely to occur to the reader. It will not simply mirror the chapter heads and subheads (although these may form the bones of the structure). Its function is to link, to connect, to show how similar topics are dealt with in different chapters.

It should be possible to read an index and acquire a good idea of the content of the book and the balance of the discussion. The main subjects, however, may not appear at all – in *The Life History of the Frog* there might be no entry for 'frog' or 'life history' but only for 'tree frog', 'reproductive cycle', etc.

Further reading

An excellent short introduction to the skills of the indexer is to be found in:

M.D. Anderson, *Book Indexing* (Cambridge University Press, Cambridge, 1971)

The British Standards Institution set revised guidelines in:

BS 3700: 1988

Butcher, *Copy-editing* gives helpful advice on the editor's role.

UNIT 30

Permissions and Libel

Although the heading picks out the two problems that loom largest, this unit aims to introduce you briefly to all the legal aspects of editing. Unlike the rest of the course, it cannot even hope to be applicable internationally, except in very general terms. Wherever you are working, find out about the copyright and libel laws, and any other laws about political and social comment, freedom of information, blasphemy, obscenity, etc. If the books or journals you work on are sold around the world you may need legal guidelines from overseas representatives.

You are not expected to be an expert on the law but simply to be alert to potential problems, so that you can bring them to the attention of the commissioning editor or author and set in train sensible precautions.

Such precautions would include:

- seeking permission to use copyright material
- asking for a **waiver** (an agreement not to sue) from someone mentioned or shown in the book
- seeking legal advice on the chances of a successful libel action against your firm

---

Now do Exercise 30.1 G

Review of Exercise 30.1

1 Names of characters are not usually patented or made into registered trade marks, which would give them incontrovertible legal protection. Similarly, there is *no* copyright in a title, so there could, for example, easily be two works entitled *New French Course* or indeed *Nouvelle Cuisine*.

There is, however, an offence called **passing off**, which the publishers of a book called *Noddy at the Races* that was not written by Enid Blyton, or *James Bond in Trouble* not written by Ian Fleming, would be committing. The point is that you and the author appear to be passing the book off as the real thing, taking advantage of a ready market you have not built up yourselves.

Even if Donald's name does not appear in the title and the character is drawn quite differently, it is certainly not worth tangling with Walt Disney. Action: change the name throughout. The drawings too (here and in general) should not look like any published character.

2 This could certainly be a problem. You or the author must check the register at Companies House to make sure that no firm of that name, or a similar name, exists in the area, especially not a firm involved in any kind of food-processing activity.

3 Edinburgh is big enough and its councillors numerous enough for this to cause no problem, *provided* the details of the fictional councillor's life or activities do not match up at all closely with a real individual's. You might require an assurance from the author on this point. Authors do naturally draw on their friends, acquaintances – and indeed enemies – for particular characteristics, sometimes even forgetting the origin as the characters take on lives of their own.

Using a real location as the setting is not uncommon. Although precise addresses will usually be fictional – tourists are often disappointed to find no 221B Baker St – a character walking down Princes St, or the Champs Elysées, harmlessly helps the reader to picture the story.

If the setting is not a city but a small town or village, the name of the place should be fictitious. Remember that *just* changing a name is not enough if the internal evidence still makes the setting unmistakable to a local person, especially if, say, a councillor, vicar or butcher is involved in murky deeds.

4 This is perfectly normal and acceptable under the **fair dealing** provision of the Copyright Designs and Patents Act 1988, which in this respect makes no alteration to the Copyright Act 1956. Provided there is sufficient acknowledgement, 'fair dealing with a work **for the purpose of criticism or review**' is not an infringement of copyright. There are similar 'fair dealing' exemptions for the purpose of reporting current events and for research and private study.

The Act itself does not impose any limit on the amount quoted under this rule. In law, therefore, the only argument is over whether the quotation is genuinely for purposes of criticism or review. So gratuitous quotation, or using someone else's words to avoid having to think up one's own, would probably be seen as unfair.

Despite its lack of legal foundation, a code of practice has, regrettably, grown up that defines what is 'fair' much more mechanically, not in terms of the use but the *length* of the extract. A common convention is to apply for permission (as discussed below) for a prose extract of more than around 400 words, and for even a couple of lines of a poem or song.

Both the restrictions and exemptions in the Act relate to 'the work as a whole or any **substantial part** of it'. By implication, therefore, a non-substantial part may be freely used for any kind of purpose. Neither law nor practice, however, offers a reliable definition of 'substantial part', except to agree that the significance of the content, not the length, would be the criterion.

(The similar copyright exemption for **fair use** in American law does spell out the criteria for fairness, including amount as well as use, but again gives no specific number of words.)

5 Permission would certainly be required for this level of quotation from one source. There is a possibility too that it would be refused because your book might be seen as competing too closely with the textbook. So you, your rights department or the author must find out at an early stage whether permission will be granted.

A much less easy problem for *you* to spot is **plagiarism**. The commissioning editor and expert readers who report on the project before acceptance should be sufficiently aware of the competing books to recognize passages that duplicate other works without acknowledging the fact. This is a serious offence, for which the publisher as well as the author can be sued: if you have any suspicions, alert the commissioning editor. An author who 'solved' the problem posed here by paraphrasing the textbook, instead of quoting it directly, would be guilty of plagiarism.

6 This doesn't come under the fair dealing rule because the passages are not being used for purposes of criticism or review, but as exercises. You would have to apply for permission for any passages within copyright (see below). In this context the length of the passages is immaterial (although something *very* short might count as 'non-substantial'). Look out particularly for genuine examination questions, which always require permission.

For an anthology or collection of readings, similarly, you must seek permission for any passages within copyright, although there are limited exemptions for collections to be used solely in schools.

A passage remains **within copyright** until seventy years after its publication, or seventy years after its author's death, whichever happens later. (The 1988 Act abolished the rule that unpublished material enjoyed copyright indefinitely; the term of copyright was raised from fifty years to seventy in mid-1995.) Note that there may be separate copyright in an edition or translation of the work of a long-dead author.

7 Although the fair dealing convention discussed above applies as much to artistic works as literary ones, it is less frequently invoked. Most publishers apply for permission to reproduce all illustrations, whatever their use. As you learned in Unit 25, 'after' implies significant adaptation of a figure. If this is extensive enough to render the acknowledgement a mere courtesy, no permission may be necessary. If, on the other hand, the adaptation changes the meaning or purpose of the original, you may need permission even to adapt it. So the appropriate action will very much depend on the circumstances. In general, it is safest to apply for permission.

8 Naturally such photos are sometimes essential but, wherever a partial photo (for example one not showing the face) would be equally instructive, crop to ensure anonymity. If a face has to be shown, a black oblong over the eyes or mouth can disguise it. (In addition, always mask a hospital number or other identification.) If any part of the subject will be recognizable (even by inference), you need written permission from both the patient and the clinician. Take similar precautions for photos of people in prison, etc.

The danger in this case is that the subject may sue for bringing into disrepute or breach of confidence:

the *subject* of a photo does not have rights under copyright law. The copyright in a photo normally belongs to the photographer. A photo library may handle the permissions administration (just as publishers or literary agents may handle such matters for an author). The copyright in an employee's work belongs to the employer but this does not cover freelance or contract work. So if a photographer is commissioned to take pictures for a project, the contract must spell out the ownership of the original material and both **economic** and **moral rights** (terms introduced in the 1988 Act). Moral rights include the right to be named as author and the right to object to derogatory treatment of the work. They apply equally to literary and artistic works.

9 Such an autobiography without a measure of revelation is hardly going to sell, and people in the public eye necessarily become more tolerant of exposure than a private individual. As far as practicable, however, you would ask for waivers from those concerned. You will certainly need assurances from the author that the stories are true to the best of his or her belief. A libel lawyer should be consulted if serious allegations are made, even where the author has evidence to support them.

10 Politicians become accustomed to being the butt of jokes and would usually find their reputations damaged more by rising to such treatment than by the publication of the satire itself. As in the case of the autobiography, the publisher has to weigh the risk, that is, the likelihood that someone will in fact sue.

Permission-seeking

In a contract with a publisher, the author usually guarantees that the work is original and/or that all necessary copyright permissions have been cleared. Your role is often therefore just to check that this has been done or advise on what permissions are needed. In an anthology (for text) or an illustrated book (for photographs), on the other hand, the publisher often takes full responsibility.

Even where fees are to be paid by the author, some publishers prefer to take on the permissions administration (writing to and chasing the relevant **copyright-holders**). This may be done by a specialist rights department or a picture researcher, but editors often become involved. Even if you are not the one actually writing for permission, you may have to pass on the appropriate source details to the person responsible.

Don't forget that *separate* permission is essential if you decide to use one of the illustrations appearing inside a book on the jacket or cover. This will almost always be at the publisher's expense, rather than the author's.

Now do Exercise 30.2   **G**

Review of Exercise 30.2

As the exercise indicates, for text you usually write to the publisher for permission in the first instance. In his or her contract an author gives the publisher the right to publish the book. **Subsidiary rights**, which include quotation, translation, serialization and film, often also become the publisher's responsibility in exchange for a share of the proceeds. (The publisher may or may not have to obtain the author's specific consent in each instance.) Alternatively, an author may retain some or all subsidiary rights, in which case they are often administered by a **literary agent**. If the publishers do not handle the relevant rights, they should forward your letter or tell you where to re-apply.

Make sure that you write to the *originating* publisher: if different firms publish **cased** (hardback) and paperback editions, the originator is normally the hardback publisher; if there are US and UK editions, you or the author should look carefully at the **copyright page** (the verso following the title page, as we shall see in Unit 31) to find out which of them originated the book. Again, this just saves time: you should be redirected if you pick the wrong one.

Frequently in the case of illustrations, and occasionally in the case of text, the work you want to reproduce does not originate in the book where the author has seen it. A poetry anthology, for example, gathers poems from many different sources. When you are asking for source details, stress that the author must look in a book's acknowledgements to find the true origin – perhaps an art gallery or photo library or (in the case of a poem or figure) an earlier book.

Under **section A**, you need to give exact bibliographical details – the author, title, date (not the publisher obviously, because that is who you are writing to), and pages on which the extract appears. All these will usually have been supplied by the author.

In addition, say approximately how many words you want to quote (in the case of poetry, how many lines) because that will affect the payment demanded. You should also mention any omissions **or** amendments that the author is proposing to make.

It is usually a good idea to attach a photocopy of the extract (or figure, etc.) to your letter. You may want to send other material too (for example critical comment on the passage), so that the copyright-holder cannot claim later that he or she didn't know how the piece was to be used.

Under **section B**, give

- the author and title of your publication
- the projected publication date (month and year)
- the editions for which you seek rights (cased and paperback, cased only, paperback only, etc.)
- the initial print run – cased and paperback as necessary
- the projected **list price** (retail price) of each edition
- the kind of book, whether educational, general, etc. (at least if you want to do any special pleading on fees)
- the rights you seek (see below)
- the market area in which it is to be sold (see below)

Usually the rights you ask for will be 'non-exclusive English language rights'. If, on the other hand, your firm wishes to translate a whole book, you need *exclusive* English language rights. (Translation involves substantial outlay and competition would be detrimental.) If the book you are originating is to appear in different language editions, ask for those (non-exclusive) language rights as well.

The market area is likely to be *either* the world *or* the world excluding the United States (*or* excluding North America) *or* the UK and the Commonwealth. Acquiring rights for the United States (or for North America, which includes Canada) can double the fee, so you need to be sure that sales there will justify the extra cost. If the book is intended for sale only within the UK, or for that matter only within India or Egypt, confine your application to rights for that market.

The initial print run, price and kind of book all help the copyright-holder to set an appropriate fee: rates are normally graduated according to the kind of project. The original permission should cover you for reprints. On the other hand, many permission-granting letters (for both text and illustrations) stipulate 'this edition only', so you have to apply all over again for a new edition. (We touched on the differences between reprints and new editions in Unit 17 and return to the question in Unit 31.)

Acknowledgements

The replies granting permission will stipulate:

- the form of the acknowledgement (and possibly its position – as we saw in Unit 28, a few copyright-holders insist on its inclusion in full on the same page as the illustration or extract)
- the fee payable (for artwork and photos, as we saw in Unit 26, there may be separate invoices – often arriving at different stages – for supply of the original and for the right to reproduce it)
- requests for complimentary copies to be sent on publication: make sure that these are noted and fulfilled

As we have seen, a source should always be given (whether or not permission is necessary). It may appear in parentheses or notes (for text and tables) or in the caption (for figures). Alternatively, all sources may be gathered together in a list of illustrations or in acknowledgements. For example, many of the exercises used in this course are based on sources other than my imagination but to state their exact origins in place might have proved distracting: the details therefore form a separate acknowledgements section at the end of the Exercises. Even when sources do appear within the text or in captions, the copyright-holders are usually also thanked in the acknowledgements where specific permission has been granted.

A general expression of gratitude is followed by a list, usually alphabetical, of those being thanked. (If both text quotations and illustrations are involved, deal with them in separate paragraphs.) The thanks to each individual copyright-holder may list several different items.

An alternative system is to follow the numerical order of the plates, exercises, etc. Again if several come from one source, they can all be grouped together.

If photos or drawings, for example, are unnumbered you may need to give the page numbers (and perhaps note 'bottom', 'top', etc.) for identification. Since acknowledgements often cannot be finalized until page proof, this is not a significant drawback.

Do, however, start the process of permission-seeking as early as possible. You may be redirected; you often have to send reminders before receiving a reply; permission may even be denied, in which case you (or the author) will have to start again with a substitute passage or illustration.

When compiling the acknowledgements, or checking those compiled by someone else, resist the urge (instinctive, I hope, by now) to standardize. Follow the *precise wording* of the credit line asked for by a copyright-holder, even if it seems repetitive or inconsistent with other copyright-holders' requests. This is particularly important in acknowledgements for works of art. Museums and galleries require full and precise compliance with their instructions: in some cases legal rights as well as benefactors' sensibilities may be at stake. You may, however, have to rearrange the order of information, for example if the permission-granter has phrased the credit line on the assumption that it will come at the end of the caption rather than in an amalgamated list. Have the actual letters in front of you as you write the acknowledgements. Never make up a form of words in the hope that the permission will arrive any day.

If you receive no reply to two reminders, or if you have failed (after reasonable efforts) to trace the copyright-holder, include a disclaimer at the end of the acknowledgements saying that you have been unable to contact the copyright-holders of (for example) Figures 6.1 and 8.7 but will be happy to include an acknowledgement in future reprints.

Now do Exercise 30.3

Remember to include an introductory sentence.

Review of Exercise 30.3

Check your work against the alternative sample answers on the next page. The handwritten figure numbers on the permissions letters show how James Francis has been keeping track of which correspondence relates to which figure. This is a great help when you are compiling the acknowledgements. (The other figures in the book are presumably the author's own.)

Spelling out 'Figure' for diagrams in *our* book and abbreviating to 'Fig.' for theirs is not essential but helps to distinguish between the two. The style is legitimate if our book spells the word out in text references to figures but abbreviates to 'Fig.' in references to other works (as discussed in Unit 14).

The exercise demonstrates the variety of forms a permission-granting letter may take. In fact the spectrum is even wider, ranging from a close-printed contract to the return of your application letter with a handwritten 'OK – £20'.

You will have noticed that Longman asks for the acknowledgement for figures to appear immediately below the figure, that is, in the caption. Since they are not specific about the form of words, giving source information there in your normal reference style should be sufficient (see Unit 28), though you would include them in the acknowledgements as well, as a courtesy. If this had been permission to reproduce a passage of text, the request for acknowledgement on the copyright page could be awkward. As we'll see in Unit 31, although some publishers do include acknowledgements there, a separate acknowledgements section is more usual. You might have to discuss with Longman whether this would be an acceptable alternative.

American permissions often give more specific instructions on the form of the acknowledgement. For legal reasons it is particularly important to include the **copyright symbol**, date and name of the copyright-holder in the credit line.

The Sage permissions form also includes a section (not ticked in this case) enjoining you to write separately to the copyright-holder. This might incur an additional fee or other conditions and you would thank both (publisher and author or literary agent) in the acknowledgement.

Further reading

A helpful but weighty volume on copyright law and practice is:

M.F. Flint, *User's Guide to Copyright* (Butterworth, London, 3rd edition, 1990)

Sample answers to Exercise 30.3

Version A - alphabetical

We are grateful to the following for permission to reproduce copyright figures:

Gerald Duckworth & Co Ltd for Figures 2.3 and 5.2 from A.E. Smith, Essentials of Management (1986), Figs 3.3 and 4.2; Longman Group UK Limited for Figure 6.2 from Henry Joseph, Business Sense and Nonsense (1988), Fig. 3.1; and Sage Publications, Inc. for Figure 5.1 from Sara Miller McCune, 'On being an evaluation publisher', Evaluation Practice, 10, 2 (1989), Fig. 2, copyright © 1989 by Sara Miller McCune.

Version B - by figure number

We are grateful for permission to reproduce the following copyright material:

Figures 2.3 and 5.2 from A.E. Smith, Essentials of Management (1986), Figs 3.3 and 4.2, by permission of Duckworth; Figure 5.1 from Sara Miller McCune, 'On being an evaluation publisher', Evaluation Practice, 10, 2 (1989), Fig. 2, copyright © 1989 by Sara Miller McCune, reprinted by permission of Sage Publications, Inc.; and Figure 6.2 from Henry Joseph, Business Sense and Nonsense (1988), Fig. 3.1, by permission of Longman Group UK Limited.

UNIT 31

Prelim Pages

The acknowledgements section we looked at in the previous unit is just one item that may be in the preliminary (prelim) pages. In this unit I introduce the others, and some of the variations you will come across in different books. The author usually sends in a list of contents; preparing the remainder of the prelims is the responsibility of the publishing firm, often in the person of the editor.

In a book going through a paste-up stage (or planned from the beginning in double-page spreads), prelims and text are often numbered in a single sequence, using arabic numbers. In other books, partly following tradition but more importantly to ensure flexibility, the prelims have roman numerals; arabic page 1 then begins the main body of the book. For both roman and arabic sequences, as we saw in Unit 3, odd numbers are always on the right (the **recto**); even numbers always on the left (the **verso**).

Half-title and title page

Many books have a **half-title** (a recto, p. i) that shows nothing but the title; frequently a blank verso follows. The reason for this apparently wasteful style is that the first **leaf** (recto and verso) of a **cased** (hardback) book is glued to the **endpapers** (the thicker paper attaching the book to the case), so that the book only falls open naturally at the *second* recto (p. iii).

In fiction the half-title is sometimes more profitably used, either for a blurb about the book or for biographical details about its author, both of which will also appear on the **jacket** (in the case of a hardback) or **cover** (in the case of a paperback). We return to blurbs in Unit 32.

In any book the **half-title verso** (p. ii, facing the title page) may be used, rather than left blank. It may record the author's previous publications or form the **series page**, listing other books in the series and perhaps giving further details about its scope and aims. (Alternatively, the name of the series, and

volume number if any, may be noted on the half-title and/or on the title page.)

Educational books frequently start more directly, with the title page. (Since they are often in paperback, the problem of the half-title sticking to the case doesn't arise.) Indeed, sometimes space is so tight that **inside covers** contain information normally included in prelims.

The **title page** (p. iii in most books) gives all the important details: title, subtitle, author(s) or editor(s), sometimes a translator or illustrator as well, publisher's name or **imprint** (many firms publish under several different imprints) and perhaps a **logo** (symbol). (Traditionally, place of publication was included too but this is less usual now.)

Copyright page

The **copyright page** or **imprint page** or **title verso** (p. iv) gives the legal and technical details about the book. These should normally include:

- the full registered name of the publisher

- the publisher's address (sometimes several addresses or a list of places)

- the **copyright notice**, that is, the name of the copyright-holder and the copyright date (see below)

- the date of first publication and **printing history**, that is, any new editions and reprints (by your firm) since that time (see below)

- a **rights clause** (usually a standard form of words reserving all rights in the work – not a legal necessity but common practice)

- the **ISBN** (International Standard Book Number) and/or **CIP data** (the British Library's Cataloguing in Publication data, supplied in response to the publisher's application)

- the country in which the book is *printed* (essential

for legal purposes) and usually the printer's name and address

The author's contract should clarify who is to be the copyright-holder. Copyright often remains with the author, or it may belong to an institution that funded the work, or in the contract an author may assign copyright – not just the right to publish – to the publisher. If the author is dead, the correct form may be 'estate of …'.

A new edition acquires a new copyright date, so the copyright notice might read:

© James McManus 1976, 1984

There is, however, no new copyright in a reprint, even a reprint with corrections. As we saw in Unit 17, reprints may include lines (or even paragraphs) with minor amendments but should always have exactly the same pagination as the original. If there are major changes, the book should be called a new edition, in which case it also has a new ISBN.

Although the *copyright* date doesn't change for a reprint, the printing history should always be updated:

First published 1976

Second edition 1984

Reprinted 1986, 1987 (twice), 1989

A translation has its own copyright notice and printing history. The copyright-holder is sometimes the translator, more often the publisher who has paid for the translation. Certain details about the original publication must also be given on the copyright page: the language, the book's title in that language, the date, publisher and place of that publication and its copyright notice.

Now do Exercise 31.1

Review of Exercise 31.1

Check your work against the sample answer on p. 182. The order in which the information appears is immaterial but all the elements (as listed above) must be included.

On the title page, 'by' is only needed after 'edited' or 'translated', not before an author's name. The typographical style of the title will be decided by the designer: don't underline it for italic as you would a book title in the text or bibliography. Similarly, as we saw in Unit 17, no colon separates title and subtitle: they are simply differentiated typographically.

A copyright page form, such as the one provided for this exercise, saves time. (For this reprint in real life, of course, you would not have to draft the page from scratch because the printer would just add '1989' to the existing film.) The layout of the copyright notice on the form is naturally geared to new books but leaves you room to insert an alternative.

For the country in which the book is printed, it is customary to say 'in Great Britain' rather than 'in Scotland'.

Other prelim pages

None of the pages we have looked at so far (pp. i–iv) bears a page number in the printed book. The next page (p. v) is usually the contents and this is where **folios** (the typesetter's term for page numbers) begin. We return to the contents list in more detail after the next exercise.

Other prelims might include any of the following.

- A frontispiece (illustration) was traditionally an art-paper plate **tipped in** (pasted in by hand), facing the title page. Although expensive, this is sometimes still done, for example in a biography. The illustration facing the title page in an **integrated book** (where text and pictures are printed on the same paper) may similarly be called a frontispiece, now occupying the half-title verso. A map relating to the whole book might appear here but would more often be put on the verso at the end of the prelims, facing arabic page 1.

- A dedication ('To my mother', etc.) usually comes before the contents, preferably on a recto with verso blank.

- An epigraph (a short poem or other quotation) sums up the book's message or subject matter.

- Lists of illustrations, tables, etc., are not essential (unless they also contain acknowledgements) but can be helpful.

- A preface (usually by the author) and/or foreword (usually by someone else and so often put before the contents list) sets the book in context.

- Acknowledgements may be either the author's own thanks to colleagues and friends, or the more formal listing of permissions we looked at in Unit 30, or both.

- An introduction is usually longer than a preface and less personal, more closely concerned with the book's subject matter. If it is really a whole chapter and essential to an understanding of the book, the introduction is often better included with the main text, starting at arabic page 1. If, however, the introduction is likely to change radically in a new edition, it is best kept in the prelims, to minimize page numbering changes.

- Explanations of the abbreviations or symbols, a chronology of events, the dramatis personae, etc., may all appear in prelims; sometimes even a glossary, although this more often goes into the endmatter, especially if long.

- Notes on the contributors give biographical details, or at least the affiliations, of the authors of chapters in an edited volume.

Now do Exercise 31.2   **G**

Review of Exercise 31.2

I hope that the books you chose showed a fairly wide range of ingredients. The order may have conformed to a more predictable pattern but that too can differ widely.

At typescript stage you (or the designer) will usually instruct the typesetter 'new recto' at the beginning of each item in the prelims after the copyright page. Exceptions might be less important items (where you may say 'recto or verso') or pages that should be on a verso in order to face the title page or arabic page 1. Remember, however, that you must never have a blank recto (either in prelims or elsewhere in the book), whereas blank versos are common.

At page proof or paste-up, as we saw in Unit 29, you often have to squeeze or stretch a book in order to make it fit satisfactorily into an even working. As well as trying (within reason) to tailor the index, you often have to adjust the prelims. The separate roman numeral system enables you to do this without affecting the body of the book. Some items may have to shift from recto to verso; others to double up on one page; *in extremis* you might even drop the whole half-title leaf. Remember to think in terms of leaves: arabic page 1 must always be a recto, so you cannot have an odd number of prelim pages. (For example, if the last numbered page is xiii, it will be followed by a blank xiv.)

Contents pages

The contents list should mention all the prelim sections that follow it, except for the dedication and epigraph; it will also include the chapter headings and endmatter. As we saw in Exercise 5.2 (Politics of Resistance), part titles and (in an edited volume) the authors of chapters should appear too. Sometimes the A subheads within chapters are listed to give a fuller flavour of the coverage; in textbooks all levels of subhead may be included.

Check the author's contents list (and any other lists of tables, etc.), as you edit the typescript, to ensure that it is complete and that the wording of headings tallies exactly. Don't forget to add the index (if any) to the contents list, even though you will not as yet have copy for it. Similarly, include any other items still to come such as acknowledgements or a list of illustrations. Once you have done all the cross-checking, you may have to decide what to use as running heads (book title left and chapter head right *or* chapter head left and A head right, etc.) and, as you learned in Unit 5, to devise shortened versions where necessary.

Page numbers may appear on the contents list in the form '00', as they did in Exercise 5.2 (Politics of Resistance), since they cannot be added until paste-up or page proof. However, folio numbers can be helpful on a contents list, both for you while you edit and for the designer: if they have been given, don't delete them but show – either by boxing the whole list or by circling each number – that they are not to be set. Notice that it is quite common to omit page numbers against the part titles. As with an entry in a table (see Unit 25), the number goes against the last line of an entry, in this case the author's name.

Write at the top of the relevant folio of the typescript 'arabic pagination begins here'.

Now do Exercise 31.3

You will need a query sheet.

Sample answer to Exercise 31.1

Title
page

The Erl King

Michel Tournier

translated by

Barbara Bray

COLLINS
London

Copyright
page

William Collins Sons & Co Ltd

London · Glasgow · Sydney · Auckland

Toronto · Johannesburg

English translation
© William Collins Sons & Co Ltd   1972

First published 1972
Reprinted 1983, 1989

First published in French under the
title Le Roi des aulnes, 1970,
by Editions Gallimard, Paris
© Editions Gallimard 1970

British Library Cataloguing in Publication data

[TO FOLLOW]

ISBN 0 002 21212 9

Printed in Great Britain
by William Collins Sons & Co Ltd, Glasgow

Review of Exercise 31.3

'Table of' now looks old-fashioned; the words 'Chapter' and 'Page' are equally unnecessary in a contents list. Omitting 'Chapter' from the contents does *not* necessarily mean you must delete it in the chapter heads themselves (although many publishers do so). Here I would just make the chapter heads consistent by adding the word in the heading of Chapter 7 and showing that the title starts on a new line.

Equally out of favour are roman numerals for chapter numbers, although they are still quite often used to number the *parts*. In some books the number may be spelt out as a word in the chapter head; it is usually still given an arabic figure in the contents list (and probably in text cross-references). Here I'd change all the roman numerals to arabic and 'Five' in the chapter head to '5'. Again, the colon after the number in the contents is much better as an em space (or possibly a full stop).

You had to add 'Introduction' at the beginning of the contents list. Such unnumbered headings may *either* be indented to align with the first word of the other headings *or* be set full left. Although the book probably contains tables, it is not essential to include a list of them. You'd have to check whether there was a bibliography or further reading list at the end of the typescript; almost certainly there will be an index.

In this case boxing the folio numbers is simplest. As we have seen, an introduction is often best in the body of the book, rather than in prelims, so here I'd confirm the beginning of arabic pagination on the first folio of the introduction and by writing the page number '1' against it on the contents list.

You should have noticed too that Chapter 1 is disproportionately long. You would have to consider whether it should be split in two or perhaps other chapters united. Such restructuring would, of course, have to be discussed with the author.

Then there were some heading discrepancies. The shorter version of the title of Chapter 3 (wrongly called 4 in the chapter head itself) seems more likely in the context of the other chapter heads: in your query list you'd ask for confirmation both of the heading and the number change. (The chapters *might* be in the wrong order.) For Chapter 12, suggest to the author deleting the subtitle in the chapter head (or perhaps converting it into a first A subhead). This is preferable to adding it to the contents list: it gives no extra information and, in general, chapter heads should follow a similar pattern throughout. Again query which form of Chapter 15's title is most appropriate.

There were rather too many 'the's' in some chapter heads. Capitals must remain for the Bank of England (4) and the City (15) (and for Euromarkets in 10 if you didn't delete 'The').

Always read through the contents list *after* as well as before (and during) editing to make sure it offers a useful summary of the book's contents. Do also make time to *re-read the introduction* once you have edited a book. On the technical level, this is helpful because, surprisingly often, you may find you've spotted the *second* instance of an inconsistency rather than the first. On the more general level, you cannot really tell whether an introduction is helpful and accurate until you have read the book.

Further reading

Useful coverage is to be found in Butcher, *Copy-editing*.

UNIT 32
Jacket Blurbs

As we saw in Unit 31, a cased book often (though not necessarily) has a **jacket**; a paperback has a **cover**. The publisher's jacket or cover **blurb** (promotional copy) is sometimes written by the promotion or marketing department, sometimes by the commissioning editor, sometimes by the desk editor. Even if you are not responsible for writing blurbs, you may be checking them against your detailed knowledge of the book or proofreading them.

What goes on the jacket and cover

The **front panel**, often illustrated, will show the title (and sometimes the subtitle) and author. The designer needs to know whether the title or the author is the major selling point. The **spine** similarly gives title and author (sometimes surname only) and publisher's name and/or logo. An eye-catching spine is as important as a striking front panel. Notice that the spine always turns the same way on English language books: if you lay the book on its side with the front panel uppermost, you should be able to read the spine. (In parts of continental Europe the opposite convention is followed.)

On the jacket, the blurb about the book often comes on the **front flap** and biographical details about the author on the **back flap**. The **back panel** is more variously used, sometimes for a photo of the author, sometimes for books of related interest, sometimes for a continuation or repetition of the front panel illustration. The publisher's name often appears here too.

Other common ingredients, variously placed, are: series title and volume number if any, picture credit, designer's credit (if out of house), publisher's full address, ISBN and/or **bar code** (for computerized bookshops), place of printing.

On the cover, space is far more limited because there are no flaps: only the back panel is available. This will certainly carry a blurb about the book or review clippings if (as is common) the paperback is published after the hardback. It may also give some details about the author. The publisher's name, picture credit, designer's credit, ISBN and/or bar code must fit in too.

If more space is needed on a paperback, information can sometimes be printed on the **inside front cover** and/or **inside back cover**. This entails additional expense, however, as the cover then has to be printed twice. We saw in Unit 31 that, when space is tight within the book, items such as the contents, acknowledgements and copyright information may appear on the inside covers.

For the remainder of this unit we concentrate on the blurb about the book.

Non-fiction

The form of a blurb, like the jacket and cover design as a whole, depends entirely on the market, the readership you are targeting.

In an educational book, the blurb will often consist of a list of selling points giving purely practical information for the teacher, for example:

- Offers full coverage of the syllabus for … [naming specific examinations]
- Comprehension exercises follow each passage

In an academic, scientific or general non-fiction book, bringing out the major selling points is just as important but they are usually wrapped up in a more discursive blurb.

Publishers often send their authors a **marketing questionnaire**, asking for biographical details, suggestions of journals that might review the book and, most important for our purposes, a summary of what the book aims to do and how it differs from others already on the market. If you, as desk editor, are writing the blurb you are likely to have this completed questionnaire to hand, and perhaps some guidelines from the commissioning editor, as well as the typescript (especially the contents, introduction and conclusion).

The principles of blurb-writing are not unlike those we looked at in Units 8 and 12.

■ Seize the reader's attention in the first para. If the book is by an academic for academics, this is usually best achieved by stressing what is new or different about this particular work:

> Mary Douglas presents the first sophisticated analysis of ...

If, on the other hand, you aim to interest general readers, you may need first to show that the subject is important by putting it into a context they already know:

> Eastern Europe has undergone dramatic changes. What are the implications for the West? This book explores ...

Most readers will not wade right through your carefully constructed blurb but will buy the book – or be put off it – on the strength of the first para, maybe even the first sentence.

■ The conventional shape for a blurb is a pithy first para, followed by a more meaty description of the book's themes and coverage (in one or two paras), with a final para that summarizes and stresses who it is aimed at (which subject areas, whether students as well as lecturers, practitioners as well as academics, etc.).

■ The struggle to write a blurb usually revolves around avoiding repetition of words and phrases ('this book', 'the author', 'shows', 'provides') and excessive use of the passive or the verb 'to be', and managing to vary the pattern of sentences sufficiently, while keeping them short and direct. Achieving a well-turned blurb can, nevertheless, bring something of the satisfaction of writing a poem.

Now do Exercise 32.1

Review of Exercise 32.1

Compare your answer with the (genuine) sample on the next page, and with other people's versions if you are doing this course in class. The answer given is by no means perfect – certainly not in the poem category – but follows the classic pattern, keeping fairly close to the author's original, while bringing out the points stressed in the commissioning editor's brief.

Questions can be effective, especially when you are attempting, as here, to present opposing views clearly. These questions repeat 'is' reprehensibly but later on efforts are made to search for other verbs – 'offers ... evaluates ... examines ... analyses ... explores' – help, is the supply of synonyms running out? The welcome change of sentence pattern comes only just in time.

The author's summary demonstrates other points to watch out for. Phrases such as 'is intended to' or 'attempts to' are unnecessarily tentative. You should always assume that the book achieves what it sets out to do. Authors are often too modest; publishers equally often unwisely oversell their books. Look for the middle way of honest praise for the good points while suppressing the short-comings.

'This book', 'the author', etc., can become extremely tedious (worst of all, 'In this book, the author ...'). Switching occasionally to the book's title or the author's name gives more immediacy. Avoid a pedestrian catalogue: 'Part one shows ... In part two ... The conclusion claims ...'.

Fiction

Have you ever had a 'whodunnit' ruined for you by the blurb? Revealing who is murdered, for example, may not matter if the event happens on p. 5 but is disastrous if the tension built up in the first three chapters depends on guessing which one of the characters will be stabbed. In blurb-writing for fiction, the whole art lies in whetting the appetite without giving away the plot.

If the book's main feature is the beauty of the language, you may want to quote a short passage in your blurb to give the flavour. Again, be sure not to destroy its impact in place.

Now do Exercise 32.2

Sample answer to Exercise 32.1

This is the definitive analysis of a question of crucial importance to Northern Ireland: why are so many Catholics unemployed or in low-paid jobs? Is it the result of discrimination by Protestant employers? Or is it determined by factors within the Catholic community, such as large families, low educational qualifications and living in areas of long-term economic decline? Challenging both these opposed orthodoxies, the book offers a convincing analysis of the present position and evaluates the available remedies.

David Eversley examines the composition of the labour force by religion and socio-economic status. He analyses the employment structure, particularly the changing relative importance of manufacturing industry and the service sector. He explores changes in fertility and migration patterns, educational provision and attainment. Using census data, supplemented by later statistics where available, he also highlights sub-regional differences for all these factors.

He finds that long-entrenched discrimination has been exacerbated by the deepening recession affecting the whole country. While progress will necessarily be slow as long as general unemployment persists, the way forward lies in determined efforts to improve education and training combined with rigorous enforcement of anti-discrimination legislation.

As a detailed case study of religious discrimination in the labour market, the book will be of interest to scholars and professionals in social demography, sociology, political science, social administration, labour economics, policy studies and geography.

ISBN 0 8039 8203 8

Consolidation and Summary

Throughout the course, points learned in earlier units have cropped up again in later ones. In this final section the interweaving process goes still further. Each exercise combines specific major topics that were previously tackled separately. At the same time, each exercise presents the features most relevant to specific, very different, areas of publishing: a travel guide, a scholarly work, an instructional text and a short story. As always, everyone should tackle everything: although mixed in differing proportions, the same skills apply across the whole spectrum of publishing.

In this section *each exercise is the equivalent of a whole unit* earlier in the course. This is partly because they are longer but also because you should be using them to refresh your memory. Before tackling an exercise, look back and revise the relevant units; afterwards, follow up any points you had forgotten. Between them, the consolidation exercises review the whole course but in a fresh way.

A TRAVEL GUIDE

Here we combine the proofreading skills learned in Units 2–3 with the knowledge of typographical mark-up gained in Units 24–5. Check back to Unit 2 for proofreading techniques and symbols and the colours to use. Remember that when you are reading proofs you must make marks both in the margin and in the body of the text. Look back too at the examples of type specs and mark-up you met in Unit 25. In this exercise you do not have to do the mark-up yourself but you need to understand what the typesetter was being asked to do, not only by the editor but also by the designer. Refresh your memory too about the different stages of proof (Unit 3) and layout in columns (Unit 24).

Now do Exercise C.1

You are given a marked typescript, relevant excerpts from the type spec, and galley proofs because the book is complicated enough to require a paste-up. (An alternative way in which many such books would now be produced would be on a DTP system, where the pasting up may be done on screen.) Much of the book will be in two columns; some sections and many of the illustrations will stretch across the two columns.

A typescale (see Unit 24) (or pica rule and depth scale) is helpful but not essential: you should be able to judge any problems by eye alone. The typeface used in the proof is as specified (Garamond).

Review of Exercise C.1

The typescript mark-up

Before you check you own work, let's look at the editor's and designer's marking of the typescript. You will notice that it has been specifically marked for type size, measure and spacing of paragraphs because these vary in quite a complicated way. However, to keep the script as uncluttered as possible, headings have just been coded generically.

If you wanted to use generic coding for type size and measure too, the best way would be to draw lines down the margin in different colours of highlighter. Similarly, as we saw in Unit 5, a boxed section may be highlighted. (You would need to explain your system for the designer.) In two-colour work (for example in school texts), highlighter is particularly helpful for showing the use of the second colour. In Unit 15 we also saw its application to marking mathematics. (But remember that highlighter does not always photocopy satisfactorily, sometimes even obscuring the words meant to be highlighted.)

The idea of making a distinction in type size in this travel guide between the general introduction and the more detailed information on what to eat and see may have come either from the designer or from the editor. Remember that the whole process works best as a cooperative effort, each feeding in ideas rather than insisting on rigid demarcation.

The horizontal rules for the box can easily be put in by the typesetter; vertical rules often have to be added later as artwork (perhaps by your design department). You would mark them on the proof only if they were to be the typesetter's responsibility. (A DTP system copes more easily with verticals.)

Note that the A and B headings are hierarchical but X (the box head) is not necessarily superior or inferior to the B level. It flags a special category and so starts a new sequence, X, Y, etc. (see Unit 5). For simplicity the lowest level in the hierarchy ('China-town', etc.) is specifically marked for bold rather than coded as a heading (see the review of Exercise 27.2, Roots).

The X head has been specified as 10/12 pt caps above text set in 12/15 pt. An alternative that would give a similar (but not identical) result would be to specify 12 pt small caps. Often **spaced small caps** (or spaced caps) are thought more attractive. When typeset, Garamond spaced 10 pt caps would look like this:

FACTS AND FIGURES

The instruction 'spaced' can be part of the specification and/or the spacing may be marked in the typescript thus:

FACTS AND FIGURES

Even though all these headings are less than a line long, the specification gives the size in the form 10/12 pt, etc. The 2 pt leading would, however, only be relevant if some headings were to go on to a turnover line. Spacing around the headings is expressed in text lines (15 pts). (See Unit 25.)

Note the two different ways in which $\frac{1}{2}$-line spaces have been marked round material to be transposed (copy ll. 22 and 42): do whichever seems clearer in the context but double-check to make sure the spaces are marked to go where you intend them. When you are transposing a phrase from one line to the next (as on copy ll. 9–10), be careful not to circle it completely, or to make it look as though you are underlining for italic.

Errors in the proof

Now check your work against the answer opposite. In one-column setting, mentally divide the text down the middle and mark corrections in the left and right margins, as you learned in Unit 2. In two-column setting with a narrow space between the columns, mark in the outer margins. In three-column work it is safest to mark all corrections in the right margin of each column.

Remember that, as proofreader, your role is to carry out the editor's system. So, for example, even if you prefer the typesetter's capitalization of East and West (proof l. 2), you should follow the typescript and mark them lower case. Nor would you dispute at this stage the clear marking to close up degrees, both of latitude and temperature (copy ll. 20–1). The typeset style is a valid option; if thin or normal spaces had been wanted, they should have been marked in the typescript (see Unit 15).

Change the editor's system only when it is plain wrong (as opposed to representing a valid alternative to what you may see as the norm) or where it has been applied inconsistently (in which case it is usually best to take the course that requires least proof-correction).

So, for example, you could not tell from this piece whether 'foodstall' (proof l. 44) occurs more frequently than 'food-stall' (proof l. 32) and would pencil queries against all the instances until you could be sure which way to standardize. For this reason it is very helpful to have the editor's style sheet (see Unit 14) to hand when you are proofreading.

When you have decided between 'food-stall' and 'foodstall', you will mark the inconsistent one in blue as an editor's (not typesetter's) error. Other blue (author's and editor's) corrections were: proof l. 2, deletion of 'e' (the word 'arrive' was carelessly deleted on copy l. 2 – always include a short upright stroke at the beginning and end of a deletion, as on copy l. 3); the space on proof l. 7 (copy l. 9); on proof l. 11 the transposition of the full stop and closing parens (copy l. 14); on proof l. 13 the transposition of 'always' and 'be' (essential but wrongly shown on copy l. 15); the second misspelling of 'aromatic' (proof l. 27; copy l. 27); on proof l. 40 the deletion of 'places' (almost certainly the editor's intention was to make the two B heads parallel – 'What to eat',

Singapore — City of Contrasts

Odd and new, East and West meet in Singapore. Arriving at the super-efficient Changi Airport you drive in along a brand-new highway lined with the beautiful maintained gardens earn Singapore the name the 'Garden city'. But a block from the towering skyscrappers of the center, the crumbling, busting shops of Chinatown epitomize exotic Asia. One night you'll dine at a ultra sophisticated gormet French restaurant, the next you'll be eating an equaly delicious rice and curry disk with your fingers of a banana-leaf plate in the street.

FACES AND FIGURES

Singapore conslists of one island and about 57 ever smaller ones, all together a making land area on about 620 sq km (or 215 sq. miles.) The impresive government land reclamation project mean than such estimates must be always approximate and rapidly become out of date. The main island mesures 42 km (26 miles) by 23 14 miles.

The climate is hot as the city lies just 1 N of the equator. The average temparature of 36.7°C (82°F) varies a little though the year and the average relative humidity in 84%.

The language of administration and business is English, official languages are mandarin Chinese, Malay, and Tamil (from Southern India), reflecting the ethic mix of the 2.5 million population.

What to eat

The hallmark of the cuisine is vargity: Chinese Malay, Indonesian, European and (more recently) Japanese restaurants as well as the unique richly aromatic Nonya or Perajakan cuisine. Dried spices and aromatic herbs are pounded together from the rempa, than fried in oil before Assam liquid or cocanut oil is added. Pork, mushrooms, soy beans, and shallots all add to the flavor.

Don't ignore the ubiquitous food stalls. They serve all kind of foods. Best loved by Singaporeans are *cha shod fun* — slices of barbicued pork coloured and served with rice and soy sauce gravy, and Hainnese chicken rice — boiled chicken served with fragranc rice and a dip consisting of chilli, garlic and ginger.

(A) salt-fish and eggs are common ingredients 0 Soy sauce, garlic.

What places to see

Chinatown typifies tradition Chinese life style, architecture, and business. Pick out souvenirs; explore the ancient temples; eat from the foodstalls.

Little Araby the Muslim district, centres on the Sultan mosque and offers and offers batiks basketware, jewellery and spices.

Raffle Hotel a still elegant reminder of British colonial days. Sample the famous Singapore sling'.

Orchard Road is known as the 'Bond St of Asia': a beautiful shady avenue, it is one of the most exclusive shopping areas of the world.

The Botanic Gardens began in Victrian times, offers a lake, masses of flowering topical shrubs and manificent specimens of tree spldes. There is also a extensive orchid collection. Open 5 am – 11 pm of weekdays; 6 am to midnight at the weekends.

'What to see' – but he or she forgot to delete the original); the deletion of stops in 'a.m.' on proof l. 61 (copy l. 52).

Some of these may seem unduly harsh on the editor (especially in the context of this abominable typesetting) but remember that typesetters are not supposed to make sense of the material but to *follow the editor's marking*.

The en rule, instead of an ordinary hyphen, in 'banana-leaf plate' (proof l. 8) would be quite wrong: it would imply a plate made of both a banana and a leaf. The form of dash marked in the typescript is a spaced em rule, necessitating corrections on proof ll. 36, 37. The spaced en rule in '5 am – 11 pm' (proof l. 60) is usual because it makes the meaning clearer than a closed-up en (as you would have in 5–11 pm).

I hope you did notice that '11 pm' had been set as two 'l's instead of two ones. They look odd because they are close together but more specifically you can see the difference between one and 'l' in this typeface by looking at proof l. 15 (compare 'lies' with '10').

In fact, of course, it should not be '10' but '1°' on proof l. 15. Strictly speaking a degree sign is not a superior (the same goes for a **prime** such as x') but it is probably safest to mark it as such here since a full-size zero has been set. It is certainly worth clarifying by writing 'deg' (circled). The same abbreviation is used to clarify this symbol where necessary in a typescript.

You would want to avoid the occurrence of the same word at the ends of proof ll. 15 and 16 but this will be accomplished anyway because of the addition earlier in the line. On proof l. 41, again because of the additions, 'lifestyle' will be taken over on to the next line: marking the close-up saves a possible error in the revise proof. Some publishers prefer to avoid a single word at the end of a para (ll. 48 and 62), counting this as much a **widow** as the short line at the top of a column or page (Unit 2).

Finally, a few points on the marking in the proof. On ll. 14 and 17 the full stop has been shown in the correction only because the text mark unavoidably passed through the existing full stop. Again for reasons of clarity, it is usually best to delete the whole double quote when replacing it with a single quote (and vice versa), as on ll. 52–3. No *margin* marks have been shown for the transposition of ll. 45–8 and 49–51, nor for cancelling the indent on proof ll. 53–5, because with so many corrections they would only add to the confusion.

In a travel guide the most important criterion will be factual accuracy. At editing stage this will mean making sure everything has been updated: prices, opening times, population (queried by the editor here as the ticked question mark on copy l. 19 shows) – and in Singapore even the current number of islands. Similarly, at proof stage getting all the names and numbers right is essential.

Layout and typography problems

A travel guide must also look attractive and treat parallel sections about different locations in similar ways. So consistent layout is vital.

Judging the type size and measure problems by eye should not have been too difficult. The measure of the first piece of text is clearly not as instructed: it should be a single column. (At paste-up this would then be divided into two even blocks and positioned above the box.) The B heads on the second galley are similar enough in wording to strike you straightaway as looking different, even if you could not tell which was correct. (When you cannot be sure, just write 'check type size' against each.)

If you are checking type with the aid of a typescale (illustrated on p. 133), compare the height of a capital with the 'H' (or on some scales the 'E') to determine (approximately) the point size of the type; then use the depth scale to check that the linefeed is as specified. For example, if 12/15 pt type is required, first compare a capital with the 12 pt 'H', then check that the baselines correspond with the 15 pt column on the depth scale.

Oddly there is no special symbol for changing unjustified to justified setting (proof ll. 56–62) and vice versa: 'correct vertical alignment' could be used but it is not as specific as the circled instruction shown.

Again, you should be able to tell by eye whether a space is a line or only half a line. (Compare by looking at the distance from baseline to baseline in the surrounding text.) Marking the reduction of space (above proof ll. 52 and 56) is not easy to do unambiguously. An alternative method to that shown is to write '– $\frac{1}{2}$ line' or '$\frac{1}{2}$ line out'.

The general principle is that, wherever possible, you should use a single standard symbol (not words) but occasionally circled instructions are indispensable for the sake of clarity.

We don't know whether these two columns will be side by side in the paste-up. If they are, even with an additional line in column 1 and cutting a line of space (in total) in column 2, you would have to add significantly to column 1, or cut column 2, in order to bring them into alignment (Unit 20).

In addition to checking for literals (typos), sense and layout in everything you proofread, remember to check that page or column depths are consistent and that running heads follow the prescribed pattern. At the final stage **correction lines** are sometimes stripped in by hand: check that they are straight, that the space between lines remains even throughout. (It is much easier to judge this on a photocopy than on the CRC or film itself.)

A SCHOLARLY WORK

Switch your mind back into editing mode: forget the symbol in the margin; return to working between the lines. In typescript all marks should come as close as possible to the word affected.

Confusion sometimes arises over whether to mark a **hard-copy printout** from an author's disk as a typescript or as a proof. Usually the author can provide double-spaced copy. In that case, I would always mark it between the lines like a typescript because it is easier to make the amendments absolutely clear that way. (This becomes especially important if the disk is to be corrected by the author.) If there are very few amendments on a page, put small crosses (in pen) in the margin against the lines requiring correction, to ensure that none of your changes is overlooked. If you have to use single-spaced copy, you have no option but to mark it as a proof.

In this exercise we revise how to handle scholarly apparatus such as notes and references (Units 17–19) and tables (Units 21 and 25). Look through those units again before you start.

The exercise also demonstrates problems of grammar (Unit 7), punctuation (Unit 9), handling quotations (Unit 11) and house style (Unit 14), including numbers (Unit 15). All these have recurred frequently in the course but do refresh your memory on any areas that you know are still hazy in your mind.

Now do Exercise C.2

*Remember to mark the passage as a typescript, not as a proof. Unlike the previous exercise, where the project was going through galleys and paste-up, this one will go straight to page proof. You are given no style guidance. For the table and references, just ensure a clear layout and consistent treatment. To keep track of your decisions on general style points (quotes, spellings, numbers, dates) and hyphenation, etc., make yourself a **style sheet** (see Unit 14 for an example). As usual you will also need a query sheet.*

Review of Exercise C.2

Check your work against the sample answer (for the first folio only) on the next page.

The table

Authors are usually asked to type each table on a separate sheet but (as here) they don't always comply. Since this book is going direct to page proof (and the heading is probably not a chapter head), we cannot be sure where the table will fall. If it occupied only four lines or so, you might leave it and hope that the typesetter would be able to position it precisely. For any longer table, as you know, you must change the text reference (l. 7) to a specific number. The more extensive change in the sample answer neatly avoids the repetition of 'show'; an alternative would be 'as Table 1 demonstrates'. (The 'T' may be either upper or lower case: note on your style sheet which form you choose.)

To match this changed text reference, you must add a main head to the table, consisting of (at least) a table number and (preferably) a table title. In your queries, *either* ask the author to suggest a title *or* (as the marginal question mark indicates here) ask for confirmation of your suggestion.

Where a table appears in the middle of a paragraph it is important to show that the text runs on (ll. 7 and 16). (As we have seen, most publishers prefer to position tables at the top or foot of a page.) However, there is no need to key in the table, as you normally would. Instead, just show where it begins and ends (as for any other displayed matter).

In column heads (where space is often tight) abbreviations such as 'rcvd' can be helpful but in the stub there is usually room to spell words out. The abbreviation '000s (beginning with an apostrophe, not an opening quote) means 'thousands' and, again, can be helpful in a column head. In this note, however, '000s cannot be meant and even 'per 1000' would be nonsense. I've suggested a solution but it must be confirmed by the author.

Similarly, it is quite common to use the symbol '%' in tables but to spell out 'per cent' in text, as in the sample answer. Certainly making the '%' a unit

Sample answer to Exercise C.2

(A) Unemployment and crime

By 1982 the number of people out of work in Britain had risen
to 3.5 million (14 per cent of the workforce) and one million of those
had been out of work for more than a year. The rise had been
phenomenal: in 1972 only 800,000 were unemployed. In the
same period, crime and imprisonment statistics show equally
significant increases (Table 1).

Table 1 Reported crime and imprisonment, 1972–82

	1972	1982	Increase (%)
Serious offences reported	3,448	6,226	80
Persons under sentence received into prison	57,739	94,377	63
Average daily prison population	38,328	43,707	14

a Per 100,000 of the population.

In the 18–20 age group figures have risen even more sharply.
The question is: are unemployment and crime causally linked?

The idea that economic conditions, in general, and unemployment,
in particular, causes crime, has a long history in criminology

below the last column head is the neatest solution for this column. The other two columns require no units. (Don't add 'no.' unless it is essential for clarity, for example where statistics for both number and percentage are given for each year. See the discussion of Exercise 21.2, Re-offending.)

On the style sheet you will have noted your decision on thousands (comma or thin space). Be sure to match the style of l. 5 with the table. In text it is legitimate (and quite common) to distinguish between four-digit and five-digit numbers: 6000 but 60 000 (or 60,000). In a table, however, as we saw in Unit 25, you must introduce a space (or comma) throughout so that the digits line up correctly.

Check the percentages with a calculator (it would probably take too long without). Make sure that you perform the calculation the right way round: 6226 ÷ 3448 % gives approximately 180%, that is, an 80% increase. In fact no queries arise.

There are several options for the table note. The indicator should not be attached (as it is in the original) to *both* the side heading and the numbers. It may be confined to the side heading, as in the sample answer. Following that logic further, you could incorporate it fully into the side heading. A third option is to keep the note indicators next to the two numbers but delete the one in the stub.

Converting the table note indicator to 'a' as shown, although not essential, helps to distinguish it from the notes in the text. You certainly wouldn't use asterisks for regular table notes in statistical material because (as we saw in Unit 21) they are reserved for levels of probability.

Since these appear to be official statistics rather than the results of the author's own research, the table should almost certainly have a source: the pencil question mark signals this query. As you are given no guidance on table layout and style, just keep it simple and consistent; do not, for example, mark the main head or column heads for italic, small caps, etc. Whether column heads are centred or left-ranged is similarly best left to a general design instruction. On the other hand, I would, as you see, mark the horizontal alignment of the column heads and the turnovers in the stub to ensure consistency.

Precisely where this dividing line falls between editor's and designer's spheres varies greatly in different areas of publishing: find out how much marking is expected of you. As we saw in Unit 21, a table style or similar book to follow is helpful.

Other points on the first folio

Since the paras are regularly typed, although in block style, it is not essential to mark them (for example on l. 18). If you decide to do so, you have to continue throughout the typescript.

In Unit 21, I mentioned that 'the UK' and 'Great Britain' strictly speaking refer to different areas. 'Britain' (l. 1), however, is widely used, particularly by Americans, as synonymous with the UK. You don't have to impose total consistency but keep a lookout for varying usage that could be misinterpreted by the reader to imply deliberate distinctions.

On l. 3 'm' is better spelt out; if left as 'm', it should be closed up. The matching change to '1 million' (identifying the '1' as 'one' because it is handwritten) is not essential but does make the relationship clearer.

The (pencil) crosses against 'workforce' (l. 3) and 'age group' (l. 16) indicate deviations from the forms recommended by the *Writers' Dictionary*. They are nevertheless common alternatives, and expressions that are likely to recur in this text. Unless a rigid house style demands it, it can be unwise to commit yourself to such non-essential alterations until you know whether the author's usage is consistent. The more changes you undertake, the greater the risk of forgetting some of them as you go along. Write the author's form in pencil on the style sheet (preferably with the first few folios) and go back to your crosses when you have decided which way to jump. You cannot, of course, change your mind half-way through the book but it may take a chapter or two to assess the author's preferences and level of consistency.

Note on ll. 18–19 that the sense is 'economic conditions ... cause' but 'The idea ... has'. The comma before 'has' *must* go because it intrudes between subject and verb. Some editors would dispense with all the commas on ll. 18–19. Instead I've added one at the end of l. 18 to make up the pair. Yet another way would be just to keep one pair of commas round 'and unemployment in particular'.

House-style points

Throughout the text you had to make or apply decisions on numbers, etc. (noting them on your style sheet). In this kind of work, percentages should certainly be given in figures, so change l. 32 to '13' (as well as making 'percent' – the American form – into two words). Ages (l. 16) are best as figures too, but you must not change l. 34 as it is part of a quotation.

On l. 40, keep 'thirty' if your general rule on numbers is to spell out below a hundred (change to '30' if your rule is below ten). The date on l. 27 should be either '10–12' or '10th–12th'.

On all such points, you may be able to follow

your own preferences or you may be required to follow a set house style – or you may be expected to follow the author's prevalent style. If the last, you would use marginal crosses in pencil in the first chapter or so, as suggested for 'workforce' and 'age group'. Do *also* skim through the typescript for such points *before you start*: the first chapter is often written last, perhaps after a considerable interval, so that it doesn't always conform with the rest of the book.

When you are typesetting from authors' disks it is particularly important to limit editorial changes, so you will often be standardizing to the author's style. For example, you might well have to accept hyphenation of 'superbly-cooked meal' if that style has been followed consistently. Advance guidelines for authors become particularly important in those circumstances.

Text editing generally

The first line of fo. 269 inadvertently repeats the last of fo. 268.

Quotations needed attention as usual. On l. 25 mark a three-point ellipsis and even spacing; on l. 26 transpose the full stop and closing quote (this is a phrase, not a sentence). On l. 33 again mark the ellipsis for spacing; on l. 34 'it' should almost certainly be in square brackets, to show it was not in the original (whereas on l. 33 the parentheses almost certainly were); on l. 35 add a closing quote before the reference. Each of these points on ll. 33–5 should be included in the queries to make sure your guesses are correct. On ll. 50–1 change to single quotes (if you opted for that style); on l. 51 again transpose the full stop and closing quote.

There were numerous problems of grammar and punctuation. On l. 25 'than' should be 'that'; insert a comma on l. 26 (or delete the one on l. 27) and a full stop on l. 29; similarly, I'd add a comma after 'however' on l. 29; transpose the apostrophe and 's' on l. 30, probably also changing 'are' to 'were'; it should be 'survey of' on l. 36.

The semicolon on l. 41 must be a colon; each 'which' on ll. 42, 45 and 48 *could* be 'that' and many editors would change them all to improve the flow (others such as myself would hesitate as this is clearly part of the author's style); certainly the commas round the 'which' clause on l. 42 are quite wrong; 'fail' on l. 43 is correct despite the singular form of 'remainder' (a word of multitude, like 'majority', etc.); add 'an' at the end of l. 43; many editors would think 'Whilst' (l. 44) old-fashioned, although a good many authors still prefer it before a vowel; 'lead' is better than 'led' on l. 46.

I'd prefer 'First' on l. 50 (if you kept 'Firstly',

follow it with 'Secondly' on l. 58); 'also' is redundant on l. 52; 'than previously' on l. 54 sounds odd and is better changed to 'than they were', also perhaps bringing 'now' forward to follow 'are'; on l. 56 delete 'essential', without forgetting to remove the 'n' from 'an'; on ll. 56–7 *either* put 'claiming against' *or* retain 'on' and delete 'company'.

On l. 62 'to' should be 'with' (because of 'inter-'); 'etc' on l. 65 usually has a stop after it, as an abbreviation (not a contraction) and commas before and after it (or you could spell it out as 'and so on').

Hyphens also required attention as usual: 'time-series' (at the end of l. 44) should be 'stetted'; on l. 45 add a hyphen to 'cross-sectional' (it is a prefix here, like 'trans-' or 'multi-', not an adjective); again note 'home-owners' (l. 55) in pencil on your style sheet – the author and/or you may later opt for two words; 'race relations' (l. 61) must certainly be two words; the *Writers' Dictionary* recommends 'interrelated' (end of l. 61).

Unless you are familiar with the subject matter, there may have been technical terms you didn't recognize – among them perhaps 'time-series and cross-sectional studies' or 'intervening variables'. As we saw in Unit 13, this needn't worry you and you would not normally query them unless they seem to be used in contradictory ways.

The word 'of' is repeated on ll. 21–2. There are misspellings, literals, etc., on ll. 22 (two problems), 23 (capital 'C' as well as missing 'm'), 28, 30 (close up), 38, 41, 42, 44, 46, 50 (space), 53 (close up 'e.g.' or, preferably, spell it out as 'for example'), 60, 62.

When you are reading for sense it is very easy to miss some of these. If the book is to be rekeyed, you will often be rescued by the typesetter. If, however, you are typesetting from the author's disk, there is no such second chance. Either way, training yourself to spot literals at the editing stage is important in order to avoid expense in proof.

Similarly, if the project is not to be rekeyed, you must be particularly alert to other minor problems such as incorrect spacing between words and round punctuation, incorrect symbols such as one and 'l', multiplication sign and 'x' – all the errors you would be looking for in proofs. On the positive side, if a misspelling or unwelcome style point occurs throughout, you can sometimes ask for it to be amended by a **global search**, in which case you don't have to mark the change all the way through the printout.

The notes and references

Handling notes and references efficiently is, as we saw in Units 17–19, largely a matter of technique.

Even though these sections were relatively short, I trust you followed the methods you learned there. So you will have marked the note indicators with a flourish as superiors (see Unit 18) and transposed the one on l. 31 to follow the full stop. You will have seen that there is no note 3 in the list. I hope you spotted too that the missing note is almost certainly note 2 (text indicator on l. 31): the note called 2 here fits quite snugly as note 3 (l. 38). You would, of course, have to query all this.

The headings for 'Notes' (if, as is likely, they are to be endnotes, rather than true footnotes) and 'References' should be treated the same. As we have seen elsewhere, they could be coded 'A' (like l. 1), or perhaps 'B'; alternatively, you could flag them as of a different order by calling them 'R'.

The references in the text and notes need the usual tidying up: an extra comma on l. 21 (assuming you opted for that style throughout); alphabetical (or chronological) arrangement of these references on l. 21; comma and colon on l. 35; space after the colon on l. 38. It is better *not* to shift the reference on l. 38 to follow the author's name (on l. 35) because it only relates to the last phrase of the sentence — never make such changes mechanically. Standardize the style of notes 1 and 4: either form is possible provided you are consistent – a comma instead of parentheses is quite common in notes (and also in table sources).

Your initial check of the reference list will have revealed the misplaced Hawkins. When matching references against the text (ticking, as in Unit 19), you will have noted queries on Bonger (a date discrepancy) and Sellin/Selin (both l. 21); and the absence of a listed reference for Dean (ll. 35–8).

Finally, you will have styled the reference list, noting further queries on Mannheim: the initial is missing and an editor's name may be needed. (The place is also missing but you could safely fill that in as London.) The lack of an editor's name is not *necessarily* a problem since such volumes are sometimes anonymous; equally this style might be followed if *Mannheim* is the volume editor.

A related point to look out for generally in a bibliography or reference list is that there are two kinds of editor, and they are treated differently. The one you are already familiar with (which might be missing here) is the compiler of an edited collection, consisting of chapters by different contributors. The other is a **textual editor** (someone annotating or commenting on an author's text). This kind of editor is usually treated in the same way as a translator (see Unit 17).

I won't go into each style inconsistency here: look again at your own work on the reference list now and see whether there are inconsistencies of punctuation, order, capitalization, etc., that you missed the first time. In real life you usually have to pick up your own mistakes: there's no one around to tell you. A rapid scan after you have finished the main work can often save proof-correction costs. Note that 'Little, Brown' (l. 73) has a comma; 'Books' (l. 80) is best omitted.

It is not normally necessary to spell out HMSO (Her Majesty's Stationery Office). The Scarman Report is unusual in having been published by Penguin, because the subject of the Brixton Riots attracted great public interest; it was also published officially by HMSO, as Cmnd 8427. Such **command numbers** are often included in the bibliographical details given for British government publications. The first series of command papers was 'C', but that reached 10 000 at the end of the nineteenth century, so they changed to 'Cd', then 'Cmd', then 'Cmnd' and now 'Cm'. Never 'standardize' these different forms in a reference list. (Since they are contractions they are often set as shown here; the *Writers' Dictionary* prefers a full stop.)

In this course the references have been confined to books, journal articles or chapters in edited volumes. However, as I warned at the beginning of Unit 17, there are many other kinds of reference, such as these command papers, newspaper reports, theses and legal cases. If scientific, academic or professional non-fiction is your field of publishing, your next priority will be to read Butcher, *Copy-editing* (and perhaps more specialist works mentioned there) to come to grips with the conventions – not just over references but on all manner of style points – in your particular subject area.

AN INSTRUCTIONAL TEXT

This exercise again combines practice of several skills: handling figures and captions (Units 26–8), structure and headings (Unit 5), and improving style, which we looked at first in Unit 8 (Meaning and Clarity), then in Units 20 (Making Cuts), 23 (Lists) and, most recently, 32 (Jacket Blurbs). Finally, some of the considerations about logical organization discussed in Unit 29 (Editing the Index) are relevant here. Before you start the exercise, look back at all those units to refresh your memory.

Now do Exercise C.3

You don't need to be an expert gardener: use the figures to understand the text and vice versa. (If you are already involved with gardening books, you'll know that the terminology has changed: ignore the problem for now.) Remember, when you are improving style, to re-read the edited sentence and (more quickly) the whole paragraph. Think about the logical presentation of information, both as you read and when you finish each section; make the necessary adjustments but ask for the author's confirmation.

Review of Exercise C.3

The objective in practical or educational books is to provide sensibly organized, unambiguous and clearly written text with helpful, accurate diagrams. We look first at the figures (since on the whole they present more straightforward problems), then at the structure and finally at style improvement.

The figures

There are two main alternatives. You could retain two figures (as in the original) by making the demonstration of the correct pruning angle into an **inset** in Figure 1. (Such an inset often does show an enlargement of one particular section of a diagram.) Alternatively (and perhaps preferably), you could renumber to create three separate figures. Their order will depend on whether and how you rearranged the text (as discussed below).

Whichever course you took, you should have added a reference to each figure *in the text* at the point where a visual explanation most helpfully reinforces the verbal one. There is already a text reference on l. 41 to the figure (or inset) showing the cutting angle. Insert a reference (by number) to the bush rose figure on l. 34, either in parentheses before that full stop or in a separate sentence. The figure showing the climber may be mentioned *either* (preferably) on l. 61 after 'new growth' *or* at the end of the relevant discussion, on l. 68.

In addition, key in each figure (but not an inset), by writing, say, 'Fig. 1 near here' in the margin close to the text reference.

You will probably need to list the captions separately (as we saw in Unit 28). If the first diagram becomes a separate figure, it too must have both a number and a title, perhaps 'How to cut' or 'Technique for pruning'. The other two captions should have parallel wording, preferably with 'Pruning' in both.

Your firm might also require you to type label copy separately (as we saw in Unit 27). Otherwise, just make clear amendments to the labels on the roughs themselves. In books at a higher level, you would avoid such extensive wording on diagrams; in practical and educational texts, such explanations can be very helpful. (An alternative would be to make more use of lists in the text; if you did that, you might dispense with some of the figure labels.)

Improve the labels by making them parallel and consistent. Standardize to *either* '3rd', '5th' and '⅔' *or* 'third', 'fifth' and 'two-thirds' (adding a hyphen as well as an 's'). Just as we saw for tables in Exercise C.2 ('%' in the table with 'per cent' in the text), figures and text (for example ll. 32–4) do not have to match up on such points as abbreviations or words versus figures (although each must be internally consistent). Add 'cut' before 'at 3rd' and 'eye' after it (this may be in pencil as the subject of a query, as we'll see below); add 'shoots' after 'weak'. It would be helpful too to add 'from ground' after '5th eye' since the scale is too small to show the eyes. (This cannot be paralleled in the '3rd eye' label because it does not apply to laterals.) 'Avoid' is used incorrectly both here and on l. 60: on the figure a better label would be 'branches should not cross'; the text could read 'don't allow branches to cross'.

The label style (all labels beginning lower case, without punctuation) is quite usual. For consistency just lower-case 'Cut' in one instance.

'Bud' and 'eye' need no **indicator lines** (connecting label to drawing) as the artist will be able to place the labels unambiguously. Add one, however, to the longer label on the climber diagram.

The key showing the symbol for a cut must *either* move to the first figure that uses it *or* be omitted (as too obvious to require explanation). The key for 'new wood' could either remain alone or (preferably) be replaced by a label and indicator line at the top of the two striped branches (keeping the helpful shading).

There is some careless drawing on the roughs. Query whether the short lines across laterals on one branch of the climber are intentional (and if so what they mean) or whether (as is likely) they should be the standard little blocks showing cuts. Notice too that, whereas other laterals are shown sprouting alternately from the main stem, those on the middle branch of the climber have only been sketched in vaguely. Add a circled instruction asking the artist to draw those laterals so that they branch alternately like the rest.

Structure and headings

You will, I hope, have noticed that some reorganization was imperative. The phrase 'The first skill to be learned' (l. 40) should have rung alarm bells: we might already have cut down the bush by this stage. At minimum, ll. 40–6 must come earlier in the discussion. Certainly too the headings on ll. 20 and 56 should be parallel. If bushes and climbers represent the main division, bushes should not be discussed under a heading about climbers, and vice versa. From l. 70 onwards, for example, none of the discussion fits under the heading 'Method for climbers': these are afterthoughts best moved to more appropriate places.

When such problems arise, analyse the content *paragraph by paragraph*, ignoring the existing headings:

1 (ll. 2–5)   introduction
2 (ll. 6–14)   kinds of rose
3 (ll. 15–19)   timing of pruning (general)
4 (ll. 21–4)   preparation for pruning bush roses
5 (ll. 25–30)   purpose of pruning (general)
6 (ll. 31–9)   technique for pruning bush roses
7 (ll. 40–6)   how to cut (general)
8 (ll. 47–55)   deadheading (general)

The next para break (on ll. 63/4) is illogical: either run on to create one para, or break after 'show' (l. 60) or perhaps after 'growth' (l. 61). If run on, this para 9 (ll. 57–68) is about the technique for pruning climbers.

Para 10 (ll. 69–71) just provides cross-references on two quite different points – training climbers and disease (general).

Para 11 (ll. 72–8) concerns fertilizing (general) (with 's' in the style of the passage, but my book uses -ize spellings).

Para 12 (ll. 79–80) is an afterthought on pruning bush floribundas (make the form of the plural consistent here and on ll. 7, 10 and 51: 's' is probably more common). (See also below on the new terminology.)

Returning to the headings, we find that the chapter head (as it probably is) on l. 1 incorrectly promises discussion of 'training', whereas all we get in the body of the piece is a cross-reference to an earlier chapter. (Also, 'for' should be 'of'.) The other topic mentioned ('care'), along with l. 73, gives a clue to one possible way (though by no means the only way) of reorganizing.

Introduce an A head 'Pruning' before para 3 and bring the substance of para 5 (the purpose of pruning) together with para 7 (how to cut) forward to follow para 3.

Make l. 20 a B head 'Bush roses' (probably not repeating the word 'pruning' since the A head already shows the subject matter) over paras 4 and 6 (using parts of ll. 25–6 as a transition) and bring in para 12.

A parallel B head 'Climbers' (l. 56) follows with para 9 (as a single para or two) under it, and l. 69 (training) as a separate final para for cross-reference.

So what happened to para 8, on deadheading? This moves down to become the first para in a new section beginning before l. 70 with an A head 'Caring for your roses' (or simply 'Care' or 'After-care'). This renders redundant such phrases as 'both bush and climbing' (ll. 48–9 and 52). The rest of para 10 (the cross-reference on disease) and para 11 (fertilizing) come in this section too. *Either* leave them in the present order, to build up to a rousing ending, *or* move ll. 70–1 to the end as a cross-reference.

When transferring sections from one folio to another (paras 5, 7 and 8), follow the method demonstrated in the sample answer to Exercise 29.2 (Choices index).

The process of logical ordering obeys principles not unlike those you learned for indexes in Unit 29: avoid split entries (part of the discussion in one place and part in another); read back each para to see whether it fits logically under its heading. Also, just as the headword is not repeated in subentries, there is rarely any need for repetition of the words of an A head in the B heads that come under it.

Such reorganizational work may be required, especially in the development stage (see Unit 3), if you are working on educational, technical or reference texts. Always take care (again as we saw for rearranging indexes) that you are not interfering with an author's deliberate structuring of material: double-check to ensure that your changes really are improvements. In particular, recheck all connecting phrases in case they no longer make sense. Do also always show the author what you have done. Usually the simplest way is by returning the typescript (or a photocopy) with a general query in the form: 'pp. 26–30 – plse chk rearrangement acceptable.' (You may also have to explain the meaning of 'A', 'B', etc.)

Recheck too that the explanation of new terms still appears at the *first* occurrence. In this passage, even before rearrangement, several terms were only explained the second time they were used: 'lateral' (ll. 34 and 66) and 'eye' (ll. 31 and 36). The switch from 'eye' to 'bud' and back again (ll. 31–4; see also the first illustration) is particularly confusing – is a distinction intended or not? Probably not, but you will need to ask the author (or find out yourself). Finally, 'deadheading' appears at l. 5 but is not explained until l. 48. In this case, an explanation at l. 5 would be inappropriate so it may be better to substitute 'removal of dying blooms throughout the flowering season' (in the context 'blooming' could be misinterpreted).

As I warned in the instructions about the exercise, the terminology has changed, a situation that can crop up in any field. Hybrid tea roses are now officially called 'large-flowered roses'; floribundas are called 'cluster-flowered roses'. If you were publishing the piece today, you would have to consult the commissioning editor on whether or not to change to the new terms throughout. Whichever terminology you use, explain the other system somewhere, since the reader will come across both variants in catalogues and other books.

Editing the text

There was much room for improvement. Retain the informal style – don't attempt to turn it into literary prose or a dry thesis – but do address the boring repetition of the same vocabulary, excessive use of the passive, loose grammatical structure, etc. Again showing the result to the author should preclude unexpected problems in proof; note specific queries only where you cannot be sure you have interpreted the meaning correctly.

Contradictions must always be queried (or otherwise checked). For example, on ll. 4–5 pruning and fertilizing are (not 'is') said to be needed in spring and autumn, but all the pruning discussed takes place in spring, the fertilizing (ll. 75–6) in spring and summer. On l. 70 'fungicide' should be 'fungi' (a mere slip probably and best corrected silently).

There were ambiguities or unclear referents (see Unit 8): 'ones' (l. 35) – better as 'plants'; 'it' on l. 44 – the stem or the eye? (the stem is meant); 'cut back' on l. 64 – *which* branch? (as it stands, it could mean the new one or even both – the figure gives the answer); 'remove the rest' on l. 80 – presumably all the other shoots.

In page cross-references (ll. 69 and 71), remember to alter the number to '000' (without obscuring the original) as well as making 'p.' and 'page' consistent. (As we saw in Unit 14, a distinction may be made between text and a cross-reference in parentheses, but that is not the case here.)

There were **dangling participles** (see Unit 7) on ll. 2 and 25. The better option on l. 2 may be 'Although they require considerable attention, roses are' because this also solves the loose construction on l. 3 ('affording ...' tacked on after a comma), which is much better as a semicolon followed by 'they will afford'. 'Riot of colour' (l. 3) is a cliché – perhaps 'glorious' would do.

By l. 6 we have had quite enough of 'requiring', 'need', etc. (see Unit 32, Jacket Blurbs) and go on to a lethal surfeit of 'different', 'treated differently', etc. An improved version might be:

~~Different~~ treatment ~~is required~~ *differs* for bush roses ~~as compared~~ *and* ~~to~~ climbers, ~~Also you need to know that~~ floribundas ~~grow~~ *for* and ~~differently to~~ hybrid tea varieties, ~~and so are treated~~ ~~differently~~ The hybrid *tea* rose has [single] [large] flowers, each growing on ~~their~~ *its* own stem; on floribundas a cluster of flowers ~~comes out of~~ *sprouts from* the same ~~spot~~ *place* on the stem. Both kinds can be bushes or climbers, ~~and are treated differently~~ ~~There can be~~ *Each category may include* weak, medium ~~or~~ *and* vigorous growers ~~in all categories~~, which are also treated differently.

When you finish editing a chapter or section, always go back to introductory remarks such as these to make sure they were followed through. Are different instructions in fact given for the different categories? (I don't think this is a problem here but it is worth checking.)

Read quickly through your own work again now to see where you might make further improvements. At the same time, look out for places where you may have made incorrect changes because you misunderstood the sense. That is a far worse offence than missing a few improvements. Make sure you have not introduced repetition of words. (The obvious word is often one that already appears in the sentence before or after.) Look too for unclear marking of an insertion or places where you amended but forgot to delete the original (as in 'making a' and 'What places' in Exercise C.1, Singapore).

The problems included 'start to be tackled' (l. 15); 'However, whenever' (l. 19); a wrong tense on l. 22; repeated 'each other' (l. 23) – solved by 'branches that cross may rub'; 'for improvement in' (l. 26) – better as 'to improve the'. In place of the dash on l. 28, you could begin a new sentence, 'You are also pruning to encourage growth: in general ...'; 'it goes without saying' (l. 29) never needs to be said.

Straightforward commands are always better than 'you are counting', 'is the right thing to do', etc.

(ll. 31–3). Move 'back' (l. 36) to follow 'Cut' (l. 35); on l. 39 ', which' is better as '; this'; for 'the way' (l. 40), try 'how'; for 'although not' (l. 42), 'without'. Avoid the repetition 'because ... disease' on ll. 43–5 by combining the subjects of the sentence; on l. 45 'are' should be 'is'; on l. 46 replace 'his' with 'a', perhaps also making 'gardener' plural (see Unit 12).

On l. 53 'as and when' is tautologous. The repetition of 'ruthless' (ll. 54 and 63) destroys its impact (one of the instances could change to 'be firm' or 'don't hesitate to'). On the other hand, I would keep the repetition of 'past its best' on ll. 50 and 55 as a change of wording might imply a change of meaning – see 'bud' and 'eye' above. Avoid circumlocutions such as 'it is essential to' (l. 53). On l. 55 'as a whole' is redundant.

I'd change ll. 57–8 to 'Do not cut climbers right back each year like bushes: you would be giving'; on l. 59 'much too much' is over-colloquial even here; 'Like' is misused on l. 60.

Replace the repetitive 'is shooting' (l. 64) – perhaps with 'starts'; integrate the parenthetic explanation (ll. 67–8) to make a single clear explanation such as 'cut back each lateral on the old wood, removing about two-thirds of its length'; the last sentence of the para (l. 68) is redundant; improve 'Aside from' (l. 73) and 'through up until' (l. 77).

Apart from inconsistent hyphenation, misspellings occurred on ll. 24, 35, 36, 50, 59, 67, 77.

A SHORT STORY

In the previous exercise you had to edit extensively because the overriding priority was clear explanation of the technique for pruning roses. As we saw in Unit 13, the approach to creative writing is very different. In particular, you must be sensitive to the rhythm of sentences as well as their meaning.

There can nevertheless be plenty to keep the editor occupied.

This final exercise concocts a wonderful goulash of many of the points you have learned throughout the course. Above all, it should reinforce the habit of *looking everything up.*

Now do Exercise C.4

---

*Apply the forms recommended in the **Writers' Dictionary** and **Hart's Rules**. If you do not recognize the specific use of a word, consult an ordinary (reasonably detailed) dictionary before you change it.*

Review of Exercise C.4

The original story is appropriately entitled 'Jots and Tittles', the minutiae important in diplomacy and the essence of the editor's trade. I hope you spotted most of the large number of errors and inconsistencies, which I am not going to explain in any

detail here because from now on you are on your own. Make time to look through the passage again tomorrow yourself: I suspect you'll find that at least a couple of howlers remain.

I will just mention a few points that may have puzzled you. You had to decide who was speaking and for how long: is this a dialogue or a monologue?

As we saw in Exercise 9.3 (Archy and Mehitabel), if a speech goes on over several paragraphs, it has an opening quote at the beginning of each paragraph; the closing quote does not come until the very end. Clearly that system has not been followed here. Nevertheless the most likely construction is that the whole passage is a monologue: I would mark on that basis but list the point as a query. (To avoid the quotes altogether, you or the designer might decide just to enclose 'said Antrobus', on l. 1, in square brackets.)

The alternative theory, that the first paragraph is spoken by someone other than the main narrator, or perhaps is an extract from some older published work (because of the capitals), doesn't really hold water. This is one of the few paras where the author has *not* put a closing quote (though that could just be carelessness). Certainly l. 16 ('But') seems to lead on from l. 15 and thereafter there is little doubt that 'I' remains the same person. Almost certainly, that person is Antrobus.

Rather than indicating a different source, the capitals in the first paragraph convey exaggerated emphasis. If you lower-cased them (as you might well be tempted to do), you should ask in your queries whether this is acceptable.

Another puzzling sentence occurs on ll. 11–12. If you have not already done so, look up 'C.-in-C.' in the *Writers' Dictionary* ('Med.' is the Mediterranean). It all makes sense if you add 'in' before 'harbour'. On l. 14 'boothook' should be 'boathook'.

Many phrases were unusual but extremely evocative: 'gnarled embryonic English' (l. 28) or 'quenched himself' (ll. 44–5) or 'irremediable huff' (ll. 101–2). On l. 34 , however, 'circling' is better than 'circulating'; on l. 48 'Georgic' is a malapropism for 'Georgian'; I'd query the meaning of 'corrupt groups' on l. 52.

I hope you did not ruin the joke by 'correcting' the quotation on ll. 106–9. Instead, 'stet' the misspelt words to make sure that the typesetter does not automatically correct them either. I would raise one query with the author, suggesting that on l. 106 'than' for 'that' may be more confusing than amusing.

We are not, of course, dealing here with a quotation that is sacrosanct because it must follow the original newspaper report: the whole story is fictional and comic effect is the only criterion. Similarly, you could just opt for one form of the various inconsistent names, organizations, etc. Check that you noticed *all* the discrepancies between ll. 20 and 73–4; also that you saw l. 80 should be 'Yugoslavs' (or 'Serbs'), not 'Czechs'.

NOT SO MUCH AN END AS A BEGINNING

Although this consolidation section primarily draws together the threads of what you have already learned, in each exercise you probably also came across something new. One of the most rewarding features of editing is that every project brings you new knowledge, often about the subject matter, but often too about your craft. Long may your learning continue.

The aim of the course as a whole has been to set you on the road; to alert you to all the minute details that absorb an editor's attention; to enable you to discriminate between subtle distinctions and inconsistencies; to give you a flavour of the wide range of expectations that publishers in different fields may have of their editors; but above all to help you to gauge, and respond to, both the author's intentions and the reader's needs. Go on building upon the skills you have learned: as in any other craft, true competence – and hence satisfaction – comes only from experience.

Further reading

All the works cited in earlier units are important but for me the key books are:

Judith Butcher, *Copy-editing* (Cambridge University Press, Cambridge, 3rd edition, forthcoming)

H.W. Fowler, *A Dictionary of Modern English Usage*, revised by Ernest Gowers (Oxford University Press, Oxford, 2nd edition, 1965)

Leslie Sellers, *The Simple Subs Book* (Pergamon, Oxford, 2nd edition, 1985)

The Chicago Manual of Style (Chicago University Press, Chicago, 13th edition, 1982; distributed in the UK by International Book Distribution, Hemel Hempstead)

M.D. Anderson, *Book Indexing* (Cambridge University Press, Cambridge, 1971)

Index